No. 2747
$21.95

# MAJOR HOME APPLIANCES
## A COMMON SENSE REPAIR MANUAL

### DARELL L. RAINS

TAB BOOKS Inc.

Blue Ridge Summit, PA 17214

FIRST EDITION
FIRST PRINTING

Copyright © 1987 by Darell L. Rains
Printed in the United States of America

Library of Congress Cataloging in Publication Data

Rains, Darell L.
Major home appliances.

Includes index.
1. Household appliances, Electric—Maintenance and repair—Amateurs' manuals. I. Title.
TK9901.R35  1987    683′.83    86-23157
ISBN 0-8306-0747-1
ISBN 0-8306-2747-2 (pbk.)

©Copyright 1984—DLR PUBLICATIONS,
P.O. Box 830-132, Richardson, Texas 75083-0132

# Contents

# Introduction

The major home appliance has always been one of the best investments for the homemaker's dollar. Stories of refrigerators that cost $250 and lasted 20 years without so much as a service call are fairly common. The automatic washer handles the toughest job in homemaking, but it runs day in and day out, month after month, year after year, with dependability and good service.

The home major appliance is smarter than ever. It has taken all the guesswork out of what used to be the most hated chore in the household — washing and drying dirty clothes. It has reduced the task to a simple matter of selecting a wash cycle and pushing a button. The dryer decides for itself when the clothes are sufficiently dry, the machines protect delicate fabrics, they do not over wash or over dry, they don't waste resources, cleaning materials, etc. Although these appliances now are taken for granted, they are an essential in any household.

Although major home appliances are very dependable and require only a minimum amount of care, they can be abused.

How do you possibly abuse a refrigerator? It is very easy to do. It is a common practice and a very costly one to the careless owner. To understand proper care of a refrigerator, you need to understand that it is a beautifully-balanced, electromechanical device that requires only a little effort on the behalf of its major working component — the compressor — to do its job properly. The compressor circulates freon through the cooling coils in the freezer portion of the refrigerator and maintains the preset temperature with very little effort. The machine will come on and operate only a dozen times a day in normal use. However, this delicate operating balance can be quickly upset by misuse.

The biggest enemy of the refrigerator is dirt. The airflow system that removes excessive heat from the area of the compressor and condenser coils causes a buildup of lint, dust, dirt that is sometimes not cleaned for many years. A dirty coil cannot dissipate heat properly and all the normal functions of the refrigerator are impaired by poor air circulation. Throughout this service guide, we will suggest ways to extend the life of your major appliance by simple preventive maintenance.

Washers and dryers can be misused, too. The washer is designed to do a very difficult job — remove imbedded dirt and grime from a wide variety of fabrics. But, like the pack horse, it can be over-loaded. This creates several problems. The machine simply can't distribute soap and clean rinse water as it is supposed to do. But the biggest problem created is excessive work load on the gears, pump, and drive motor. Overloading a washer or dryer will shorten its life and result in poor performance as well.

Lint buildup in the back of a clothes dryer restricts its performance and should be cleaned out periodically as we suggest later in this guide.

The dishwasher is also misused. The homeowner will often, without thinking, cram the dishwasher full of dishes — and after the cycle completion wonder why the dishes are not clean. Dishwashers, like other appliances, are designed to be work horses when used properly, but the dishwasher is not capable of distributing the proper spraying pattern when overloaded. Homeowners are not aware that HOT WATER is necessary for the proper cleaning of the dishes. Water that is not "piping hot" will not properly dissolve the detergent as it goes through the cycle. It is wise to always "prime" the hot water line at the kitchen sink before using the dishwasher. This little trick will allow the hot water to dissolve the soap detergent properly. After completion of the cycle, the dishes look like new.

Take care of your major appliance and it will very probably serve you better than any other major investment you make. Misuse it and you may be in for some costly repairs.

In developing this service guide we chose to show only one type of major appliance, since it would be virtually impossible to illustrate and describe repair procedures for the dozen or more different brands of washers, dryers and refrigerators. The brands we selected represent almost one-half of all the major appliances in use today.

If you do not own this particular brand of appliance, the pictures and step-by-step instructions will not apply directly to your machine, but the techniques and general repair procedures should still prove very helpful.

# 1

# General Information

## PRODUCT WARRANTY

Homeowners who have home appliances in warranty should have a clear idea of what is covered by their product warranty. Most new appliances have a one-year parts and labor warranty, which means the manufacturer of the appliance will furnish parts and labor at no cost to you to restore the appliance to working order. Most homeowners do not call a factory service center when they discover a problem with a machine under warranty. This is a mistake because the dealer warranty service is included in the price of the machine. So, when you first notice a problem, call a factory-authorized service center and they will take care of the problem at no charge to you. Remember, any unusual squeaks, rattles, or intermittent problems need to be serviced during the first year of ownership. The manufacturer's obligation is for the time as specified, usually one year, in the product warranty booklet. You must pay all repairs, whether minor or extensive, for equipment out of warranty.

## EXTENDED WARRANTIES

Some independent appliance service centers offer extended product warranties or service contracts. It is our opinion that these benefit no one but the service center that writes them. A random study of our files on repair of automatic washers showed most washer repair costs were less than $65. Depending upon the age of the washer, the extended warranty contract costs $65 to $75 per year. On the surface, this sounds like a good deal until you consider that the automatic washer is a very reliable appliance and its likelihood of needing repair is one in five for a one-year period. By comparing the relatively low costs of repairs per year and the low likelihood of requiring any repairs or service at all, the dollars that the homeowner spends for service contracts over a 10-year period is a very poor investment.

## PARTS REPLACEMENT SOURCES

All home appliances listed in this service guide - automatic washers, clothes dryers (electric and gas), refrigerators, compact ice makers - if they are used day in and day out will eventually experience a failure. When this happens, you will have to decide whether to repair the appliance or replace it with a new model. Faced with the high cost of new appliances, many homeowners elect to repair their existing machine.

When you need a replacement part to restore a nonoperational appliance, there are two sources to consider: the factory parts distributor and the factory authorized service center. To save money, you can buy replacement parts from the factory parts distributor at a better price than you can buy the part from the factory authorized service center. The service center is independently owned and will mark up the price of parts approximately 40 to 60 percent over the factory parts distributor. Factory outlets may be available only in large cities however.

When you order a replacement part from a factory outlet and the part is not a stock item, you will normally have to pay by cash or money order before the distributor will order the part. Most will not accept a personal check. This payment also covers the cost of mailing the part to your residence. It will take approximately ten to fourteen days for delivery.

When ordering parts from a distributor, you must know the model number (eight to ten numbers) so the clerk can identify and order the correct replacement part of the appliance. When you return a part to the parts distributor, for whatever reason, there is usually a fifteen to twenty-five percent restocking charge. So, be sure to furnish the parts distributor with the proper model number or other information when ordering replacement parts.

As mentioned earlier, you can save money by going to a factory parts distributor. However, there are advantages to buying from an authorized service center:

- It isa locally owned business which probably has courteous and friendly personnel.
- It has factory-franchised parts and service.
- You may reduce driving time to the parts distributor to pick up ordered parts.

When you order parts at a service center, it is usually a policy of the company that parts be paid for before being ordered.

## ELECTRONIC AGE APPLIANCES

Automatic washers and clothes dryers that use electronic control assemblies are now available to the American homeowner. Electronic circuitry in home-entertainment equipment such as TVs, radios, and stereo equipment have been available for years. However, washers and dryers that use electronic circuit boards are relatively new to the industry. Manufacturers hope that, with the growth of these products, future manufacturing costs can be reduced.

Electronic controls offer convenience in operating an appliance by offering a combination of options. For example, the preprogrammed cycles of the electronic control automatic washer simplify program selections. If the user forgets to fully program the unit, the washer has its own brain and will automatically switch the cycles and complete the wash. Electronics also has the potential for conserving energy. Cycle selection and options can be preprogrammed for energy efficiency. For example, the electronic control washer automatically programs the selection of warm wash and cold rinse in all cycles. If the user selects another wash option, the electronic control automatically programs the energy-saving setting for the next wash cycle.

Competent service technicians can diagnose and replace electronic controls quickly with the help of diagnostic features built into the electronic control. The tested longevity rate of electronic control assemblies have shown a life span approximately 30 percent longer than the older electro-mechanical control.

The first decision that a potential buyer must make is whether the electronic control circuitry is worth an additional $200 per-pair cost difference as compared to a conventional washer and dryer. The standard washer will fill, agitate, drain and spin exactly like the electronic control model. For the most part, both types use the same drive motor, gear case assembly, water inlet valve and water pump assembly. The main difference is the programming of the unit, controlled by the electronic or solid-state circuitry.

Another concern the potential buyer must consider is the replacement cost of components that make up the electronic control assembly. These assemblies are expensive to replace when a failure occurs.

Service of the electronic assemblies is far beyond the reach of the reader of this service guide. A factory-trained technician must be called in to service the electronic unit.

## ELECTRICAL TESTING

Because all major appliances require electricity as an energy source, you should have a basic knowledge of the relevancy of electricity to appliance servicing. This includes a knowledge of circuit breakers or fuses when the source of electricity fails, and a knowledge of how to use simple electrical test equipment for minor electrical diagnosis.

If an appliance does not appear to be receiving power, check the electrical distribution panel (circuit breaker box). *(Figure 1)*. Circuit breakers consist of an electromagnet that breaks the current when its magnetic field has been stretched to its maximum allowance. Circuit breakers act as ON-OFF switches for the flow of electricity to

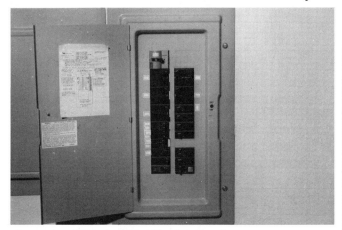

Figure 1 — Electrical Distribution Panel

specific electrical outlets. An electrical contractor will normally mark the switches at the time of installation to indicate which switch controls which electrical outlets. Therefore, when an appliance totally fails, check the circuit breaker box to see if the switch is OFF. Then correct the cause of the overload and manually reset the switch to the ON position.

Some older homes have fuses to serve the same purpose as circuit breakers. Fuses protect the house wiring system and appliance overloads and short circuits. Fuses are devices that consist

Figure 2 — Screw-in and Cartridge Type Fuses

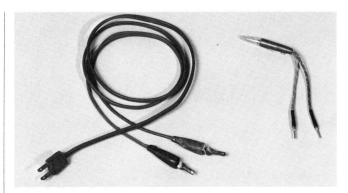

Figure 3 — Homemade Electrical Test Cord and Neon-Bulb Test Light

of a metal strip that melts at a very low temperature. When a fuse is in proper working order, current flows through the metal. If a surge of current occurs due to current overload or a short circuit, the flow of electricity through the metal strip generates heat to melt the metal strip, thus breaking the current and creating an open circuit. Then you must replace the fuse. Fuses are of a screw-in or plug type, and the cartridge type *(Figure 2)*. Usually screw-in fuses are used in 120-volt lines, while cartridge fuses are used in 240-volt applications.

Test equipment can be an important aid in finding the cause of trouble in a failed home appliance. The main purpose of testing is to find out whether current is flowing through a particular component without being "leaky" or "open." The normal procedure is to disconnect the component from the line, connect the leads from the test equipment to the component terminals, plug in or switch ON the test equipment to the component terminals, and then plug in or switch ON the test equipment to get a reading on the dial.

For minor electrical diagnosing and troubleshooting, you need two inexpensive pieces of test equipment: a homemade electrical test cord *(Figure 3)* and a neon-bulb test light. You can make the electrical test cord from an old discarded appliance cord. You simply attach two alligator clips to the exposed wires at the end of the cord. You can use this cord to make live electrical checks and to check refrigerator compressors. The neon-bulb tester is used for making live voltage checks. This tester is a very simple device that is available in most hardware stores. It cannot be used for checking electrical components of an appliance. The test cord will be discussed in more detail later in this service guide.

Professional appliance technicians use a

variety of sophisticated testing tools to determine power breaks and to analyze an appliance for defects. You would probably use this test equipment only if you had a greater-than-normal aptitude to challenge difficult repair problems. However, the following simple testing devices may be helpful to you:

Volt/Ohmmeter *(Figure 4)* - A volt/ohmmeter set on the VOLTAGE scale measures the voltage across an electrical line and determines if the proper voltage is available. The OHMMETER scale of the volt/ohmmeter allows you to locate breaks in circuits and make continuity checks to switches, thermostats, elements, motors, capacitors, etc.

The volt/ohmmeter is mentioned several times throughout this service guide as a necessary tool to test home appliance components. If you do not have this test equipment, you can purchase it for less than $15 in do-it-yourself centers and electronic stores. These economical versions are capable of performing almost any check and test that is mentioned in this service guide. The volt/-ohmmeter is very easy to use, and there is no reason to be afraid of using it. In fact, when making a continuity check between one contact to another on an appliance, you always unplug the appliance first. Voltage or electrical checks would damage the meter movement of the volt/-ohmmeter.

In checking a suspected defective switch, for example, you unplug the appliance and set the volt/ohmmeter selector switch to the RX-1 scale. Place one probe of the volt/ohmmeter on one terminal of the switch and place the remaining probe to the other terminal of the switch. With the

Figure 5 — Ammeter Used in Checking Electrical Appliances

switch depressed (pushed in), you should see continuity, or 0 ohms, (full meter deflection) on the volt/ohmmeter scale. This procedure will be used many times throughout this service guide.

Ammeter *(Figure 5)* - Amperage is the current at which electricity flows through a conductor. An ammeter measures the current flow. It is effective in checking appliance motors and refrigerator compressors.

Wattmeter *(Figure 6)* - Wattage is the product of volts times amperes. A wattmeter measures the frequency at which sixty-cycle alternating current changes direction 120 times each second. This determines how effectively the mechanical system of an appliance is functioning.

Switches - You check switches with a volt/-ohmmeter to test for electrical continuity across

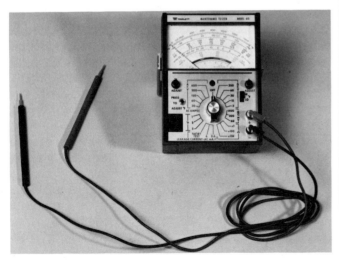

Figure 4 — Volt/Ohmmeter Used in Checking Electrical Appliances

Figure 6 — Wattmeter Used in Checking Electrical Appliances

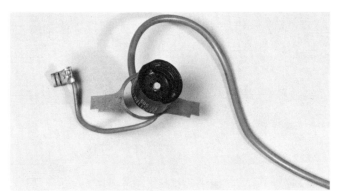

Figure 7 — Refrigerator Overload Protector

the terminals of each switch setting. You always disconnect the appliance before checking any switches with the volt/ohmmeter. Live voltage checks will damage the meter movement.

Overload Protectors *(Figure 7)* - An overload protector is a bi-metalic device that consists of two types of metals. One metal expands more than the other as heat is applied or as they are cooled. As the temperature changes, the uneven expansion of the metal causes them to bend. As they bend, the contact points in the bi-metal will make or break the circuit. In the case of a refrigerator, the overload protector is attached to the compressor housing and senses unusual temperature conditions as well as excessive electrical loads, thus breaking the circuit.

Overload protectors can be checked with a jumper wire and a volt/ohmmeter. When using the jumper wire method, you place the jumper between terminals one and two of the protector. If the compressor will run with the wire jumper in place but fails when jumper is removed, a faulty overload protector is indicated. A safer (and easier) way to check a protector is to use a volt/ohmmeter. Across terminals one and two; there should be continuity (meter swing to 0 ohms) if the protector is good, and no continuity (no meter swing) if the protector is defective. *(Figure 8)*.

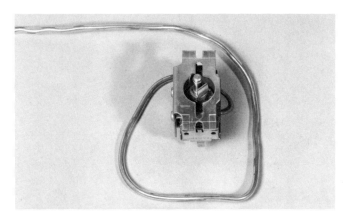

Figure 9 — Refrigerator Thermostat

Thermostats *(Figure 9)* - In a refrigerator, the thermostat opens the circuit and shuts off the compressor when the preset temperature of the thermostat is reached. When the thermostat contacts close, the compressor starts up again and continues running until the unit has again reached the desired temperature. This process maintains a constant coolness inside the refrigerator. The thermostat can be checked with the volt/-ohmmeter by removing the thermostat from the refrigerator cabinet and warming the sensing bulb with your hand. You should achieve continuity (0 ohms on the RX-1 scale) with the ohmmeter across the thermostat terminals *(Figure 10)*.

Start Capacitors - Most compressors in refrigerators, freezers, air conditioners and a variety of common electric motors must have high starting torque in order to begin rotation under load. To obtain this torque, a starting capacitor *(Figure 11)* is placed in series with the start winding circuit of the electric motor. When the start winding is engaged by electricity, the capacitor builds up voltage and then discharges via the same winding in the form of a power surge.

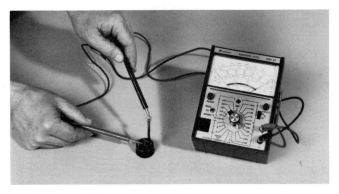

Figure 8 — Checking For Continuity in the Overload Protector

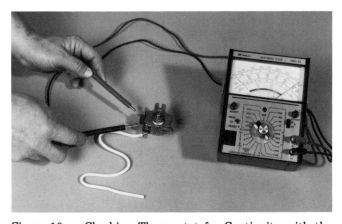

Figure 10 — Checking Thermostat for Continuity with the Volt/Ohmmeter

Figure 11 — Starting Capacitor Used in Refrigerator Compressor Starting Package

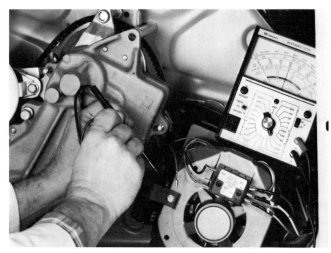

Figure 13 — Checking the Starting Capacitor with Volt/Ohmmeter

This power surge from the capacitor gives the electric motor or compressor motor the added torque it needs to begin running under a loaded condition.

WARNING: A charged capacitor is extremely dangerous. A capacitor will hold a charge indefinitely even while not in use. If a person were to touch the terminals of a charged capacitor, the build-up of high voltage would give him a shock that could result in bodily injury or be fatal.

You discharge a capacitor by shorting the two terminals together (*Figure 12*). This can be done by using a screwdriver with an insulated handle. The best method is to use a 20k ohm (20,000) resistor that is rated at 2 watts or higher. This method eliminates the hazard of high-voltage arc that will occur when discharging a start or run capacitor using the "screwdriver short" method.

After the capacitor has been fully discharged, check the capacitor by using the following procedure and the volt/ohmmeter. Set volt/-ohmmeter to the RX10 scale and connect the leads to the capacitor. The meter should swing full scale momentarily before starting a slow motion in the opposite direction as the capacitor discharges. If the meter fails to swing full scale on contact with the terminals, the capacitor is open and must be replaced. Also, if the volt/ohmmeter remains in the full-scale position and does not begin to move in the opposite direction, the capacitor is shorted and must be replaced (*Figure 13*).

Relays (*Figure 14*) - The function of relays used in refrigerators is to energize the start winding in the compressor motor until the unit comes "up to speed." At this point, the relay breaks

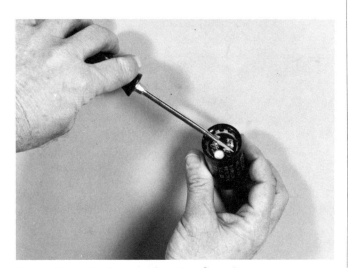

Figure 12 — Discharging Starting Capacitor

Figure 14 — Typical Relay Used in Refrigerators

Figure 15 — Solenoids Used in Automatic Washer

the circuit to the start winding and the run winding takes over, allowing the motor to continue to run. If the relay is not dropping out or sticking, the compressor runs hotter than usual and, in most cases, shuts off via the overload protection circuit described earlier. A relay is on the verge of failure if the unit is "struggling" — trying to start several times before actually beginning to run. When you find this condition, replace the relay. Low-line voltages will cause the refrigerator relay to "chatter." This does not happen very often, but when it does you must find the low-voltage source.

Solenoids *(Figure 15)* - The purpose of solenoids, used mainly in the automatic washer, is to convert electrical energy into mechanical energy. A solenoid is basically a wire coil that produces a magnetic field. When energized by electrical current, it acts like a magnet. A plunger assembly inside the coil is pulled into it by magnetism. When the solenoid is de-energized, the plunger moves out of the coil by gravity, or by spring pull. There are several applications of solenoids in home appliances, including water inlet valve, bleach dispensing, end-of-cycle signaling, lid latch control and agitation control.

Check solenoids for defect by using the volt/ohmmeter. Place the volt/ohmmeter probes between the two terminals, with the meter set on RX10 scale or RX100. The meter should show a half-scale or less deflection, which indicates the solenoid coil is good *(Figure 16)*. No meter movement indicates an open solenoid, and the defective component should be replaced.

Timers *(Figure 17)* - You can check timers in the automatic washer and some refrigerators with a volt/ohmmeter across the contact points in the same manner as described for switches. Timers frequently have dirty contacts that fail to make a circuit. In this case, you should clean the timer contacts with a small file.

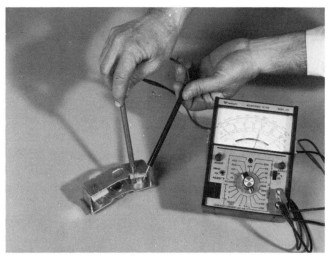

Figure 16 — Check Automatic Washer Solenoid for Continuity with the Volt/Ohmmeter

## PERSONAL SAFETY IN WORKING WITH APPLIANCES

Personal safety is the primary consideration in working with an electrical home appliance. To ensure your safety, observe the following rules:

- Never attempt to work with live electricity when servicing an appliance. Always disconnect the appliance cord from the appliance outlet or turn the electrical power OFF at the electrical distribution panel (circuit breaker box). To make certain that the proper circuit breaker has been turned OFF, test the line by turning the appliance ON and make sure that the appliance line is dead.

- Never work near live electricity where

Figure 17 — Automatic Washer Timer

the floor is wet. If necessary, place an empty box on the floor to avoid the danger of electrical shock.

• Make sure that all appliances in the home are properly grounded at all appliance receptacles. Electricity follows the path of least resistance. If an appliance has been properly grounded — then insulation has worn off an electric wire and the bare wire touches the metal cabinet in which the appliance is housed — the flow of electricity will find its way to the ground through a ground wire. If a body were to come in contact with the appliance cabinet, it will have no current flow through it because the body would offer more resistance than the ground wire. If no path to the ground exists, however, the electricity would flow through the body and result in bodily injury, or even death.

• Never work with loose wires. You should secure loose connections so that they do not vibrate and work loose during normal operation of the appliance. When replacing worn or stripped-out screws, be sure to use the right size. Never use a longer screw than the original because the longer screw might penetrate the appliance wiring harness and cause a short to the cabinet.

Throughout this service guide, the terms NOTE, CAUTION, and WARNING have specific meanings. A NOTE provides additional information to make a step or additional procedure easier and clearer to understand. Disregarding a NOTE could cause you additional problems in diagnosing and servicing of an appliance problem. A CAUTION emphasizes areas where equipment damage could result. Disregarding a CAUTION could cause your equipment electrical or mechanical damage. Personal injury, however, would be unlikely. A WARNING emphasizes areas where personal injury or even death could result from negligence by the homeowner. Mechanical damage could very easily occur. You should take WARNINGs seriously. Neglecting to do so can cause serious bodily injury or even death.

## INSTALLATION AND PROPER CARE OF REFRIGERATORS

If a moving company has installed your refrigerator, check their work carefully before you put the refrigerator back into service. If you move yourself, you should use the manufacturer's appliance installation instructions.

Never lay the refrigerator on its side in a moving van or truck. When a refrigerator is lowered to horizontal, the compressor oil leaves the compressor housing. In most cases, the refrigerator will not run when put back into service. Refrigerators use very low horsepower motors that have a history, after they are laid on their sides, of never running again. If, for some reason, you cannot follow this advice and you must lay the refrigerator on its side, be sure to let the unit sit in an upright position for at least ten hours before turning the unit ON. This will enable the unit to be properly balanced out before starting. Follow the above steps or you will be a prime candidate for a compressor changeout.

When refrigerators are moved, the bumps and rough handling can cause electrical problems such as loose or broken wires. Often these electrical problems are simple in nature and can be solved by removing the back of the unit and checking for loose wires that have fallen off the spade connectors of the terminal block or that lead to the compressor starting package.

On refrigerator doors that use magnetic gaskets, I have received many complaints about the freezer door coming open by itself and spoiling all the food. In many cases, the homeowner is slamming the refrigerator door too hard, which causes the freezer door to break its seal and come open. The solution is to gently close the door so the door gasket can seal properly and the freezer door has no chance of falling open.

Another common complaint is that the refrigerator door is out of alignment and not closing properly, causing an accumulation of frost inside the door. It is true that refrigerator doors sometimes get out of alignment, — often as a result of someone leaning on the door while the door is open, or children swinging on the door. When a refrigerator door is out of alignment, inspect the door to see if the gasket is mating at the top and bottom of the refrigerator cabinet. If there is a gap, open the door and loosen all the screws that hold the gasket to the door liner. (There may be as many as twenty to twenty-five of these screws attached to the door liner, but they should be loosened to relieve tension on the door liner to keep it from breaking or cracking.)

Refrigerator doors, as a rule, have no crossrails, so to align the door you need to use a popping action to bring the door back in align-

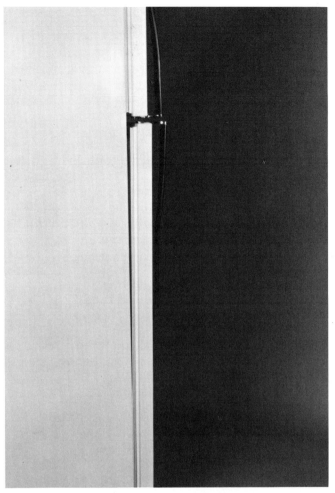

Figure 18 — Refrigerator Door Out of Alignment

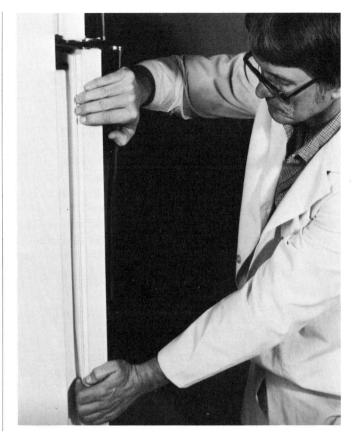

Figure 19 — Alignment of Refrigerator Door

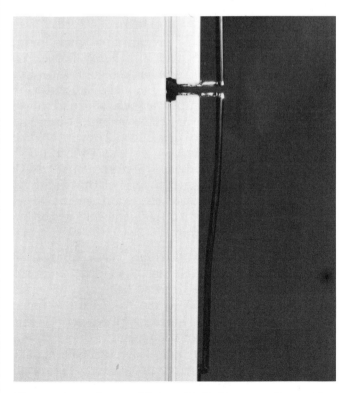

Figure 20 — Proper Mating of Refrigerator Door After Alignment

ment. If the door has a gap at the top *(Figure 18)*, apply pressure by placing one hand in the center of the door and the other hand at the top of the door, and popping (not too hard) the door and then checking for proper fit. Continue this procedure if the door still does not seal properly *(Figure 19)*. After final adjustment, tighten all the screws that hold the gasket to the door liner and check for the proper closing of the door *(Figure 20)*.

For years, I have made service calls to fix refrigerator door handles that are loose. Most homeowners have looked for screws to tighten and found none, so they call the service center. The trim, door panel, door gasket, and door insulation have to be removed to fix the handle. For this so-called simple repair, the bill is very costly because of the time and labor involved. Manufacturers, for the most part, use special nuts on door handles, which are usually attached to screws inside the door panel. In time, these nuts work loose and the homeowner has a loose door handle, and a costly repair job, unless he can fix it himself.

For a refrigerator to give many years of trouble-free service, it must have some preventive maintenance. One necessity is to clean the condenser regularly. A dirty condenser can cause high cabinet temperatures, which lead to higher operation costs. Dirt and debris can enter the housing of the condenser fan motor and cause early failure. Refrigerator manufacturers recommend that the condenser be cleaned every two to three months with a vacuum cleaner or long bristled brush. To gain access to condenser coils, simply remove the grill on the bottom front of the refrigerator. By following this procedure at least twice a year, you may eliminate future repairs and your refrigerator will work more efficiently and economically.

## INSTALLATION AND PROPER CARE OF THE AUTOMATIC WASHER

If a moving company has installed your automatic washer, check the installer's work carefully before resuming use. A very common complaint after a homeowner has moved, is water leaking on the floor or the washer is filling with water improperly. Usually the problem is embarrassingly simple - the installer simply failed to put the drain hose into the drain standpipe. So, check their work very carefully before using your major appliance.

You should follow precautions when installing an automatic washer in a NEW home. You must thoroughly flush the hot and cold water lines at the washer station. To flush the hot water line (Figure 21), you simply attach one end of the washer fill hose to the hot water faucet and then place the other end of the fill hose down the drain or basket. When performing this procedure, be sure to hold the fill hose when you turn ON the water; otherwise, the pressure of the water will force the fill hose out of the drain and water will go all over the floor. To flush the cold water line, use the same procedure.

The purpose of flushing these lines is to eliminate contaminants such as dirt, mud and solder flux from the lines so that no debris will stop up the washer hoses and block valves. Before attaching the washer hoses check to see if a small screen is at the end of each hose. If these screens have been installed by a previous technician, make sure they are clean before reinstalling (Figure 22).

The next step is the proper set up of the washer self-leveling legs (Figure 23). This feature

enables the installer to level the washer on a level or slightly shifted foundation. This feature also keeps large capacity automatic washers from walking and vibrating excessively. Most washers spin at the rate of about 500 to 750 RPMs. If a wash load is slightly out of balance, a washer not properly leveled will vibrate and cause the washer basket to bang against the washer cabinet. Damage to the washer can result.

The next step in washer installation is proper cabinet alignment. With the rear legs leveled, all you need to do is position the front legs properly (Figure 24). When aligning the front legs, simply adjust the legs so that they are not higher than the rear legs. You can usually adjust the front legs with a crescent wrench. Use a small level to perform the adjustment (Figure 25). Always level your machine, because with proper alignment most of the wash water will drain out of the tub to the water pump. This gives the tub a chance to dry

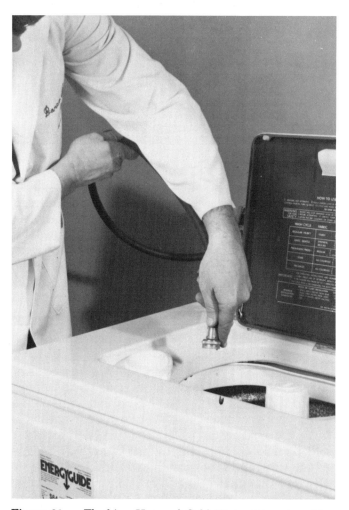

Figure 21 — Flushing Hot and Cold Water Lines in a New Installation

14

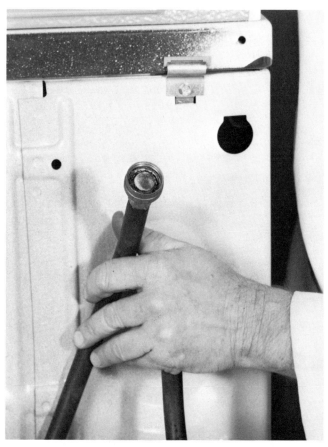

Figure 22 — Checking for Restriction in Inlet Screen of Automatic Washer Fill Hose

out when not in use. If the washer is higher in the front than the back, wash water will stand in the back of the outer tub and eventually cause rust spots and holes to develop.

The final step in washer hookup is proper positioning of the washer drain hose *(Figure 26)*. When connecting the drain hose, insert the end in the drain and then wedge the drain hose under the hot or cold water inlet hose. This will ensure that the drain hose will not jump out of the drain. The water pump of an automatic washer disposes of drain water with great force, which can flood a laundry room very quickly if it isn't securely locked into the drain standpipe.

Proper use and care of an automatic washer can eliminate most service calls. The automatic washer is not only the most complicated of the major home appliances, it can also be the most fragile. The washer timer *(Figure 17)*, is the brains of the appliance. It consists of a box containing electrical timing switches that tells the washer what to do during the various cycles. The timer can be damaged easily and the most common cause of timer failure is "fanning" the dial while the unit is ON. This rapid spinning of the dial will lead to early failure of the contact switches in the timer by erratic electrical power surges to the switches. The washer would fail. To prevent this

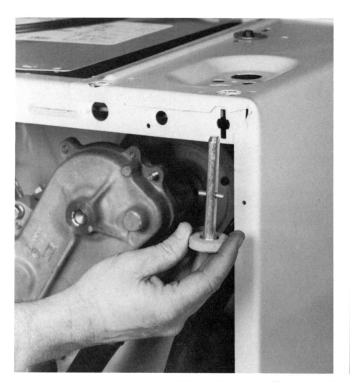
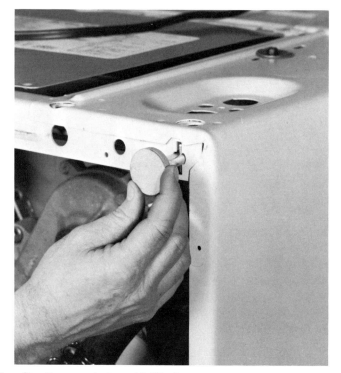

Figure 23 — Installing Rear Self-Leveling Legs on Automatic Washer

Figure 24 — Positioning Of Automatic Washer Front Legs

needless failure, never make a timer selection while the unit is ON. Always turn dial clockwise and slowly while making cycle selections.

Another cause of unnecessary service to the automatic washer is using too much laundry detergent. It is not true that the more detergent you use, the cleaner the clothes will be. Excess detergent and water go over the washer tub ring and get into the washer drive motor, which could lead to a motor burnout. The filler in the soap can also push clothes to the top of the washer basket where the agitation will pull them into the washer outer tub. They will eventually end up in the water pump.

Automatic washer drive motors are very reliable over the years, but water can be damaging and motor burnout is an expensive repair. To help eliminate this failure, use the minimum amount of detergent necessary to get your clothes clean. Not only will you avoid an expensive service call, you will cut down on detergent cost.

From location to location, detergents will react differently, so you will have to experiment as to which detergent will give the best results. If you move to a new location, consult the home economist at the local power company. He or she will be most helpful in recommending a washer detergent for your area.

Certain detergents that contain low phosphate have a history of causing unusual odors and souring in an automatic washer. This is caused by low phosphate and fillers in the detergent, which forms a sediment build up in the washer outer tub. If the washer is not used for three or four days, the unusual odor can become quite noticeable. The remedy for this problem is to mix two gallons of vinegar to about twelve gallons of very hot water and let this set in the tub for fifteen minutes. Then fill the washer with warm water and agitate with no clothes in the tub for fifteen minutes. Then turn washer OFF, and let it set with the vinegar mixture in the outer tub

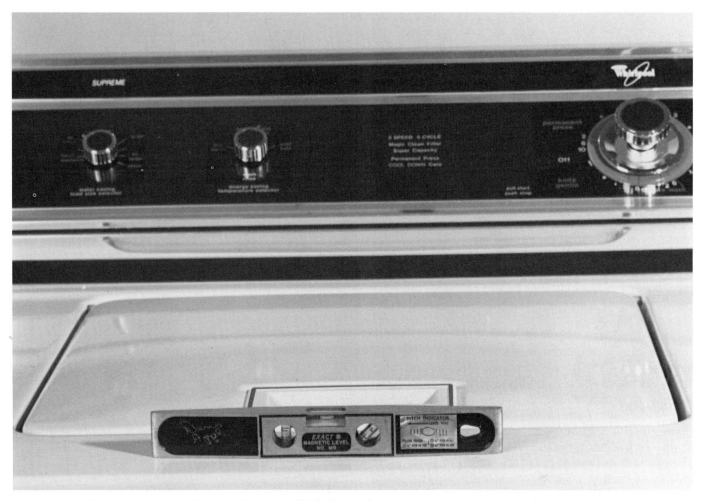

Figure 25 — Check Automatic Washer Alignment With A Level

for eight hours before pumping the mixture out. This remedy will usually work for most odors. If odors still exist, the washer will have to be

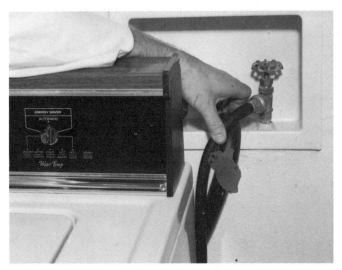

Figure 26 — Positioning of Automatic Washer Drain Hose in Wash Station Standpipe

disassembled and the excess sediment must be scraped off the tub post and the wall of the outer tub.

There are two popular types of lint filters in automatic washers: the self-cleaning *(Figure 27)* and the manual filter *(Figure 28)*. Most common is the self-cleaning, which means that you never have to clean it. The wash lint is deposited in the filter, which acts like a magnet during the wash cycle. When the washer enters the pump-out cycle, the wash lint is flushed through the water pump and then down the drain. The major disadvantage of this filter is that some homeowners get careless by washing fabrics that shed quite heavily. This can clog the filter with lint and lead to washer failure. You should not wash items that shed large amounts of lint, like shag rugs and fuzzy blankets, if you are using a washer with a self-cleaning filter. This filter is superior to the manual filter because it traps smaller pieces of lint that show up on dark fabrics. With a manual filter, you clean it after each wash load.

17

Figure 27 — Self-Cleaning Lint Filter Used in Automatic Washers

Another area of potential trouble is the drain system of the automatic washer. Frequently, it can clog up and the wash water will back up the drain and leak onto your floor. Surprisingly, one source of the problem is coffee grounds in the disposal. They form a varnish that will migrate through the pipes and cause clogging of the drain. To kill bacteria in the pipes, pour a solution of one half gallon of muriatic acid and one half gallon of water into drain standpipe and wait eight hours before using the washer. This solution is very toxic, so apply in a well-ventilated area. CAUTION: Never spill any of the liquid on the floor because it will damage the carpet or tile. WARNING: If spilled on the skin, rinse under cold water for five minutes because severe skin irritation could result.

Automatic washers take a lot of abuse by the laundry detergent splashing on the washer lid and top. Most detergents, in time, will cause the top or lid to develop splotches or form a film that is nearly impossible to remove. After trying several miracle cleaners over the years with no results, I have found the following procedure to be successful in removing most detergent film: Thoroughly clean the surface with steel wool and water to remove any traces of oil, and let dry. Brush a mixture of three parts muriatic acid to one part water and scrub vigorously. WARNING: Do not let this mixture come in contact with the skin, severe skin irritation could result.

You may apply a second application if the area is not clean, using the above procedure. Obtain muriatic acid at your local swimming pool supply store or use isopropyl alcohol as a substitute cleaner.

## INSTALLATION AND PROPER CARE OF CLOTHES DRYERS

Just as with automatic washers and refrigerators, you should check the installer's work very carefully before resuming use of a clothes dryer. Also, if you install it yourself, check the manufacturer's appliance installation instructions.

When installing the clothes dryer, the main thing to remember is not to jam the dryer against the wall. The exhaust tubing will usually kink and the dryer has restricted flow of exhaust air. A good rule of thumb when installing dryers is to leave a hand's length from the wall to the console of the dryer. After installation, again check to see that the exhaust tubing has no kinks or crimps because this would add to the time it takes for clothes to dry.

### BASIC TOOLS THAT YOU WILL NEED

Listed below are some basic hand tools that you will need for servicing home appliances *(Figure 29)*.

### TEST EQUIPMENT

Listed below is test equipment that is used when servicing home appliances *(Figure 30)*.

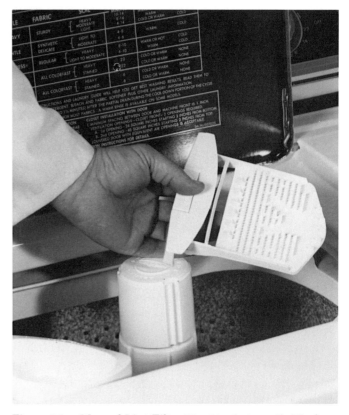

Figure 28 — Manual Lint Filter Used in Automatic Washers

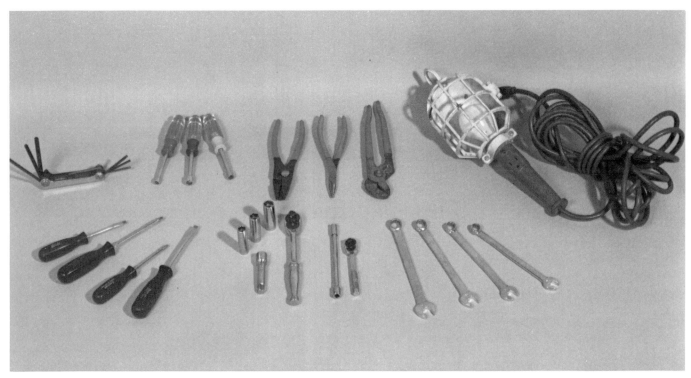

Figure 29 — Basic Hand Tools Used in Servicing Home
Appliances

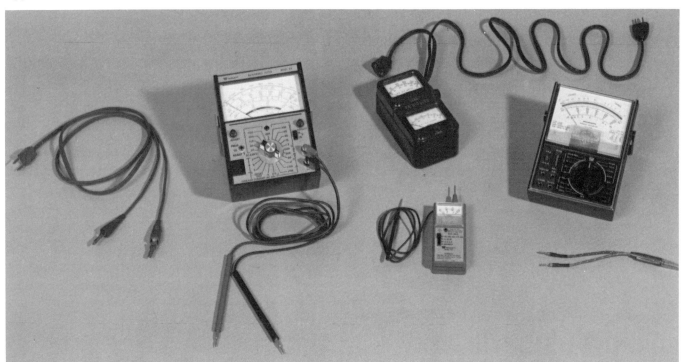

Figure 30 — Test Equipment Used for Servicing Home
Appliances

# 2

# The Automatic Washer

We felt that the simplest way to organize this guide to help the do-it-yourselfer solve a problem was to organize it in the following manner:

- Show pictures of and describe all the components that make up the system.
- List specific problems (or failures) and suggest other symptoms that will help isolate the problem.
- List components to be checked in the proper sequence to isolate the faulty part.
- Give step-by-step replacement instructions for removing and replacing the faulty part.

If the guide seems a bit complicated, it's because we are dealing with a fairly sophisticated electro-mechanical device.

But don't be intimidated by the system. It is well engineered to be easily disassembled and repaired—if you have a little good advice before you start.

For example, most homeowners give up before they ever get started. They can't figure out how to get inside the automatic washer. It is so very simple. Just open the lid, grip the opening with both hands, and pull up. Two spring clips hold the top on the washer. No screws. No magic locks. No special tools needed.

Once a washer is emptied of water, you can move it out from the wall, remove the access panel on the back of the unit, and visually inspect the machine. Such simple problems as a broken belt or loose hose are immediately obvious. Leaks are fairly easy to find, although you may need to run the washer through a partial cycle to spot the source of the leak.

When the machine is empty of water it can be unplugged and laid on its front for easy access to the lower components. Repair is often very simple and inexpensive. BUT ALWAYS REMEMBER THAT YOU ARE DEALING WITH DANGEROUS LEVELS OF ELECTRICITY, AND OFTEN THERE IS WATER ON THE FLOOR...A DEADLY COMBINATION THAT REQUIRES EXTREME CAUTION ON THE PART OF THE HOME REPAIRMAN.

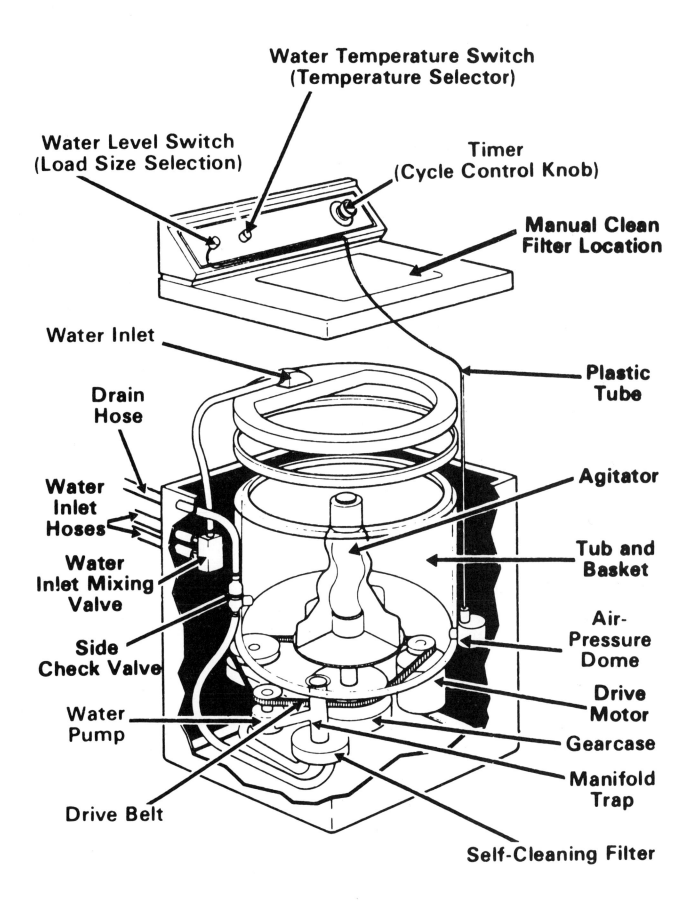

Water Temperature Switch
(Temperature Selector)

Water Level Switch
(Load Size Selection)

Timer
(Cycle Control Knob)

Manual Clean
Filter Location

Water Inlet

Drain
Hose

Water
Inlet
Hoses

Water
Inlet Mixing
Valve

Side
Check Valve

Water
Pump

Drive Belt

Plastic
Tube

Agitator

Tub and
Basket

Air-
Pressure
Dome

Drive
Motor

Gearcase

Manifold
Trap

Self-Cleaning Filter

## THE AUTOMATIC WASHER - HOW IT WORKS

An automatic washer is probably the most sophisticated appliance in your home. It is complicated because it performs a variety of functions in the course of performing the complete wash cycle: It fills with water, agitates the clothes, pumps out the wash water, and spins the clothes dry.

The washer drive motor in automatic washers is coupled to the agitator and the water pump assembly. A circuit in the washer electrical system distributes electricity to the timer motor, which controls all of the operations of the washer during the wash and spin cycles. When you turn the various washer dial selections for the type of washing desired, a set of cams in the washer timer are aligned and contact switches in the timer supply the electrical power to drive the motor, water temperature selector, water inlet valve, and control solenoids.

Automatic washers use water level controls or fill switches, which offer a choice of water levels: extra small, small, medium or regular, large, and extra large. These settings vary depending on the amount of clothes to be washed. When you make a selection, the water level control is set to open when the proper water level has been reached. In this manner, the selection of hot, warm, or cold wash water involves opening or closing the water inlet valve by means of electrically operating the solenoids. When you set the water level control and timer selection, electrical power is then supplied to the water inlet valve, which allows water to enter the washer. If, for example, you select a hot water wash cycle, a solenoid is energized to open the hot water inlet bypassing the cold-water solenoid valve or vice versa for a cold wash.

If you select a warm wash, both solenoids would be energized. The fill water is cut off by the water level control by pressure when the proper water level in the washer tub has been attained. When the water level control has been satisfied, electricity is now supplied to the washer drive motor by a set of contacts in the timer assembly. The timer also supplies electricity to other solenoids, which causes the washer gearcase to engage. The solenoid causes the drive clutch to engage and the agitator begins to oscillate in the wash cycle.

The washer agitator is driven either by a gear train or a clutch-driven method. The gear train is the most popular among the manufacturers of automatic washers. As a washer is agitating in the wash cycle, it is driven by either the gear train — consisting of a pinion gear, drive gear, connecting rod and a sector gear — or rack and pinion method.

These mechanical assemblies convert the rotary motion of the drive motor to an oscillating motion that drives the agitator through an arc of about 180 degrees and approximately sixty to seventy strokes per minute. The automatic washer basket will move slightly while the washer is in the agitation cycle. The brake assembly, which is a mechanical part of the basket drive assembly, is responsible for this action. If there were no way to hold the basket while the washer is agitating with a full load of clothes, the tub basket would revolve and the end result is that the clothes would possibly tear and become entangled in the basket. However, during the spin cycle, the agitator is locked in with the washer basket so that both are turning during the spin cycle.

After the agitation or wash cycle, the timer assembly closes a set of switch contacts which, in turn, energizes a solenoid, allowing a shifting of the arm of the water pump assembly, which further allows the wash water to be drained from the washer outer tub. During the drain portion of the cycle, the motion of the agitator stops under the control of the water level control, which does not allow the washer drive motor to start until all of the water has been removed from the washer outer tub. A short spin cycle follows to remove all excess soap suds in the tub and the clothes. During the spray rinses, the water pump assembly remains open so that the spray rinse water is removed from the outer tub by the water pump assembly and pumped out of the washer and down the drain standpipe.

The timer cam assembly now closes another set of contacts, which opens the water inlet valve and, at the same time, opens the circuit to the spin solenoid, thereby causing the washer basket to come to a stop. After a pause, the timer motor advances, which closes switch contacts in the timer assembly. The outer tub again refills with water. In some cases, you can preselect this water fill temperature at the start of the wash cycle from a selector switch — from which you can select various combinations of hot, warm, or cold wash, and warm or cold rinses.

In the deep rinsing cycle, the washer agitates for a short period of time. After the agitation time, the washer comes to a stop and the water pump again empties all of the wash water from the outer tub. The washer then enters the final rinse and spin-dry cycles. Final rinsing consists of a spin, which is accompanied by one to five brief spray rinses. The purpose of these spray rinses is to remove all residue of soap and dirt that may have accumulated in the outer tub basket and the clothes during the washing cycle. After a series of spray rinses, the basket continues to spin at a high rate of speed for several minutes, to remove the water from the clothes by centrifugal force. For the final segment of the cycle, the washer timer motor again advances to where all of the circuits are opened in the timer assembly and the washer then shuts OFF.

## WASHER MECHANICAL SYSTEM

### Gear Train

Although the homeowner will probably never do a major teardown of a washer gearcase, it is worthwhile to understand its function. The gear train of the automatic washer consists of a sector gear, connecting rod or possibly the rack and pinion gear type. In this type drive, the pinion gear drives a larger main-drive gear. A connecting rod is attached to both ends of the main-drive gear and the sector gear, which pivots on a stud through an approximate 180-degree arc. A more common type is the sector gear *(Figure 31)*. This gear meshes with the agitator gear to accomplish the washer oscillation. The washer drive belt is turning in a clockwise rotation while the drive motor is energized by the timer assembly. To disengage the gear train at certain segments of the wash cycle, a solenoid is used to convert an electrical impulse into a mechanical action *(Figure 32)*. The force exerted by the solenoid plunger is nowhere near enough power to disengage the gear train of a mechanical system which is powered by a 1/3- or 1/2-horsepower electric motor. Some help is needed to extract the gear from the train. To achieve this, the agitator gear is positioned on the agitator shaft by means of a shaft pin. A spring that is attached to the agitator shaft exerts pressure, which keeps the gear from locking with the agitator shaft. In this position, the agitator oscillates with no resistance. A solenoid assembly that is mounted to the sector gear is designed so that the assembly trails from left to right as the sector gear oscillates.

A cam bar is mounted between the solenoid assembly and the agitator gear. The solenoid plunger is slotted so that the plunger rides the cam bar. A drive pin connects to the two ends of the cam bar by the slot in the plunger which passes through a two-level slot in the cam bar.

Figure 31 — Automatic Washer Gearcase Showing Sector Gear

Figure 32 — Automatic Washer Control Magnet Mounted On Gearcase

When the solenoid is energized by electrical current from the timer, the coil is pulled upward by magnetism. As the magnet assembly travels back and forth, the plunger is pulled up into the second level of the cam bar slot. This slot is located so that the traveling action, which is powered in part by the washer drive motor and not by the solenoid coil, pushes the cam bar forward. This action causes the agitator fork assembly to travel upward, which now engages with the pin in the agitator drive and, in turn, the agitator begins to oscillate.

## Clutch-Basket Drive And Brake Assembly

A combination clutch and brake assembly is the most common method used to enable the washer to spin. This assembly serves as a brake that holds the washer basket firmly in place while the washer is agitating. It also acts as the clutch or basket drive assembly that enables the washer

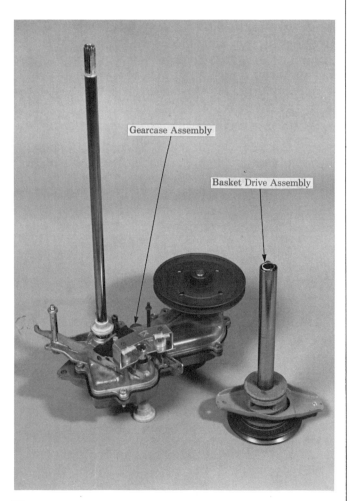

Gearcase Assembly

Basket Drive Assembly

Figure 33 — Basket Drive Assembly Used on Gearcase of Automatic Washer

to spin the clothes during the spin cycle. *Figure 33* shows a typical clutch and basket drive assembly used in automatic washers.

The agitator passes through a drive tube on which the washer basket is secured by a lock or a securing nut. As the drive tube rotates, the washer basket rotates also. The agitator shaft and the drive tube rotate independently during the agitation cycle, and as the washer is spinning they are mated together. The basket drive pulley is always turning whenever the drive motor is running. Located above the basket drive pulley is the basket drive disc that is attached permanently to the drive tube. This disc contains a special lining that is attached to the top of the basket drive pulley. The brake yoke is mounted above the clutch disc which is a stationary part. A tension spring pulls the brake yoke to a downward position, which exerts pressure against the clutch disc, thereby causing it to engage the clutch lining on the basket drive pulley.

Directly above the brake yoke is mounted a brake assembly that is pressed against the brake linings on the bottom of the tub and the top of the brake yoke. A solenoid assembly is mounted to the sector gear, which is a part of the gear train. When the solenoid is not engaged, the solenoid plunger pin rides in the lower level of the spin cam bar, which allows the thrust to hold the basket clutch.

When the solenoid is energized, the plunger is pulled upward by magnetic force of the solenoid coil, and the pin travels back and forth in the upper slot of the spin cam bar. This action pulls the spin cam bar backward from the basket clutch shaft, which allows the bar to slide downward toward the clutch lining.

A tension spring forces the brake yoke downward, pressing the basket drive clutch disc against the clutch lining on top of the basket drive pulley. The clutch lining is now engaged, and the basket drive disc and the washer basket begin to rotate and spin. As the basket gets up to full-speed momentum, from power transmitted from the washer drive motor, the basket continues to spin for the time span of the spin cycle.

When the solenoid is de-energized, end of cycle, or opening washer lid, the plunger drops into the lower slot of the spin cam bar. This action pushes the end of the bar into the basket clutch shaft and forces the brake yoke upward against the force of the tension spring to disengage the clutch from the clutch lining. As the brake yoke is forced upward, it closes the distance between the brake drums and the brake linings, which assures that the washer basket will come to a quick and smooth stop.

## Water Inlet Valve

Water enters the washer outer tub through the water inlet valve, which mixes the hot and cold water. Water inlet valves used on automatic washers are operated by solenoid coils that permit hot and cold water to enter the washer outer tub. There are two basic water inlet valves used in the manufacture of automatic washers: The single solenoid valve and the double solenoid valve.

The single-solenoid valve has only one function — mixing the incoming hot and cold water for the desired wash and rinse temperatures. This type of valve is most commonly used in low priced automatic washers.

The double-solenoid valve *(Figure 34)* offers three temperature selections: hot, warm, and cold. Energizing the cold-water solenoid allows cold water only to enter the washer outer tub. The hot-water solenoid allows only hot water. When both water inlet valve solenoids are energized, both hot and cold water enter the outer tub — which results in a warm wash. This type of valve is most commonly used by washer manufacturers on their middle and top-of-the-line model washers.

## Washer Water Pump

The water pump in an automatic washer operates continuously while the washer is in the ON position. The water pump recirculates wash water by syphoning it from the bottom of the outer tub and channeling it through an inlet at the side of the tub. On command, the water pump also

Figure 35 — Water Pump Used in the Automatic Washer

pumps out the wash water. It receives its power from the washer drive motor via a drive belt. Most automatic washers use a water pump that rotates the drain impeller in only one direction for both the recirculation and discharge of the wash water. The recirculation impeller and the drain impeller are located at opposite ends of the pump body. The impeller shaft drives both the recirculating and the drain impeller. *Figure 35* shows a typical water pump assembly.

## Filters

Several types of lint filters are used in different makes of automatic washers. All filters, regardless of type, are designed to strain and remove lint and other particles that are loosened from the clothing by the washer during the agitation cycle. On some models, the filter can be removed for cleaning and removing the lint

Figure 34 — Double-Solenoid Water Inlet Valve

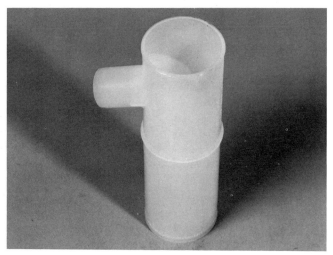

Figure 36 — Filter Trap Assembly Used in the Automatic Washer

*(Figure 28)*. On the other models (self-cleaning type), you must dispose of the filter and install a new one when a restriction forms in the filter and it becomes clogged. *Figure 27* in Chapter 1 shows a typical self-cleaning filter used in an automatic washer.

## Filter Traps

Some automatic washers use a filter trap assembly *(Figure 36)*. The purpose of this trap is to catch foreign objects and debris that could cause damage to the water pump or filter.

## WASHER ELECTRICAL SYSTEM

All automatic washers employ a 110-volt, A/C (alternating current) electrical power source. This power source is used not only to power the washer drive motor, but also the various electrical components such as timer, solenoids, valves, water level control, and switches. Listed below are components and their functions, which will help you in understanding, diagnosing, and repairing common electrical and mechanical failures.

## Timer

The automatic washer timer is an electro-mechanical (or solid-state) assembly that is the "brains" of the automatic washer. This assembly consists of a small electrical motor that drives a pinion gear meshed with a drive gear in the timer assembly. This assembly consists of the cam wheels that rotate slowly, causing the cam to make contact with switch levers which, in turn, "opens" and "closes" electrical circuits to perform the various functions of the automatic washer. *Figure 17* of Chapter 1, "General Information," shows a typical automatic washer timer assembly.

## Water Level Control

Most automatic washers use a pressure-activated switch to control the amount of water that is to enter the washer. This pressure-activated switch *(Figure 37)* consists of a plastic tube that is connected to an air dome assembly, which is attached to the washer outer tub. As the water level rises, air is trapped in the air dome and the connecting plastic tube. A diaphragm in the water level control senses the air pressure that builds up in the plastic tube, and causes electrical contacts to open the circuit to the water inlet valve, thereby cutting OFF the water supply to the washer.

Figure 37 — Water-Level Control Switch

## Lid Switch

The washer lid switch, which is a safety feature, is inserted electrically between the timer and the spin solenoid. The purpose of the lid switch is to shut OFF the washer if the lid is opened. Closing the lid would allow the washer to resume its normal spin operation. *Figure 38* shows a typical lid switch used in automatic washers.

## Solenoids

Solenoids are simply a means of converting electrical energy to mechanical energy. This energy opens and closes valves, activates mechanical components and operates switches. A solenoid consists of a coil of wire around which a magnetic field is developed when electrical current passes through the coil. This magnetic force is very powerful in its role of moving a

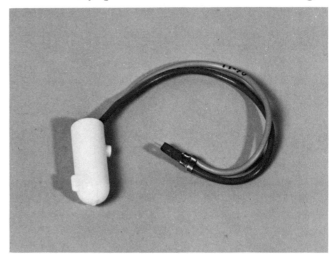

Figure 38 — Typical Lid Switch Used to Shut Off the Automatic Washer

Figure 39 — Drive Motor Used in the Automatic Washer

plunger inside a coil, etc. *Figure 15* of Chapter 1 "General Information" shows a typical solenoid.

## Washer Drive Motor

Most automatic washers use electric motors that are rated from 1/3 to 1/2 horsepower. The 1/2 horsepower capacitor-start motor is the most popular used in washer applications. The capacitor merely creates a higher starting torque in the motor. Washer drive motors are also of the one- and two-speed types. The most common is the two-speed type, which has added motor windings in the motor to provide the cycle selections — such as normal wash and gentle wash. These motors are thermally protected, which means that the motor circuit will open (the machine will not run), if overheating occurs. *Figure 39* shows a typical drive motor that is used in automatic washers.

## Electrical Connections

Most modern homes today are equipped with three-prong receptacles that accommodate the three-prong plug of the automatic washer. The third prong (bottom round) is connected to ground. To be sure a receptacle is grounded properly, insert one probe of a volt/ohmmeter in one hole of the outlet. Touch the other probe of the volt/ohmmeter to the receptacle cover plate screw. The volt/ohmmeter should show full-scale deflection on the 150-volt scale. *Figure 40* shows a receptacle being checked for a ground.

If you determine that the outlet is not grounded, you will have to install a ground wire to the nearest COLD-WATER PIPE. You can then use the three-prong plug with a two-prong outlet by the use of a special adapter *(Figure 41)*. Electrical codes from location-to-location will determine the use of these adapters.

## DIAGNOSING PROBLEMS

The most common washer problems and their most obvious failing sequence are covered in the following discussion. This discussion should aid in diagnosing and pinpointing exactly what is wrong with your automatic washer. Also listed are repair procedures to correspond to the failure symptom.

## WASHER WON'T PUMP OUT WATER

Specific failure symptoms include: 1) Washer has burning smell when running or labors excessively when running. 2) Wash water does not drain from the machine either at the end of the cycle or

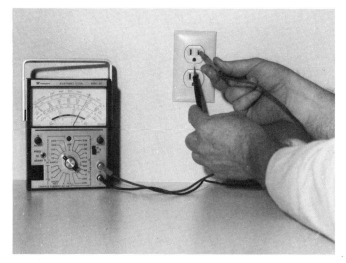

Figure 40 — Receptacle Being Checked for Ground with the Volt/Ohmmeter

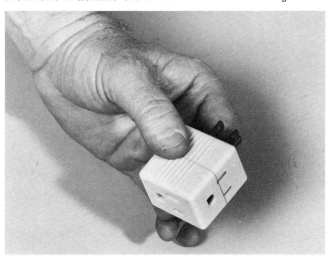

Figure 41 — Three Prong Special Adapter

when the washer enters pump out phase of the cycle. To find the cause of the problem, remove the washer drain hose from the drain standpipe and check for a kinked hose and start the washer. If water now pumps out of the washer, the problem is a kinked drain hose. If little or no water is being pumped out of the washer, the problem is either the washer self-cleaning filter, timer assembly, a filter trap restriction, or a non-operating water pump.

## Using Test Equipment

To avoid any incorrect readings when using the volt/ohmmeter, always "zero" the ohmmeter scale of the volt/ohmmeter before making any continuity checks on components. See the operating instructions.

When making continuity checks with the volt/ohmmeter, always unplug the washer power cord from receptacle because live voltage checks will damage the meter movement and ruin your volt/ohmmeter.

## Check Self-Cleaning Filter

Most modern-day washers use a filtering device in the water circulating system. These devices, which are called self-cleaning or manual filters, in some cases will become embedded with lint. This prevents the washer from pumping out the wash water. Tilt the washer against wall or lay washer on side and locate the filter *(Figure 42),* and check for lint in the filter to see if it has an obstruction.

To be certain that the problem is a defective filter, you can easily bypass the filter by

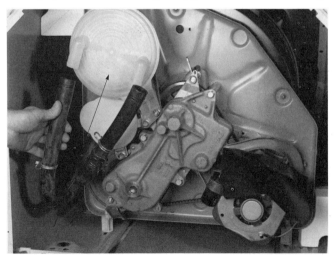

Figure 42 — Location of Self-Cleaning Lint Filter (Hoses Removed)

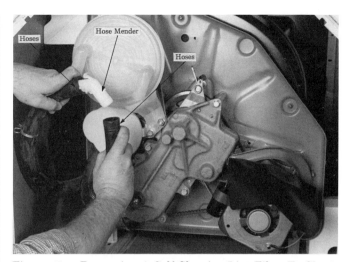

Figure 43 — Bypassing A Self-Cleaning Lint Filter To Check for an Obstruction

removing the two hoses (inlet and outlet) from the filter and joining the hoses using a hose mender, which can be purchased in most appliance and hardware stores *(Figure 43).* After bypassing the filter — if the washer now pumps out the water, the problem can be diagnosed as a defective filter. NOTE: A blocked filter can be prevented if certain types of materials are kept out of the washer. For example, fabrics that tend to shed and become stringy should never be washed in a washer that uses a self-cleaning lint filter. Shag rugs, particularly with rubber backing, will come apart and block a self-cleaning filter.

## Check Filter Trap Restriction

Some automatic washers are equipped with a filter trap or pin trap assembly *(Figure 36).* This unit is a protective device that traps objects such

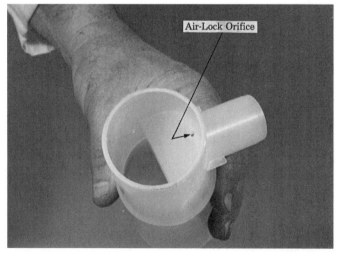

Figure 44A — Check the Automatic Washer Filter-Trap Assembly for a Restriction in the Air Lock Orifice

Figure 44B — Check Filter-Trap Assembly for a Restriction in the Air Lock Orifice

as hair pins, currency, jewelry, etc., that could damage the pump assembly. If the filter trap is totally blocked, the washer will not pump out. It is possible that the filter trap assembly air lock orifice *(Figure 44)* could be stopped up by debris or possibly soap filler. If a restriction has formed, it could prevent the washer from pumping out the water.

NOTE: Some automatic washers employ a combination filter trap and filter assembly. When a failure occurs on washers that use this type filter, the filter is replaced as a part replacement.

## Check Water Pump

When you have bypassed the filter and checked the filter trap, and still the wash water does not pump out, the next probable cause is the water pump. To check the pump, move the washer out from the wall, remove water, and tilt against the wall or lay on its side. Using hand tools, remove the bolts that secure the water pump to the washer gearcase and remove the pump to the washer gearcase and remove the pump *(Figure 45)*. Turn the pump pulley by hand in a clockwise direction. If the pulley turns freely with very little drag, the water pump should be in working order *(Figure 46)*. If the pump pulley appears to be frozen, this would be an indication that there is an obstruction in the water pump or the pump shaft is frozen. A replacement water pump would have to be installed to restore the washer to proper operating condition.

**Locate the washer tub outlet hose that is connected from the filter trap assembly to the water pump. By using hose clamp pliers, remove** the clamp from the water pump assembly. If you observe an obstruction such as underclothes or socks when removing outlet hose from water pump, you must remove the restriction to restore the washer to proper operating order. An obstruction in the water pump will cause the drain impeller to jam so that the water pump cannot pump the water out of the washer.

**If you find an obstruction, you must either repair or replace the water pump. Normally it is cheaper and faster to replace the water pump rather than try to repair it. Most water pumps are joined by a rubber gasket(s) and an assortment of screws and clips. In time, gaskets will swell and distort, particularly when a pump has been**

Figure 45 — Remove Bolts that Secure Water Pump to the Automatic Washer Gearcase

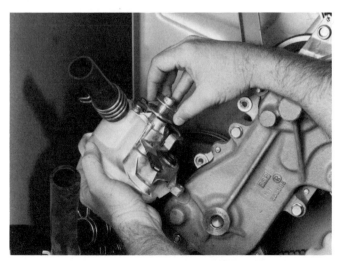

Figure 46 — Check Automatic Washer Water Pump for an Obstruction by Turning Pump Pulley by Hand

Figure 48 — Adjusting the Drive Belt on An Automatic Washer

tension by manually turning the drive belt in a clockwise or counterclockwise direction. If the belt has stretched or lost its tension, it could probably be tightened to restore the washer to

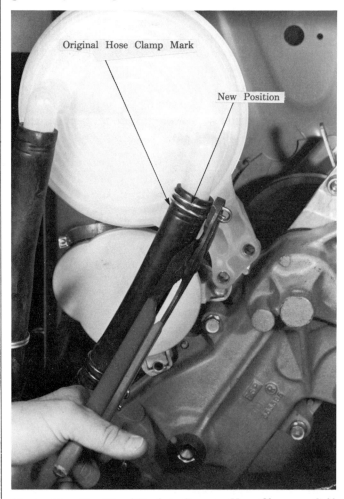

Figure 49 — Use Hand Tools to Remove Hose Clamp on Self-Cleaning Filter

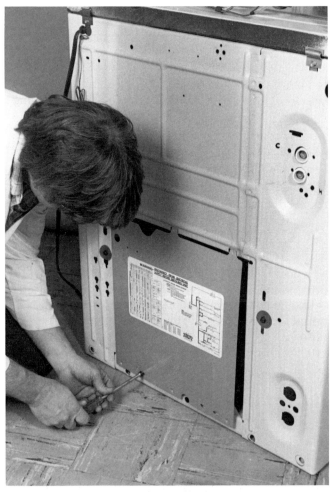

Figure 47 — Remove Access Back Panel of Automatic Washer

disassembled. When the pump is reassembled, there is a good chance that the pump would leak water.

## Check Washer Drive Belt

A final condition that could cause weak pump-out is a loose drive belt that doesn't rotate the water pump. A sure and quick check that involves no hand tools is to turn the timer knob to a cycle where there is a motor function such as spin or agitate. With the timer dial on spin cycle, the washer should begin to spin the clothes. If you hear the sound of the motor running, but the washer tub is not moving or attempting to spin the clothes, then it can be assumed that the washer drive belt is slipping on the drive motor pulley or the belt is broken.

To check the physical appearance of a washer drive belt, unplug the washer power cord and remove the back from washer *(Figure 47)*. Using a drop light or flashlight, check the drive belt

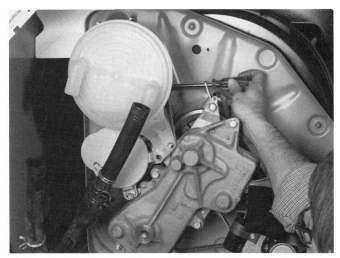

Figure 50 — Removing Outlet Hose Clamp On Self-Cleaning Filter

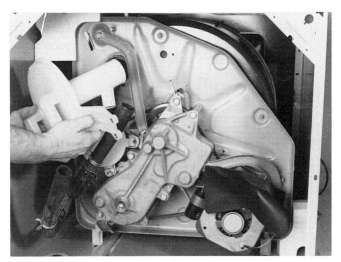

Figure 51 — Removing Self-Cleaning Filter from an Automatic Washer

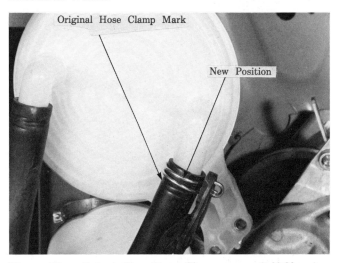

Original Hose Clamp Mark

New Position

Figure 52 — Reinstalling Hose Clamps on a Self-Cleaning Filter

proper operating order *(Figure 48)*. On the other hand, if the drive belt has burned spots in the webbing or if the belt is broken, the cause is usually a mechanical problem in the washer. A defective clutch assembly, broken teeth on gears of gearcase, and frozen shafts of water pumps can cause this problem. The problem would have to be repaired in order to restore the washer to proper operating order.

## REPAIR PROCEDURES

Unplug the washer power cord before servicing the automatic washer. Exercise care when moving the washer from its original position because the washer legs can damage the floor.

### To Replace Self-Cleaning Filter

To remove a faulty self-cleaning filter, remove water, tilt the washer against the wall or lay on its side. Then locate the filter. Using hand tools, remove the hose clamps that are attached to the defective filter *(Figure 49)*. Next, remove the tub outlet hose that is secured to the filter assembly *(Figure 50)*.

Using standard handtools, remove the nuts that secure the filter to the washer chassis and remove the filter from the washer *(Figure 51)*. Install the replacement part filter by mounting it in the same position as the defective filter that was removed. Follow the remounting and installation steps provided in the filter replacement part kit. If no installation steps are provided in the replacement part kit, reverse the above steps.

NOTE: When reinstalling the hose clamps on a replacement part filter, do not install the hose clamps in the original grooves or indentions in the hoses. Installing the hose clamps in their original position on the hoses could easily cause a water leak *(Figure 52)*.

### To Remove Filter Trap Assembly

To remove a restricted filter trap assembly, remove water, tilt the washer against the wall, or lay on its side. Locate the filter trap assembly and remove the hoses that are attached to the filter from the water pump. Remove the clamp that secures the tub outlet hose to the filter trap assembly and remove the filter trap *(Figure 53)*.

When replacing the filter trap assembly, install the replacement part filter trap assembly by mounting in the same position as the filter trap that was removed. Follow the remounting and installation steps that are provided by the

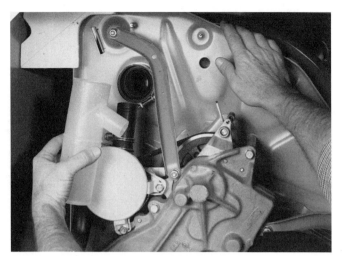

Figure 53 — Removing Filter-Trap Assembly from an Automatic Washer

Figure 54 — Removal of a Water Pump Assembly from an Automatic Washer

Figure 55 — First Step in Replacing Drive Belt is to Loosen Drive Motor Nut

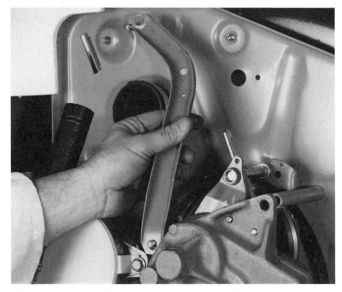

Figure 56 — Remove Gearcase Support Braces

manufacturer. If no installation steps are provided, reverse the above steps.

## To Replace Water Pump Assembly

Locate the washer water pump assembly and remove bolts — with standard hand tools — that secure the water pump to the gearcase. You may want to remove the filter assembly first to make it easier to remove the pump. Remove the tub hoses that are attached to the water pump by using hose clamp pliers, then remove water pump. *Figure 54* shows the washer water pump being removed from a typical automatic washer. (Filter assembly is also removed.)

Install the replacement water pump by mounting it in the same position as the faulty water pump that was removed. NOTE: When reinstalling the hose clamps on a replacement water pump, do not reinstall the hose clamps on hoses in the original position as removed as a leak could result *(Figure 52)*. Follow the installation steps that are provided in the replacement water pump kit. If no installation steps are provided, reverse the above steps.

## To Replace Washer Drive Belt

Using hand tools, remove the screws that secure the washer back panel *(Figure 47)*. Loosen the nut holding the motor bracket and slide the drive motor toward the gearcase *(Figure 55)*. This relieves belt tension, which will make replacement of the drive belt easier. Next, remove all the braces that are secured to the washer cabinet *(Figure 56)*. Remove the mounting bolts that attach the water pump to the gearcase *(Figure 57)*. Rotate the gearcase drive pulley until the spin cam bar is at its lowest point of travel.

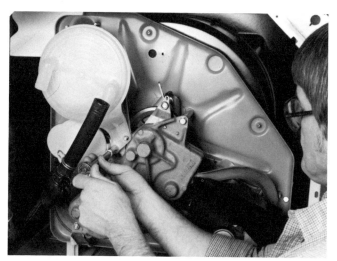

Figure 57 — Remove Mounting Bolts that Secure Water Pump to the Gearcase Assembly

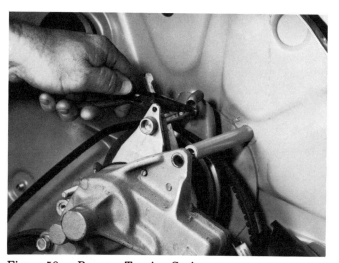

Figure 58 — Remove Tension Spring

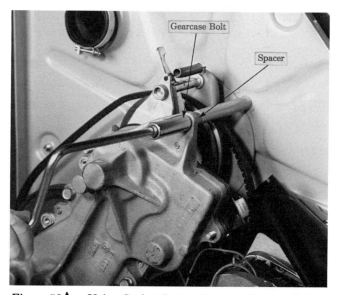

Figure 59**A** — Using Socket Drive, Remove Gearcase Mounting Bolt

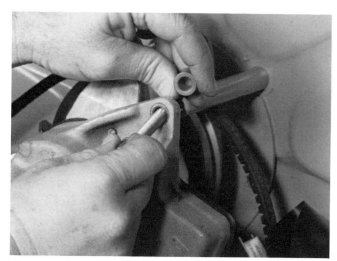

Figure 59B — Remove Gearcase Mounting Bolt with Spacer to Allow Gap for Removing Drive Belt

Remove the gearcase clutch spring *(Figure 58),* and with hand tools remove the gearcase mounting bolt that has a spacer attached *(Figure 59).* Use socket drive to loosen the remaining mounting bolts a minimum of six turns *(Figure 60).* Next, position replacement drive belt over gearcase *(Figure 61).* This enables the washer gearcase to drop down so that the part replacement drive belt can be slipped between the yoke and the basket drive pulley *(Figure 62).* If the faulty drive belt is still attached to the washer gearcase, note how the drive belt is routed around the gearcase drive pulley, water pump, and basket drive pulley. Install the replacement drive belt in the same sequence as the faulty drive belt that was removed. Now, reverse the disassembly steps to reassemble the washer. NOTE: After installation of the replacement drive belt, be sure the belt tension is not

Figure 60 — Loosening Other Gearcase Mounting Bolts To Replace Drive Belt

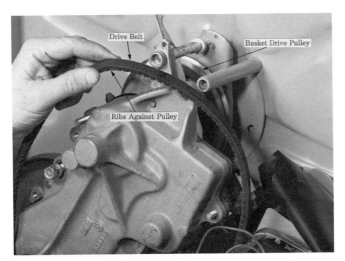

Figure 61 — Positioning of Replacement Drive Belt Over the Gearcase

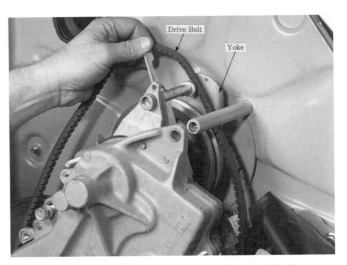

Figure 62 — Position the Replacement Drive Belt Between the Yoke and Basket Drive

too tight. There should be some slack in the drive belt to avoid noisy operation.

## WASHER LEAKS WATER ONTO FLOOR

Specific failure symptoms include: 1) Washer begins to agitate or spin and water spills or leaks onto the floor. 2) After the washer has completed its cycle, water appears on the laundry room floor. To locate the cause of the problem, first look behind the washer at the wash station stand pipe. Check the washer water inlet valve, which has two hoses (hot-cold) attached, for deterioration of the hoses *(Figure 63)*. If a hose has a leak, replace it.

### Using Test Equipment

To avoid any incorrect readings when using the volt/ohmmeter, always "zero" the ohmmeter scale of the volt/ohmmeter before making any continuity checks on components. See operating instructions.

When making continuity checks with the volt/ohmmeter, always unplug the washer power cord from receptacle because live voltage checks will damage the meter movement and ruin your volt/ohmmeter.

### Check Manual Lint Filter

Next, check the manual lint filter for restrictions that would cause water to leak on the floor *(Figure 28* in Chapter 1, "General Information"). Some automatic washers use a manual lint filter that is attached in the circulation system of the washer. On

these type filters, you must clean the lint from the screen each time the washer is used. If the filter is not cleaned frequently, the filter screen will clog with lint *(Figure 64)* and the wash water will go over the splash rail and onto the floor.

### Check Washer Drain Standpipe

If you notice a large amount of water at the front or back of the washer, check for a possible backed-up drain standpipe at the wash station. *Figure 26* in Chapter 1, "General Information," shows a typical wash station standpipe. As the washer switches to pump-out cycle, the wash water will slowly back up the drain standpipe and spill water onto the floor. If you diagnose the problem as a backed-up drain standpipe, call a qualified plumber. If you do elect to use commercial chemicals to unstop the drain, exercise extreme caution; these chemicals are very dangerous.

### Check Water Inlet Valve

If you find the washer drain standpipe to be in operating order, the next component to check is the washer water inlet valve. Recall from the earlier discussion that this is the twin solenoid valve that the washer inlet hoses attach to. You can easily check the water inlet valve for proper operation using the washer timer. Select a cycle where the washer fills with water and pull or push the timer knob to turn the machine ON. The washer should now fill with water. If you suddenly pull or push the timer control to turn the machine OFF, the water should stop entering the washer. If water continues to flow through the valve for four to six seconds, you can assume that the water inlet valve is faulty.

One final check should be made before replacing the valve. Open the washer top and check the water inlet valve to see if water is leaking through a hairline crack in the valve body (see Repair Procedures of this section). NOTE: In some cases, where the washer is exposed to seasonal temperatures of 36 degrees F or lower, and the washer is not protected, place a small wattage light bulb (15-40 watts) near the inlet valve. This precaution keeps the valve from freezing and reduces the possibility of damage such as hairline cracks or a broken valve body *(Figure 65)*.

A water inlet valve will sometimes leak, and water will collect in the basket if the washer sits idle for a long period of time. It may be only a drip, but surprisingly, it doesn't take long for the tub to fill with water and leak onto the floor. When you notice the sound of water dripping into the washer basket, it is a sure sign that the water inlet valve is defective and that must be replaced.

## Check Tub Seal

If you have determined that the water inlet valve is in working order, next check the outer tub post seal as the cause of the water leak. When diagnosing a water leak in a washer outer tub, you must first fill the tub with warm or hot water and run the washer for ten to fifteen minutes. When making this check, be patient because the washer may or may not leak the first time you check it. Look for water either at the front, left or right hand side or at back of the washer. Washers use a seal (or seals) around the tub center post. As hot or warm water enters the washer outer tub, the hot water softens the tub seal, which allows water to leak on the floor. If you diagnose a water leak as a faulty tub seal, you should call an authorized technician on the washer being serviced. NOTE: All water, whether it is fresh water or salt water, will always leave a water residue or stain on a component. If you notice stains, replace the suspected component because this will eventually cause a water leak and damage to the floor.

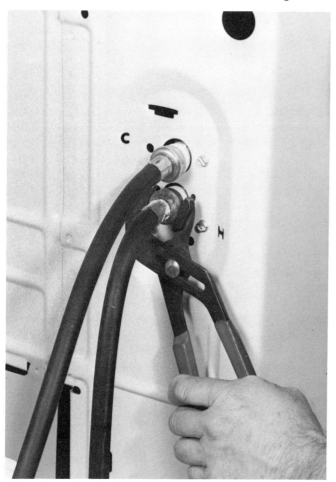

Figure 63 — Replacement of Deteriorated Fill Hose

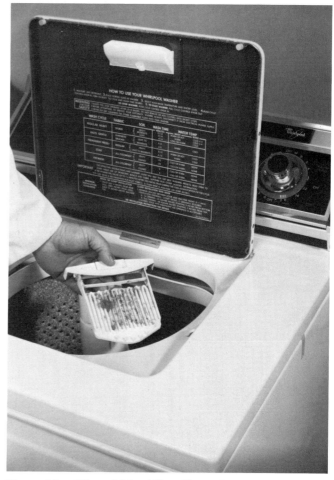

Figure 64 — Manual Lint Filter Clogged with Lint

Figure 65 — Use a Light Bulb Against Water Inlet Valve During Cold Weather if the Machine is Exposed to the Elements

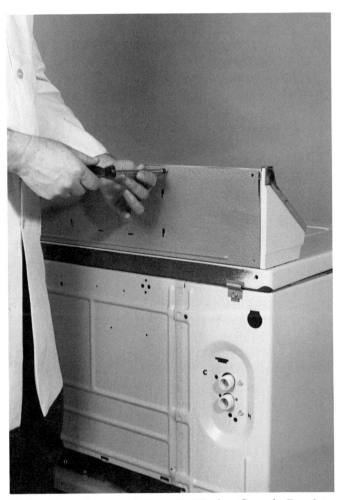

Figure 67 — Remove Automatic Washer Console Panel to Check Water Level Switch Pressure Hose Connection

## Check Washer Outer Tub

With the washer filled with either hot or cold water, remove the washer back panel *(Figure 47)* and look for traces of water around the washer base plate assembly and washer chassis *(Figure 66)*. If water is found in this area, the washer outer tub is possibly the source of the washer leaks.

A leaking outer tub can usually be repaired with a Fiberglas® repair kit. Only minor rust holes should be repaired using Fiberglas®. Follow the manufacturers instructions carefully when making repairs to the washer outer tub or other components using Fiberglas®. Tubs that require excessive repair should be replaced instead. To replace the outer tub requires removal of the washer basket first. (See Repair Procedures in this section.)

## Check Water Level Control

Another component that can cause water

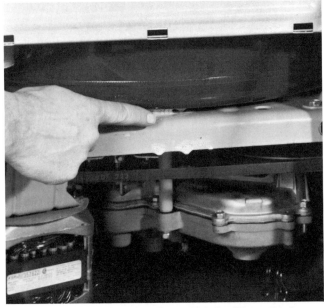

Figure 66 — Check Washer Outer Tub for Water Leaks

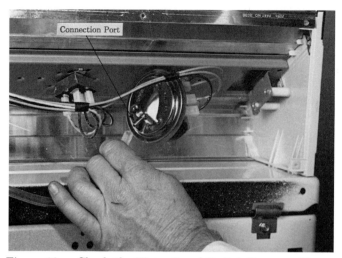

Figure 68 — Check the Water Level Switch Pressure Hose

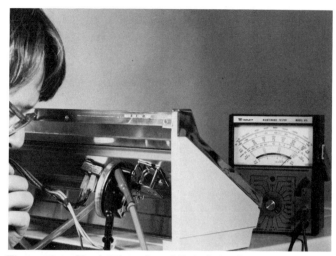

Figure 70 — Check Water Level Switch for Continuity Using the Volt/Ohmmeter

spillage is the water level control. Turn the washer timer to a cycle where the washer begins to fill. NOTE: Be certain that all water has been removed from the washer before running this test.

Set the load-size selector to the small setting on the washer console panel. As the washer is filling with water, check to see if the water cuts OFF at the proper level. If the water fails to cut OFF, the problem may be the water level control.

Before replacing the water level control, remove the washer console back panel *(Figure 67)* and check the pressure hose to the water level control. Sometimes the hose works loose and causes the washer to overfill or operate erratically. Therefore, all you need to do is reinstall the water level pressure hose *(Figure 68)*. to restore the washer to proper operating order.

If the hose does not correct the problem, a

simple check can be made to determine whether the water level control is defective. Unplug the washer power cord and remove the plastic pressure hose that is attached to the water level control *(Figure 68)*. Attach a small-diameter hose to the connection port on the water level control . Blow into the hose with the mouth and listen for a click in the switch *(Figure 69)*. If there is no click, the water level control diaphragm is defective internally and must be replaced.

A suspected water level control can also be checked with the volt/ohmmeter. Before making this check, you will notice that on most washers there will be three terminals on the water level switch. Mark and remove the wires noting the wiring sequence as the wires are removed. On the outside terminal of the switch, place one probe of the volt/ohmmeter and the remaining outside terminal place the other probe. Set the volt/ohmmeter to the RX-1 scale and with the hose attached, as described above, blow into the hose and you should see continuity (or 0 ohms) on the volt/ohmmeter *(Figure 70.)* This would indicate that the switch internally is good. If no continuity (meter swing) is noticed on the volt/ohmmeter, the switch is defective and will have to be replaced.

## REPAIR PROCEDURES

Unplug the washer power cord before servicing automatic washer. Exercise care when moving washer from its original position, or the washer legs might damage the floor.

### To Replace Water Inlet Valve

To remove a water inlet valve, you must first

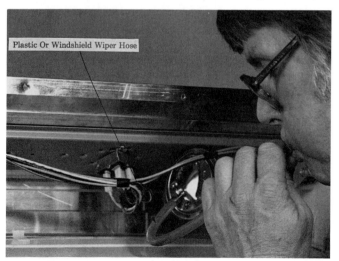

Figure 69 — Check the Diaphragm of the Water Level Switch by Blowing into the Port Connection

Figure 71 — Remove Screws from Water Inlet Valve From Outside the Washer

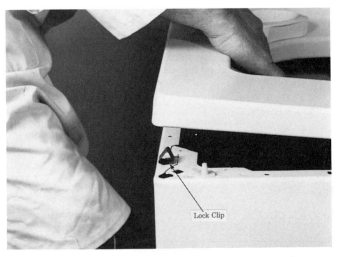

Figure 72 — Opening the Top of the Automatic Washer

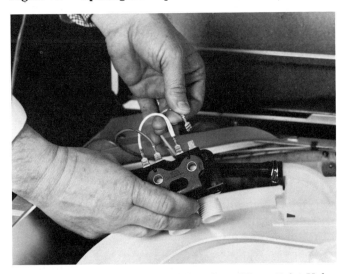

Figure 73 — Remove Harness Wires from Water Inlet Valve

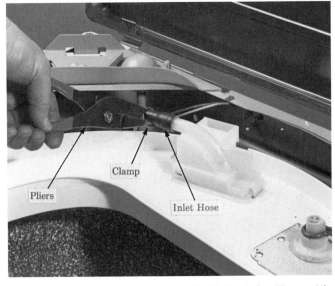

Figure 74 — Removal of Water Inlet Valve Inlet Hose with Hose Clamp Pliers

turn OFF the hot and cold water at the wash station. Remove the two fill hoses with water pump pliers *(Figure 63)*.

Remove two to four screws that secure the valve to the washer cabinet *(Figure 71)*. To remove the water inlet valve from the washer cabinet, open the washer top *(Figure 72)*.

Remove wires from the water inlet valve and note the sequence in which the wires are removed *(Figure 73)*. You will have to reinstall the removed wires to the replacement part valve in the same order as they were removed.

Using hose clamp pliers, remove two clamps that are attached to the inlet valve hose and tub ring *(Figure 74)* and remove the faulty water inlet valve. *Figure 75* shows an inlet valve being removed from an automatic washer.

NOTE: When reinstalling the hose clamps on the replacement water inlet valve, do not install the hose clamps in the original grooves from

Figure 75 — Removal of Water Inlet Valve From An Automatic Washer

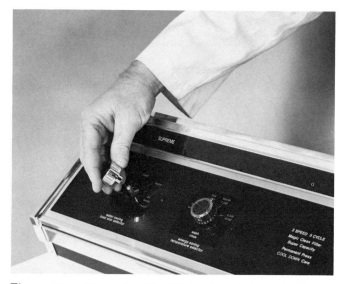

Figure 76 — Removing The Water Level Control Selector Knob From The Control Console.

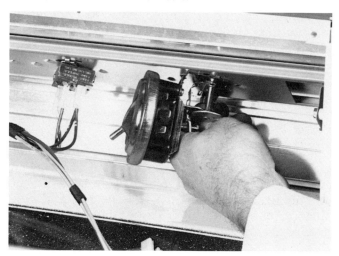

Figure 77 — Removing Screws and Pressure Hose from the Water Level Control Switch

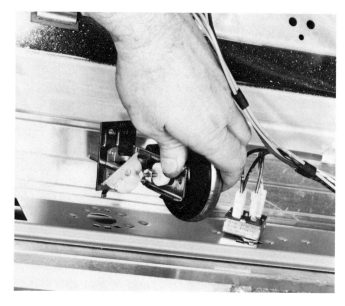

Figure 78 — Removal Of The Water Level Control From An Automatic Washer

which they were removed.

Install the replacement water inlet valve by mounting in the same position as the faulty inlet valve that was removed. Follow instructions that are provided in the replacement part kit. If no installation steps are provided, reverse the above steps.

## To Replace Water Level Control

To gain access to the water level control of the automatic washer, you must remove the screws to washer console back panel with hand tools (Figure 67). Remove the water level control selector knob from the control console of the washer by pulling it forward (Figure 76). Remove the screws and pressure hose that secures water level control to washer console (Figure 77).

Remove and discard the defective water level control. Figure 78 shows a typical water level control being removed from an automatic washer. NOTE: Upon examination of the faulty water level control, it may appear that the control can be adjusted for the proper water level setting. This control is calibrated by the manufacturer and under no circumstance should you tamper with the adjustment screw. Simply replace the unit.

Install the replacement water level control by mounting it in the same position as the defective unit that was removed. Follow the instructions that are provided in the replacement part water level control kit. If no installation steps are provided , reverse the above steps.

## To Remove Washer Basket

Raise the washer top *(Figure 72)* and lean top against a wall. Remove cap and agitator. Using a socket drive, remove the screw and nut that secures the snubber arm to the washer tub ring *(Figure 79)*. Using hose clamp pliers, remove the clamp that secures the hose to the water inlet valve *(Figure 74)*. Next, remove the tub ring clips *(Figure 80)* that secure the ring to the washer basket. Using a hammer and a socket extension, turn the basket lock nut in a counterclockwise direction and remove lock nut *(Figure 81)*. The washer basket can now be removed by pulling straight up over the agitator shaft.

Reinstall the washer basket by reversing the above steps. NOTE: When reinstalling the water inlet hose clamp to the tub ring, do not install the clamp on the inlet hose in the grooves set in the hose.

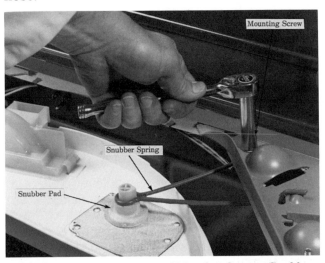

Figure 79 — Remove Screw and Nut that Secures Snubber to Tub Ring

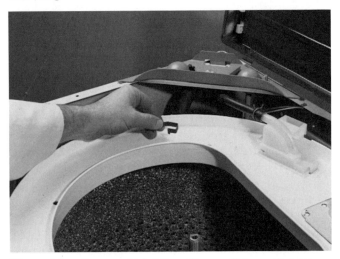

Figure 80 — Remove Tub Ring Clips to Release Tub Ring

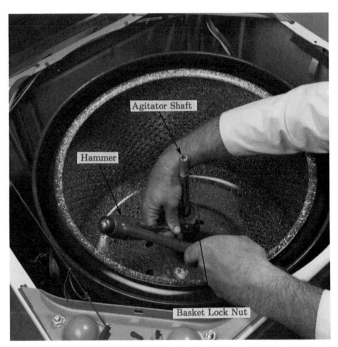

Figure 81 — Use Hammer and Socket to Remove Lock Nut and Allow Washer Basket to be Removed

## WASHER DOES NOT FILL WITH WATER

Specific failure symptoms include: 1) Little or no water enters the washer. 2) The washer does not complete the washing cycle. 3) The washer drive motor does not run during cycle. To find the cause of the problem, first check to be sure both the hot and cold water faucets are turned on at the wash station.

### Using Test Equipment

To avoid any incorrect readings when using the volt/ohmmeter, always "zero" the ohmmeter scale of the volt/ohmmeter before making any continuity checks on components. See operating instructions that came with the volt/ohmmeter.

When making continuity checks with the volt/ohmmeter, always unplug the washer power cord because live voltage checks will damage the meter movement.

### Check Water Inlet Valve Screens

Turn off the hot and cold water at the wash station. Remove the fill hoses from the washer water inlet valve, and place each hose in the washer basket. Then turn ON the hot and cold faucets, one at a time. There should be water flowing freely into the washer basket *(Figure 82)*.

If no water enters the washer basket, turn OFF hot and cold valves, remove the washer fill

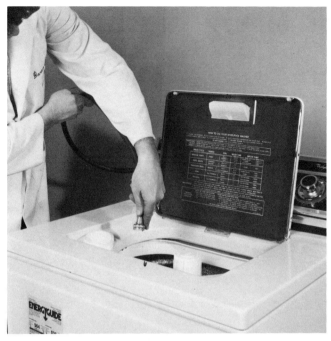

Figure 82 — Check Hot and Cold Water Source by Removing Fill Hose from the Machine and Turning on the Faucets One at a Time

hoses at the wash station and check for a restriction in the inlet valve screen(s). Remove the screens from the valve body with a small screwdriver and clean them in hot water, or replace the screens as necessary.

## Check Water Inlet Valve

Next, test for electrical power to the water inlet valve from the washer timer assembly. Using the volt/ohmmeter, set the meter on the 150-volt scale and attach the two test leads of the volt/ohmmeter to the two terminals of the water inlet valve solenoid coil to be checked. Turn the hot and cold valve OFF and plug the washer power cord into the washer receptacle at the wash station. With the test leads attached to the solenoid terminals, select a cycle on the washer timer dial to where the washer starts to fill with water. Push in or pull out the washer timer dial. You should get a voltage reading of 110-125 volts A/C on the volt/ohmmeter scale. If you do get a reading, this would indicate that electricity is available from the washer timer assembly to the washer water inlet valve. You would have to replace the water inlet valve to restore the washer to proper operating order. *Figure 83* shows a volt/ohmmeter being used to check for voltage to the water inlet valve.

If you get no voltage reading, you will have to check both the water temperature selector switch

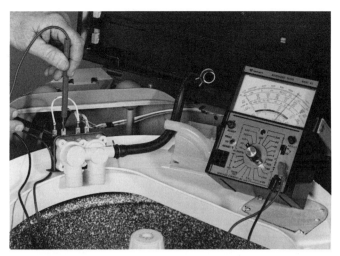

Figure 83 — Check for Voltage to the Water Inlet Valve with a Volt/Ohmmeter

and the timer assembly to determine which of the two is at fault.

## Check Water Temperature Selector Switch

You can easily check the water temperature selector switch with the volt/ohmmeter by measuring for continuity.

With the volt/ohmmeter set on the RX-1 scale, connect one probe from the volt/ohmmeter to another terminal of the selector switch. Attach the remaining probe to another terminal of the selector switch. Check the switch at each temperature setting for continuity *(Figure 84)*. For example, as you turn the selector switch knob to the hot/cold setting, the volt/ohmmeter should show full-scale deflection (0 ohms) and you should

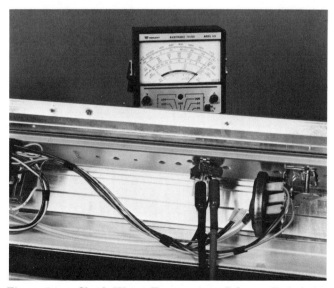

Figure 84 — Check Water Temperature Selector Switch for Continuity with the Volt/Ohmmeter

get the same reading for hot/warm, warm/cold, cold/cold, and warm/warm, if used. In any of these settings, if you do not get a continuity reading, you must replace the switch.

NOTE: Probes placed incorrectly on the switch terminals will result in inaccurate readings leading to a misdiagnosis of the switch.

## Check Timer Assembly

The washer timer switch contacts can be checked by using a volt/ohmmeter. Set the meter on the RX-1 scale and place one probe of the volt/ohmmeter on one terminal of the timer and the other probe of the volt/ohmmeter on the remaining switch terminal that supplies voltage to the selector switch. The timer switch contacts are not defective internally if continuity (0 ohms) is shown on the volt/ohmmeter *(Figure 85)*. If there is no continuity, the washer timer assembly is faulty and must be replaced.

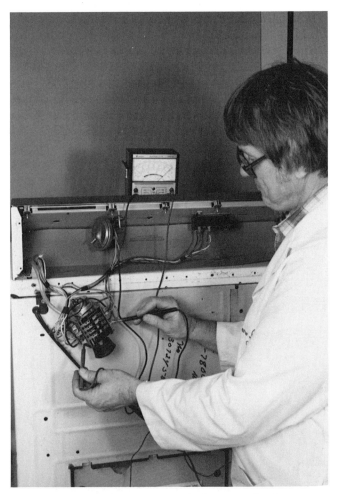

Figure 85 — Check Timer Switch Contacts for Continuity with a Volt/Ohmmeter

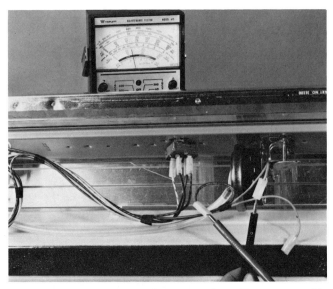

Figure 86 — Check for Broken Wires from Timer Assembly to Temperature Selector Switch

## Check For Burned Or Broken Wires

If the timer contact terminals show continuity and you find no voltage at the temperature selector switch, then you must make a continuity check for burned or broken wires from the timer assembly to the temperature selector switch. With the volt/ohmmeter dial set on the RX-1 scale, disconnect one wire from the terminal of the selector switch and attach a probe. Touch the remaining probe to the other end of same wire *(Figure 86)*. If the wire you are checking is good, continuity (0 ohms) will be measured on the volt/ohmmeter.

## REPAIR PROCEDURES

Unplug washer power cord before servicing the automatic washer. Exercise care when moving the washer from its original position, or the washer legs might damage the floor.

### To Replace Water Inlet Valve

See Page 37.

### To Replace Water Temperature Selector Switch

To remove the water temperature selector switch, use hand tools to remove the screws that secure the washer console back panel.

Remove the selector switch knob from the switch *(Figure 87)* by pulling forward. Remove the screws that secure the switch to the washer console and remove water temperature switch from the washer console *(Figure 88)*. Most knobs that are used on selector switches are made of a

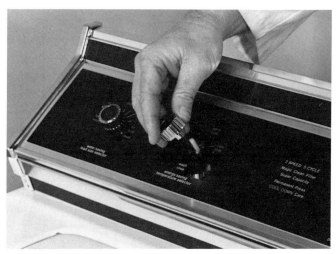

Figure 87 — Remove Water Temperature Selector Switch Selector Knob. Note Slotted Fit

plastic material and are push fit onto the switch shaft. However, this switch is a slotted shaft that serves as an alignment mark for the installer to use when a knob has to be replaced. If you do not align the knob onto the shaft of the replacement switch, the washer will not correctly fill the basket with water.

Remove the harness wires *(Figure 89)* that attach to the temperature selector switch terminals. Note the sequence in which they were removed, because they are to be reinstalled on the same terminals of the new temperature selector switch.

Install the replacement water temperature selector switch by mounting it in the same position as the defective part. Follow the instructions provided by the manufacturer or reverse the above steps.

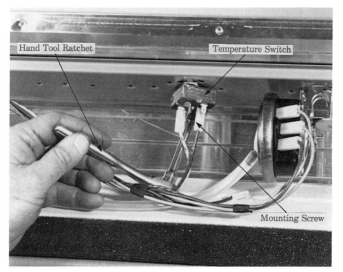

Figure 88 — Use Socket Tool to Remove Water Temperature Selector Switch from Control Console

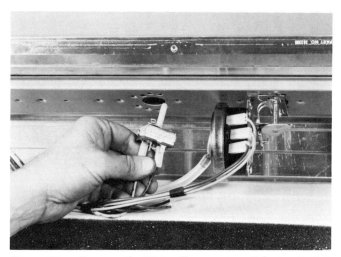

Figure 89 — Remove the Water Temperature Selector Switch Harness Wires

## To Replace Washer Timer Assembly

Remove screws that secure the back of the washer console. Remove the timer assembly knob by unscrewing it counterclockwise, and remove the timer dial from the washer console *(Figure 90)*. Remove the screws that secure the timer assembly to the washer console and remove timer assembly *(Figure 91)*. *Figure 92* shows the timer assembly connector block being removed from a late-style timer.

The homemaker may encounter two types of timers in automatic washers. The old-style timer assembly *(Figure 93)*, is the most complicated to install because the timer wires must be placed individually on a separate terminal connector on the timer. Depending on the application of the timer, there might be

Figure 90 — Unscrew Selector Knob of Timer Assembly by Rotating Counterclockwise

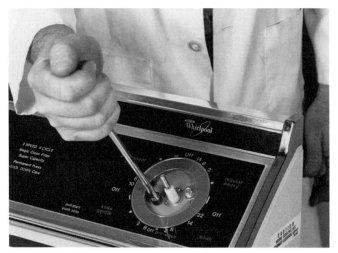

Figure 91 — Remove Screws that Secure Timer Assembly to the Control Console

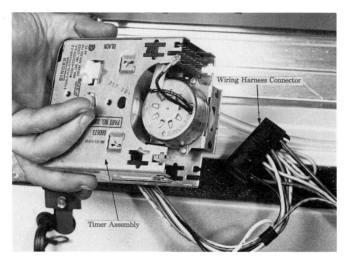

Figure 92 — Removal of Late-Style Timer Assembly from an Automatic Washer.

as many as eighteen wires that would have to be installed. When removing wires from an old-style timer, note the sequence in which they are removed so they can be reinstalled on the same terminals of the replacement timer. The newer timer is the least complicated to install as the timer wires are not individually installed on the timer terminals. Instead, a connector block is used that attaches the wiring harness to the timer connector.

Install the replacement timer assembly by mounting it in the same position as the defective timer that was removed. Follow the instructions and synchronization procedures, if any, that are provided in the replacement part timer assembly kit. If no installation steps are provided, reverse the above steps.

## WASHER STOPS IN CYCLE

Specific failure symptoms include: 1) The washer won't complete the wash or spin cycle. 2) The washer has a burning smell during the wash and spin cycle. 3) The washer leaves water in the tub at the end of the cycle.

Check the washer power cord for a possible loose connection at the wall plug receptacle.

Check to see if the wall receptacle is defective or has burned or oxidized contacts. If so, the repair should be made by a licensed electrician.

### Check Timer Assembly

Check the washer timer assembly for erratic operation. If the washer suddenly starts when the timer dial is pushed to the OFF position, the timer assembly ON-OFF contacts are defective internally and you will have to replace it. Also, with the

washer timer assembly pushed or pulled out to off, slowly turn the washer timer dial clockwise. If the washer starts a cycle, the timer assembly is faulty and you will have to replace it.

The timer switch contact that supplies voltage to the washer drive motor can easily be checked with the volt/ohmmeter. With the dial set on the RX-1 scale of the volt/ohmmeter, place one probe of the volt/ohmmeter on one terminal of the timer and the other probe on the terminal that supplies voltage (see wiring diagram) to the drive motor. With timer ON, there should be continuity (0 ohms resistance) on the volt/ohmmeter *(Figure 94)*. If switch continuity is not indicated, the washer timer assembly must be replaced to restore the washer to proper operating order.

### Check Washer Drive Motor

With the washer timer assembly pushed in or

Figure 93 — Typical Old-Style Timer Assembly for Automatic Washer

pulled out, to ON, slowly move the timer dial in a clockwise direction. If the washer runs, but after a period of five to fifteen seconds starts to smoke, very probably there is internal damage to the motor. To restore the washer to working order, you would have to replace the drive motor. NOTE: Washer drive motors have an internally-mounted overload protective device. These devices are sensitive to heat and will electrically break the circuit to the drive motor when the motor is subject to extreme high temperatures.

Before assuming that the washer drive motor is faulty, the motor can easily be checked using an electrical test cord. Unplug the washer power cord and remove the lower back panel from washer. Locate the drive motor on either the left-hand or right-hand side of the washer *(Figure 95)*. Next, tilt washer against wall or lay on its side and remove the motor wires *(Figure 96)* and note the sequence in which they were removed, because they are to be reinstalled on the same terminals as they were removed. Locate connector "W" (white) on connector block and

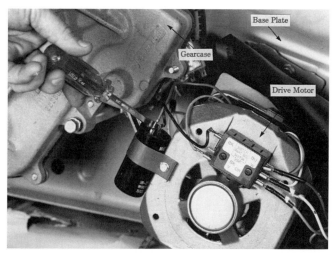

Figure 95 — Location of Drive Motor On a Typical Automatic Washer

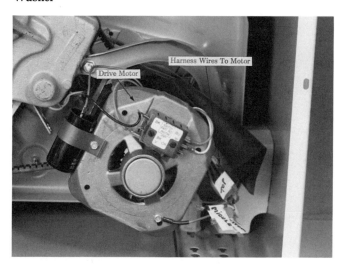

Figure 96 — Remove Harness Wires from the Drive Motor and Mark with Tape

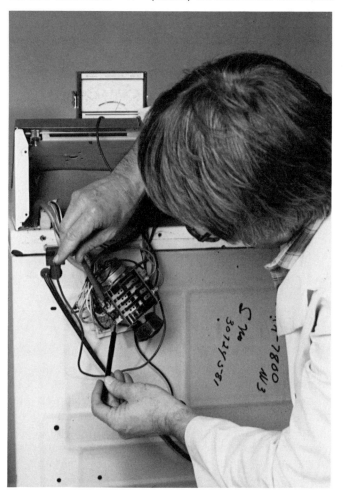

Figure 94 — Check Timer Assembly Contacts for Continuity with Volt/Ohmmeter

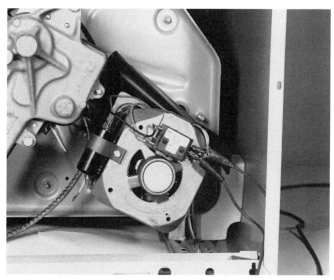

Figure 97 — Check Automatic Washer Drive Motor with 110-125V Electrical Test Cord.

attach one lead of the test cord. The remaining lead should be attached to another terminal of the terminal block. With the test cord plugged in a 110-volt receptacle, the drive motor should start to run *(Figure 97)*. Leave the motor running for a period of about ten minutes. Check the motor for excessive heat or smoke. If the drive motor runs with no problems, then it can be assumed that the drive motor is in good condition.

If, during the above check the drive motor has a humming sound while the motor tries to start, the drive motor start switch could possibly be the problem.

## Check Drive Motor Capacitor

Some large-capacity automatic washers require the use of a starting capacitor so that the drive motor may start smoothly. Checking a

Figure 98 — Check Automatic Washer Drive Motor Windings with a Volt/Ohmmeter

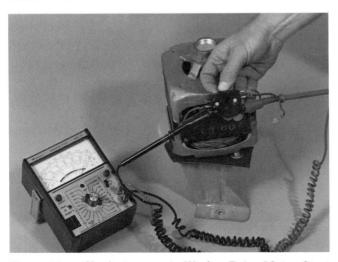

Figure 99 — Check Automatic Washer Drive Motor Start Switch for Continuity

motor start capacitor was described in Chapter 1, "General Information, Electrical Testing."

## Check Drive Motor Windings

The drive motor start and run windings can be checked with a volt/ohmmeter. Set the volt/ohmmeter on the RX-1 scale and place one probe on the white lead of the drive motor terminal block, the remaining probe is placed on the blue lead of the drive motor terminal block. The volt/ohmmeter should show continuity (or approximately four ohms resistance) if the motor winding is good *(Figure 98)*. No continuity would suggest an open or burned-out winding. If the drive motor has a humming sound when the motor tries to start, the start switch must be checked.

## Check Drive Motor Start Switch

The drive motor start switch is a component that supplies the required voltage to the drive motor start and run windings as the motor is started. As the motor reaches operating speed, the start switch drops out of the circuit. A continuity check will quickly determine if the start switch is OK. With the volt/ohmmeter set on the RX-1 scale, place one lead on the terminal that supplies line voltage to the drive motor (see wiring diagram). The remaining lead is connected to terminal 6 or 7. (See wiring diagram.) With the start button depressed, the volt/ohmmeter should show continuity (or 0 ohms), *(Figure 99)*. If the meter shows no deflection, or partial meter movement, this would be an indication that the start switch is faulty and it will have to be replaced.

## Check Washer Drive Belt

Refer to "Washer Won't Pump Out Water" Section (Page 27) of this service guide for checks to be made on the automatic washer drive belt.

## Check Wiring

If the above checks have not isolated the problem, visually check the washer console for burned electrical wires or terminals that could have worked loose. You should also check the washer console for loose connections in the wiring connector block. This check is to determine if any wires that connect to the timer have burned or jarred loose, causing a faulty connection.

You should make a final check of the electrical wiring harness that is attached to the washer drive motor connector terminals. Often during

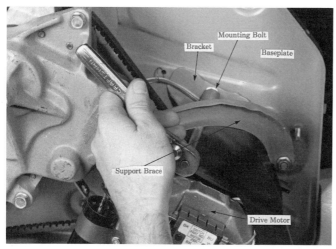

Figure 100A — Remove Automatic Washer Drive Motor Bolt from Baseplate

Figure 100B — Remove Automatic Washer Drive Motor Braces from Baseplate

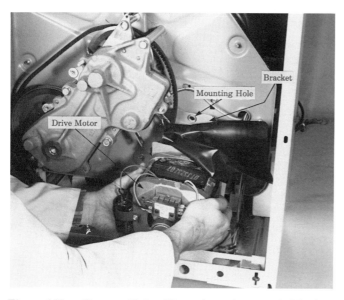

Figure 101 — Remove Drive Motor from Automatic Washer

washer operation, the vibration of the washer during agitation and spin cycles will cause wires to work loose. This condition will cause faulty electrical contact and, in some cases, the drive motor wires will become burned or broken.

## REPAIR PROCEDURES

Unplug the washer power cord before servicing the automatic washer. Exercise care when moving the washer from its original position, or the washer legs might damage the floor.

### To Replace Washer Timer Assembly

To replace the washer timer assembly, refer to "Washer Not Filling With Water" section of this service guide, Page 40.

### To Replace Washer Drive Motor

Move the washer out from the wash station and tilt against the wash station wall or lay washer on its side. Remove lower back panel and using standard hand tools, sockets or ratchet, remove the bolts and braces that secure the drive motor to the washer chassis *(Figure 100)*. Remove motor wires from the motor and remove the drive motor *(Figure 101)*. After removing the drive motor, remove the belt pulley from the shaft as the pulley is to be reinstalled on the replacement drive motor *(Figure 102)*. WARNING: The drive motor is extremely bulky and heavy. To avoid personal injury, handle the drive motor with care.

When removing the motor pulley from the defective drive motor, mark the position on the motor shaft for alignment of the motor pulley on

Figure 102 — Remove Drive Motor Belt Pulley for Use on Replacement Motor

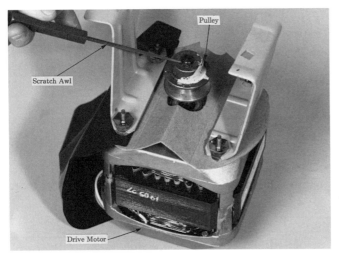

Figure 103 — Mark Drive Motor Shaft Before Removal of Belt Pulley

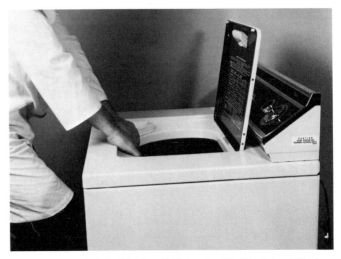

Figure 104 — With Washer Lid in the Up Position Washer Will Not Spin

the replacement drive motor *(Figure 103)*. The motor pulley must be aligned on the replacement part drive motor in the same position as it was on the faulty part. Improper alignment can cause premature wear of the washer drive belt.

Install the replacement part drive motor by mounting in the same position as the faulty drive motor that was removed. Follow closely the installation steps and instructions that are provided in the replacement drive motor kit.

NOTE: The wiring sequence of the replacement motor will vary from one motor manufacturer to another. Failure to wire the drive motor properly will result in no agitating or spinning, or erratic operation.

### To Replace Washer Drive Belt

To replace washer drive belt, refer to "Washer Won't Pump Out Water" section of this service guide, Page 27.

### WASHER DOES NOT SPIN IN CYCLE

Specific failure symptoms include: 1) Washer advances through the cycle but leaves water in the tub, or 2) The washer pumps all of the water out of the tub but clothes are wet at end of the cycle.

Check to be sure the washer lid is securely closed. Most automatic washers are designed to shut OFF if the washer lid is in the "up" position *(Figure 104)*. This is a safety feature designed to prevent injury if the lid is opened while the washer is running and spinning.

Check to make sure that the washer power

cord has not worked loose in the wall receptacle. A faulty connection could be the cause of washer failure.

### Using Test Equipment

To avoid incorrect readings when using the volt/ohmmeter, always "zero" the ohmmeter scale of the volt/ohmmeter before making continuity checks on components. See operating instructions that came with the volt/ohmmeter.

Before making continuity checks, always unplug the washer.

### Check Timer Assembly

Check to be sure the timer assembly dial is advancing as the washer is agitating. If the timer dial is sticking as it moves through the cycles, the problem is a faulty timer motor. There are some washer timer motors that can be disassembled,

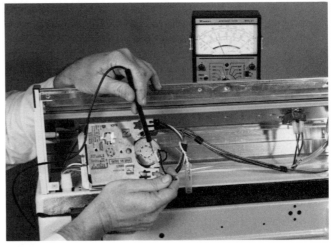

Figure 105 — Washer Timer Motor can be Checked with the Volt/Ohmmeter

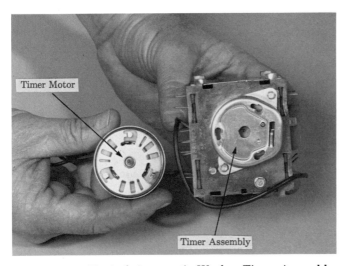

Figure 106 — Typical Automatic Washer Timer Assembly Motor Disassembled

lubricated, reassembled, and reused on the washer. Most timer motors fail due to lack of lubrication. You can lubricate the motor bearings with a solution of hi-temp oil such as sewing machine oil or light-weight motor oil. NOTE: Oils that have a silicone or detergent base should never be used in small motor bearings. Timer motors can be checked with the volt/ohmmeter and electrical test cord *(Figure 105)*.

With the dial set on the RX-1 scale, place one probe on one terminal of the timer and other probe on the terminal that supplies voltage (see wiring diagram) to the drive motor. With the timer ON the meter should read 0 ohms resistance if the motor windings are good. If no continuity is indicated on the volt/ohmmeter scale, then the timer motor is bad and should be replaced.

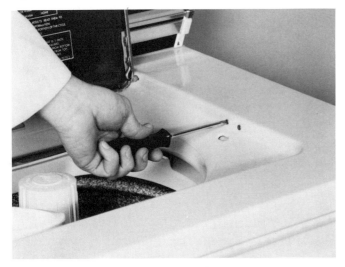

Figure 107 — Location of Lid Switch

Figure 106 shows a typical timer motor removed from the timer assembly.

## Check Washer Lid Switch

Raise the top of the washer and locate the lid switch *(Figure 107)*. This switch is a safety feature inserted between the timer assembly and the spin solenoid. It is designed to shut off the washer if the lid door is opened. When the lid door is closed, the washer will resume its normal spin operation.

There are two electrical tests you can use to check the washer lid switch: Voltage measurement and resistance.

Voltage — You can easily make this check by setting the volt/ohmmeter to the 150 A/C scale and measuring the voltage across the wires (two to three) from the timer assembly. When making a voltage check to the washer lid switch, set the dial on the timer assembly to a cycle that requires the washer to spin. The timer must be ON, of course.

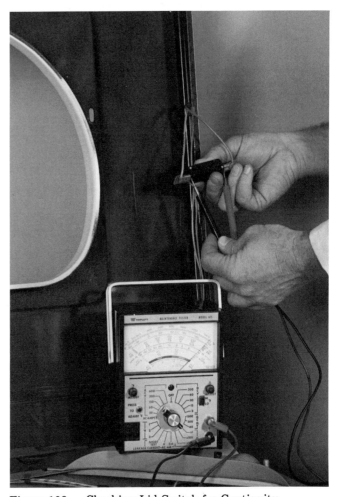

Figure 108 — Checking Lid Switch for Continuity

To make the voltage measurement, place one probe of the volt/ohmmeter on one terminal of the lid switch and the other probe to the remaining terminal. A reading of 110-125 volts should be indicated on the meter.

Resistance Check — To use the volt/ohmmeter to check for continuity of the washer lid switch, set the meter on the RX-1 scale. Place a probe on each terminal of the lid switch. With the volt/ohmmeter leads connected, depress the switch button until a click is heard. The meter should show a full-scale reading (or 0 ohms) *(Figure 108)*.

If the above test shows that voltage is available to the washer lid switch, then you know the washer timer assembly is functioning properly and that there are no burned or broken wires from the timer. If, however, there is no continuity when the switch is depressed, then the component must be replaced. If the washer does not spin in the cycle, even after replacing the switch, the problem is burned or broken wire(s) from the lid switch to the washer gearcase, faulty timer, or a faulty control magnet.

### Check Washer Control Magnet

If the washer is not spinning, the next check is of the washer control magnet. Washers use a control magnet, an electrical-mechanical component, to enable the gearcase to shift into the spin cycle. You can easily check the control magnet by using the volt/ohmmeter set on the RX-10 scale. With the volt/ohmmeter on RX-10 scale, connect the probes to both terminals of the control magnet. NOTE: When checking a suspected faulty control magnet, remove the wires from the washer wiring harness to avoid an inaccurate reading.

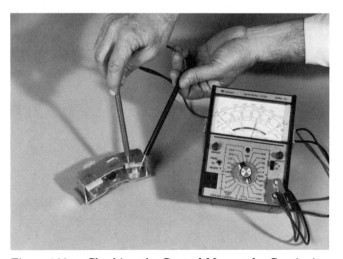

Figure 109 — Checking the Control Magnet for Continuity

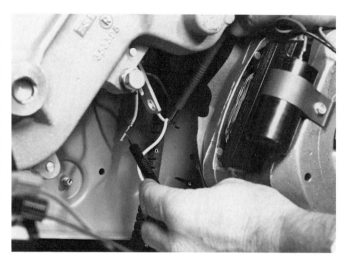

Figure 110 — Check for Voltage from the Automatic Washer Timer Assembly to the Control Magnet Using a Volt/Ohmmeter

With the volt/ohmmeter probes connected to the suspected control, a reading at least mid-scale or 100-180 ohms *(Figure 109)* should be indicated. If no meter deflection is registered, the control magnet is faulty and will have to be replaced.

To check for proper voltage to the control magnet, set the meter on the 150 A/C scale and place the probes on the wiring terminals of the control magnet. Set the timer dial to a spin cycle, and you should get a reading on the volt/ohmmeter of 110-125 volts *(Figure 110)*. A reading of 110-125 volts means electricity is available from the timer, through the lid switch, to the control magnet. Remember, in this check you are measuring voltage from the timer to the wires that connect to control magnet. The resistance check above is used to check the coils of the control magnet.

If voltage is available and the washer still does not spin in the cycle, the problem is probably in the washer gearcase or superstructure assemblies. A factory-trained technician should be called if you diagnose a malfunction in the gearcase.

### Check Washer Drive Motor

Refer to "Washer Stops In Cycle" section of this service guide for the checks to be made for the washer drive motor, Page 44.

### Check Washer Drive Belt

Refer to "Washer Won't Pump Out Water" section of this service guide for the checks to made for the washer drive belt, Page 27.

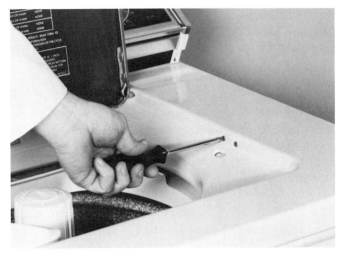

Figure 111 — Remove Screws that Secure Lid Switch to Top of Washer

## REPAIR PROCEDURES

Unplug the washer power cord from the washer receptacle before servicing washer. Exercise care when moving the washer from its original position, or the washer legs might damage the floor.

### To Replace Lid Switch

Locate lid switch and remove, with hand tools, the screws that secure the lid switch to the washer top (Figure 111). Remove the wiring harness wires from the terminals and remove the faulty lid switch. Figure 112 shows a typical lid switch being removed from an automatic washer.

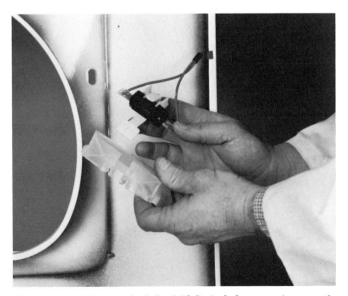

Figure 112 — Removal of the Lid Switch from an Automatic Washer

Install the replacement lid switch by mounting in the same position as the faulty lid switch. Follow closely the installation steps and instructions that are provided in the replacement lid switch kit. If no installation steps are provided, reverse the above steps.

### To Replace Washer Control Magnet

Remove screws that secure the washer back panel with hand tools (Figure 47). Locate the control magnet and remove the harness wires and screws that secure the control magnet to the washer gearcase. Next, remove the control magnet (Figure 113).

Install the new part control magnet by mounting in the same position as the faulty magnet that was removed. Follow instructions that are provided with the part. If no installation steps are provided, reverse the above steps.

### To Replace Washer Drive Motor

Refer to "Washer Stops In Cycle" section of this service guide for the replacement of the washer drive motor, Page 44.

### To Replace Washer Drive Belt

Refer to "Washer Won't Pump Out Water" section of this service guide for the replacement of the washer drive belt, Page 27.

## WASHER DOES NOT AGITATE IN CYCLE

Specific failure symptoms include: 1) Washer fills with water, and motor starts to run, but the

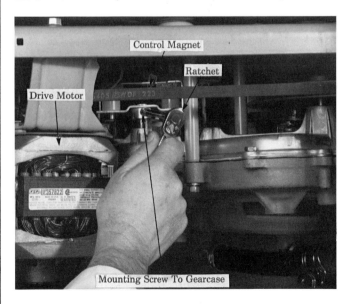

Figure 113 — Removal of Control Magnet

washer agitator does not turn in either a clockwise or counterclockwise direction, or 2) At end of cycle, clothes are gritty and soapy with water.

To find the cause of the problem, first check to make sure that the washer power cord has not worked loose in the wall socket.

Remove the back washer panel and check drive belt tension. If the belt is loose or broken, tighten it *(Figure 55)*. Set the washer cycle selector to the position where the machine begins to fill with water. Check to see if the washer begins to agitate, after the water cuts OFF. Washers will fill with water only when the timer selector dial has been set on a number, usually 2 through 14. If the timer dial is set on the number "2", for example, the washer would agitate in the cycle for two minutes before the washer drains and goes into spin.

If the washer fills with water, cuts off, but does not start to agitate, check the water level control.

## Check Water Level Control

To check the water level control, set the volt/ohmmeter on the RX-1 scale. Place one probe of the volt/ohmmeter on one terminal of the water level control, and place the other probe on the remaining terminal. With the plastic pressure tube removed and a substitute hose installed in its place, blow through the hose. The meter should show full-scale deflection (or 0 ohms). If no meter swing is evident, the water level control is faulty and will have to be replaced. For a further explanation, refer to "Washer Leaks Water Onto Floor" section of this service guide. *Figure 70* shows a water level control being checked with volt/ohmmeter.

## To Check Washer Timer Assembly

Refer to "Washer Does Not Spin In Cycle" section of this service guide for the checks to be made for the washer timer assembly, Page 48.

## Check Lid Switch

If the above volt/ohmmeter checks indicates that the timer assembly and the water level control are OK, check the wiring from the water level control and electrical components such as lid switch and control magnet. Some automatic washers use a lid switch as a safety feature in BOTH the agitation and spin cycles. On machines that use a lid switch in the agitation cycle, check the switch using a volt/ohmmeter

and the same procedures as previously described in the "Washer Does Not Spin In Cycle" section of this service guide, Page 48.

## Check Washer Control Magnet

As discussed earlier, the washer control magnet is an electrical component that is responsible for switching the machine to spin cycle. It also enables the washer to agitate in the wash cycle. Test the washer control magnet by using the volt/ohmmeter as described on Page 50, to determine if the component is the cause for the washer not agitating.

## Check Washer Agitator

Next, open the washer lid and look in the basket when it is fully loaded with clothes and the timer is ON. Check to see if there is any slipping of the agitator while the clothes are washing. Almost all washers use an agitator that is made of a plastic material which rests on an agitator shaft. In time these parts wear out, and the washer will not agitate.

Often, a washer that will not agitate has suffered a gearcase malfunction. If you determine that the gearcase box is faulty, call a factory-trained technician, or replace the machine if it is several years old.

## REPAIR PROCEDURES

Unplug the washer power cord from washer receptacle before servicing the washer. Exercise care when moving the washer from its original position, or the washer legs might damage the floor.

## To Replace Water Level Control

Remove the washer console back panel and remove the screws that secure panel. Remove the water level control selector knob from the front of the console by pulling it forward *(Figure 76)*. Remove the screws that secure the water level control to the washer console *(Figure 77)*. Remove the pressure hose from the water level control by pulling from the control connection port.

Remove and discard the faulty water level control *(Figure 78)*. Install the replacement water level control by mounting in the same position as the faulty water level control that was removed.

## To Replace Washer Timer Assembly

To replace the washer timer assembly, refer to "Washer Not Filling With Water" section of this service guide, Page 40.

## To Replace Lid Switch

Refer to "Washer Does Not Spin In Cycle" section of this service guide for the part replacement of the washer lid switch, Page 48.

## To Replace Washer Control Magnet

Refer to "Washer Does Not Spin In Cycle" section of this service guide for the part replacement of the washer control magnet, Page 48.

## Replace Washer Agitator

The washer agitator is easily accessible from the top of the washer. Normally, the washer agitator is splined onto the agitator shaft. Remove the agitator cap. Some washer agitator caps are removed by unscrewing the cap from the shaft in a counterclockwise direction. No tools are required *(Figure 114)*.

After the removal of the cap, remove the agitator by pulling in an upward direction *(Figure 115)*. In stubborn cases where the agitator is difficult to remove, you can loosen the agitator by applying penetrating oil to the shaft and tapping gently with a rubber hammer on all sides.

After removing the agitator from the washer, if you notice that the agitator shaft is eroded and

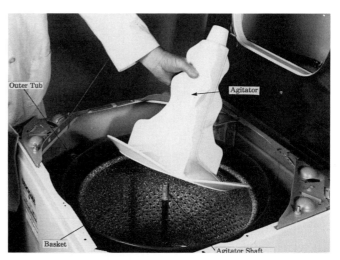

Figure 115 — Remove Agitator from Splined Shaft

worn out, you must replace the shaft in order for the washer to agitate in the wash cycle. This is not a task for the amateur, because it requires disassembly of the gearcase. Call a factory technician or replace the machine.

Install the replacement part agitator by mounting it onto the agitator shaft in the same position as the defective agitator that was removed. Follow the installation steps that are provided in the replacement part agitator kit.

## WASHER WON'T START IN CYCLE

Specific failure symptoms include: 1) When the washer is turned ON, nothing happens. 2) When the washer is turned ON you hear a faint "buzz."

To find the cause of this problem, first check to be sure that the washer is plugged in a working power source.

## Check Washer Receptacle

Make a line voltage check at the washer receptacle to determine if the problem is a faulty power receptacle or a problem within the washer. Make a voltage line check by setting the volt/ohmmeter on the 150 A/C scale and placing the probes in the holes of the wall receptacle. The meter should read 110-125 volts. *Figure 116* shows a line voltage check being made at the washer receptacle.

## Check Power Cord

If the above checks show no voltage at the power receptacle, the problem may be in the receptacle, house wiring, fuse, or circuit breaker(s). If voltage IS available at the power

Figure 114 — Typical Automatic Washer Agitator and Cap

Figure 116 — Line Voltage Check of Washer Receptacle

receptacle, but the machine still does not work, check the washer power cord. Remove the cord from the receptacle and set the volt/ohmmeter on the RX-1 scale. Place one probe on one prong of the power cord, and place the other probe on the other end of the washer power cord. (Check both wires.) If the cord has no burned or broken wires, the meter should show continuity (0 ohms) *(Figure 117)*. Perform the same procedure on the other side of the power cord. If there is a continuity on both prongs of the power cord, the cord is not faulty.

To Check Timer Assembly

With the washer plugged into a 110-125 volt receptacle, pull out or push in the timer knob with the washer ON. Turn the timer knob to various cycle selections and try to detect any buzzing sounds. If the washer does not start and you hear no noises in the timer assembly you will have to

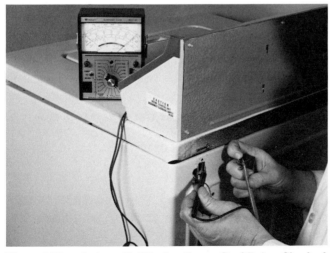

Figure 117 — Automatic Washer Power Cord Being Checked for Continuity with the Volt/Ohmmeter

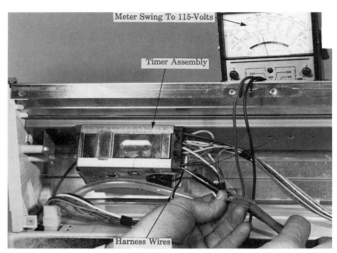

Figure 118 — Checking for Line Voltage to the Timer Assembly

determine if line voltage is available to the timer and if the contact switches in the timer assembly are in good condition.

Set the volt/ohmmeter on the 150-V A/C scale. Place one probe on the hot wire (usually black) that leads from the power cord to the BK terminal on the timer. Place the other probe of the volt/ohmmeter on the W, or neutral, terminal of the timer. With the washer ON, you should get a reading of 110-125 volts *(Figure 118)*. If you do get this reading, but the machine does not work, then replace the timer assembly. If line voltage is not available, you should isolate the problem to the electrical wires, washer power cord or wall receptacle.

The above checks are only examples. If available, you should use the wiring diagram of your automatic washer for the proper timer terminals when making line voltage checks.

Use the volt/ohmmeter to check the ON-OFF contact switch and timer function switches within the timer assembly. To check the timer ON-OFF contacts, set the volt/ohmmeter on the RX-1 scale and with timer side plate removed, the ON-OFF contacts are located as the timer knob is pulled out or pushed in. Place one probe of the volt/ohmmeter on one terminal of contacts and place the other probe of the volt/ohmmeter on the remaining terminal of the ON-OFF contacts. As the timer assembly knob is pulled out or pushed in, the scale on the volt/ohmmeter should show full-scale deflection (0 ohms), which would indicate that the contact switch (ON-OFF) is good. Thus, you could assume that the timer is not faulty. *Figure 85* shows washer timer contact switches being checked with volt/ohmmeter.

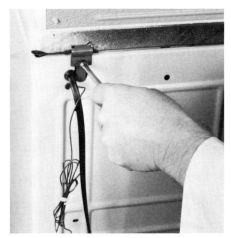

Figure 119 — Remove Screw that Secures Hinge to Washer Top

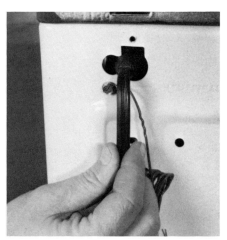

Figure 120 — Remove Washer Power Cord Grommet so Power Cord can be Removed

Figure 121 — Remove Power Cord From Automatic Washer

With timer ON, and in any cycle where the washer fills with water, listen for water trying to enter the washer tub. If you do not hear water entering, look behind the washer to see if the washer's hot/cold connections have been turned OFF accidentally. Washers are designed so that water must enter the washer tub and fill to a certain level (as selected on the load-size selector) before the washer will begin agitating.

With the timer knob turned ON and the washer hot/cold connections turned OFF, you should hear a small buzz or hum at the left or right side of the washer. If you do not hear this hum or buzz, you must make a wiring and component check from the timer assembly to the water inlet valve. Washer components that could cause the above problem such as water level, inlet valve and timer have previously been discussed in "Water Leaks Onto Floor" section of this service guide.

Remove the washer console back *(Figure 67)* and check to see that there are no loose or broken wires to the water level control and water temperature selector. Raise the washer top and locate the water inlet valve and determine if any wires may have been burned or loose or fallen off the water inlet valve. Automatic washers, during the agitation and spin cycles, produce an excessive amount of vibrations. These vibrations, in time, will cause wiring connections to become loose or dislodged from a component terminal, which can cause the above symptoms.

## REPAIR PROCEDURES

Unplug the washer power cord before servicing the automatic washer. Exercise care when moving the washer from its original position, or the washer legs might damage the floor.

### To Replace Washer Receptacle

It is recommended that a qualified electrician perform all electrical work in the replacement of a defective washer receptacle.

### To Replace Washer Power Cord

First, you must unplug the washer power cord from the wall receptacle. Next, raise the washer top *(Figure 72)* and remove the wiring harness wires that are connected to the washer power cord. Use hand tools to remove the screws that secure the hinge to the washer top *(Figure 119)*. Remove the top hinge and slide the washer power cord grommett away from its original position *(Figure 120)*. The washer power cord can now be removed from the washer cabinet *(Figure 121)*.

Install the replacement power cord by mounting in the same position as the faulty power cord that was removed.

### To Replace Timer Assembly

To replace the washer timer assembly, refer to "Washer Not Filling With Water" section of this service guide, Page 40.

# 3

# The Automatic Dryer

We felt that the simplest way to organize this guide to help the do-it-yourselfer solve a problem was to organize it in the following manner:

- Show pictures of and describe all the components that make up the system.
- List specific problems (or failures) and suggest other symptoms that will help isolate the problem.
- List components to be checked in the proper sequence to isolate the faulty part.
- Give step-by-step replacement instructions for removing and replacing the faulty part.

The automatic dryer is probably the least complicated of the major appliances, and probably the easiest to repair.

When an electric dryer doesn't heat, there is a high probability the heating element is open, or one of several thermostats is cutting off the circuit.

When it doesn't tumble, the motor is dead or the drive belt is broken. Sometimes the timer fails.

If the unit starts squeaking or banging, don't give up on it just because it is old. Usually, it can be returned to good operation by replacing an idler pulley and a drive belt.

From the pictures and descriptions in this chapter, it appears that our demonstration machine must be totally disassembled to work on it. And, yes, it is a major teardown, but it takes only a few minutes to do if you follow the repair instructions.

The heating element and most thermostats can be tested, removed, and replaced by removing only the back of the machine.

The drive motor and drive belt (that circles the dryer tub) require disassembly and removal from the front of the machine.

CAUTION: MOST ELECTRIC DRYERS USE 220 VOLTS TO POWER THE HEATING ELEMENT. ALWAYS DISCONNECT THE DRYER POWER CORD FROM THE WALL RECEPTACLE BEFORE DOING ANY TESTS OR REPAIR WORK.

56

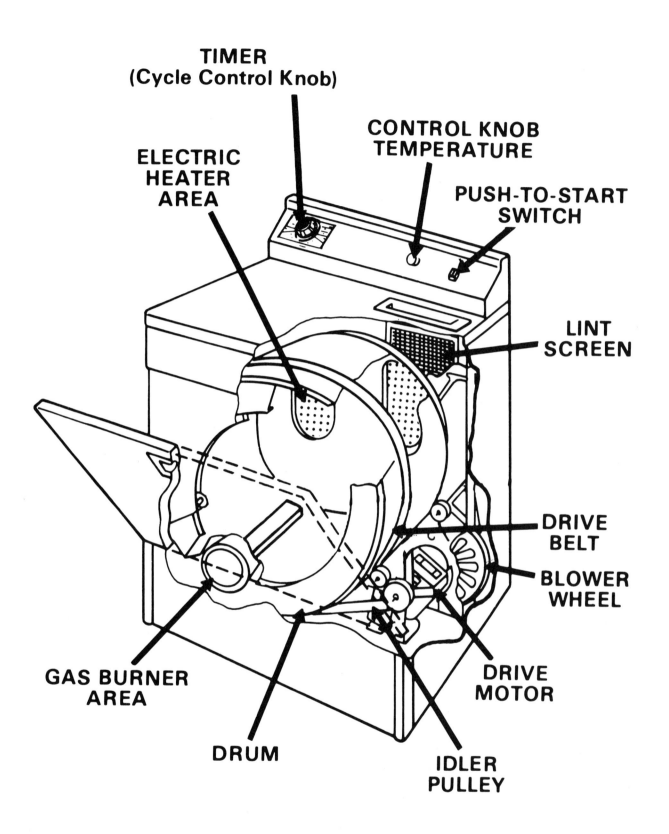

**TIMER**
(Cycle Control Knob)

**CONTROL KNOB TEMPERATURE**

**PUSH-TO-START SWITCH**

**ELECTRIC HEATER AREA**

**LINT SCREEN**

**DRIVE BELT**

**BLOWER WHEEL**

**GAS BURNER AREA**

**DRIVE MOTOR**

**DRUM**

**IDLER PULLEY**

## THE CLOTHES DRYER-HOW IT WORKS

Clothes dryers accomplish their task by furnishing heated air in large volumes to the interior of a rotating drum where the clothes are tumbled and tossed while being exposed to the passing air. For the clothes dryer to work, the machine needs a source of heat, tumbling capability, large volumes of fresh air, and the ability to remove large amounts of moisture-laden air from the interior of the dryer cabinet.

Air that is drawn from inside the house enters the dryer cabinet through vents that are in front and back of the dryer. A blower system then forces the air through ducting where the air is heated and then funnelled into the rotating drum of the dryer. Air circulates throughout the drum and eventually passes through the tumbling clothes. Air in the interior drum eventually is saturated with moisture from the clothes. The dryer blower system then forces the moisture-laden air out of the dryer through a vent located outside the dryer cabinet.

## GAS DRYERS

The gas dryer differs from the electric dryer only by the energy source used to heat the air. A gas dryer is more complicated than an electric dryer because of the pilot flame, and the ON-and-OFF cycling of the gas flow to the main burner. Components of a typical gas dryer are described below.

## Dryer Power Cord

The gas dryer power cord is a three-pronged type in which the third prong represents cabinet ground. Most appliance manufacturers include in

Figure 122 — Typical Drive Motor for Gas Dryer

Figure 123 — Timer Assembly Used in a Gas Dryer

the dryer installation kit a ground wire or harness for attaching to the nearest ground, such as a cold-water pipe. Wiring codes differ from location to location as to whether adapters for wall outlets or receptacles may be used with the alternate ground wire.

## Motor

Gas dryer drive motors are usually rated from 1/4 to 1/3 horsepower. Gas dryers require only household electricity, which is 110-125 volts for dryer operation. The dryer drive motor is a double-shaft type. One end has a pulley that attaches to a drive belt to rotate the dryer drum. The other end attaches to the blower wheel *(Figure 122)*.

## Timer

The timer assembly consists of a small motor that drives a pinion gear that meshes with a drive gear. The timer assembly contains cam wheels that raise and lower switch levers, which in turn open and close circuits to the drive motor and heating component *(Figure 123)*.

## Thermocouple

When a gas dryer pilot burner is lighted, the metal in the thermocouple bulb creates a current. This current is measured in milliamps. This current is strong enough to open a plunger, which is made of a lightweight material. You must, however, press a button (usually red) to hold open the plunger against the resistance of a spring until the thermocouple warms up (approximately 15-30 seconds). The current generated by the thermocouple is then sufficient to hold open the gas solenoid in order for the main burner to

Figure 124 — Thermocouple Used in Gas Dryer Burner Assembly.

come on. *Figure 124* shows a typical gas dryer thermocouple.

### Glow Coil Ignitor

Some gas dryers use a glow coil as an igniter. *(Figure 125)*. A 24-volt transformer supplies current to another small transformer, which causes the glow coil to heat up. Electrical current causes heat from the wire of the glow coil to ignite gas coming from the pilot burner. Once the gas is ignited, the gas flame heats a bi-metal strip which causes current to be broken or cut OFF to the glow coil.

### Gas Pressure Regulator

These devices regulate the "escape" pressure of the gas entering the dryer. Adjustments on this component are set at the factory. If an

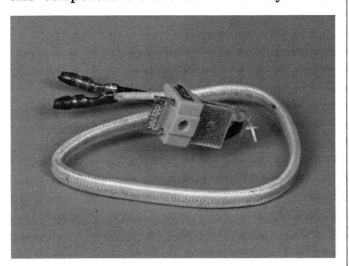

Figure 125 — Glow Coil Ignitor Used in a Gas Dryer Burner Assembly

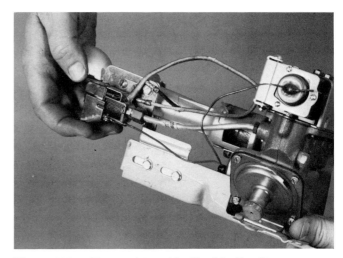

Figure 126 — Burner Assembly Used in Gas Dryer

adjustment is necessary, you should call a qualified technician.

### Main Burner Gas Valve Assembly

This valve assembly is probably the most important component of the gas burner assembly. The valve assembly controls the flow of gas to the main burner from the gas supply line *(Figure 126)*.

### Cycling Thermostats

Cycling thermostats *(Figure 127)* are bi-metal devices or thermo-discs that are designed to cut the main burner OFF when a pre-determined temperature has been attained in the dryer drum. There is no adjustment of the temperature response of these thermostats.

### Adjustable Thermostat

Some gas dryers use an adjustable thermostat *(Figure 128)* that does not use a bi-metal disc

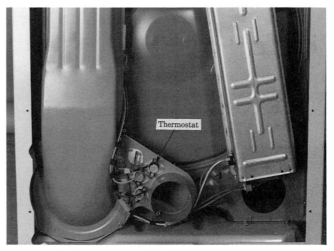

Figure 127 — Cycling Thermostats Used in a Gas Dryer

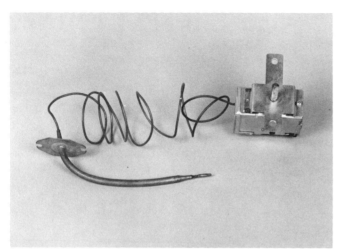

Figure 128 — Adjustable Thermostat Used in Gas Dryer

to open the circuit to the burner when a certain temperature has been attained. Instead, the adjustable thermostat uses a feeler bulb containing a mercury charge to sense the temperature of the discharge air.

### High-Limit Thermostat

This thermostat interrupts electrical power to the gas burner valve if the temperature of the burner housing exceeds a critical temperature *(Figure 129)*. In some models, the high-limit thermostat also shuts OFF electrical power to the dryer drive motor. You must restart the dryer after the drive motor cools to normal temperature. This thermostat is a safety feature that prevents dryers from overheating.

### ELECTRIC DRYERS

The electric dryer differs from gas models mainly in design of the heating element. The

Figure 129 — High-Limit Thermostat Used in Gas Dryers

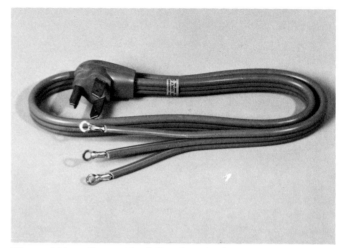

Figure 130 — Power Cord Used with Electric Dryer

electric dryer requires a three-wire 220-to 240-volt power source to operate. The two incoming lines to the dryer terminal block each represent 110-125 volts of power. Electricians refer to these as line one, L1, and line two, L2. L1 connected to the neutral wire is the power source required to run the drive motor. It requires only 110-125 volts. However, the electric dryer requires 220-240 volts of power across the line to drive the heating element. Components of a typical electric dryer are described below.

### Dryer Cord

Electric dryers use a heavy-duty, three-wire cord that is usually designed to operate in unison with a minimum 30-amp circuit breaker. A ground wire usually is not required in the installation of an electric dryer. *Figure 130* shows a typical electric dryer cord.

### Drive Motor

Electric dryer motors are usually rated from 1/4 to 1/3 horsepower, and require only household current (110-125 volts) *(Figure 122)*. The dryer motor is a double-shaft type. One end contains a pulley that attaches to a drive belt to rotate the drum. The other end of the motor attaches to the blower wheel *(Figure 131)*.

### Dryer Timer

The electric dryer normally uses the same type timer assembly that was previously described in the "Gas Dryer" section Page 58.

### Cycling Thermostats

The electric dryer normally uses the two types of thermostats that have been previously described in the "Gas Dryer" section *(Figures 127, 128)*.

## High-Limit Thermostat

The electric dryer normally uses the same type of high-limit thermostat previously described in the "Gas Dryer" section *(Figure 129)*.

## Heating Element

A coiled wire heating element is the heat source used to dry clothes in the electric dryer. This element is designed to operate on 220-240 volts of power. *Figure 132* shows a typical heating element used in electric dryers.

## Door Switch

Most electric dryers use a door switch designed to shut OFF both the heat and the dryer drive motor when the door is opened *(Figure 133)*. When the door is closed, the dryer will resume normal operation. Most late model dryers require a "push-to-start" switch to be activated before normal operation resumes.

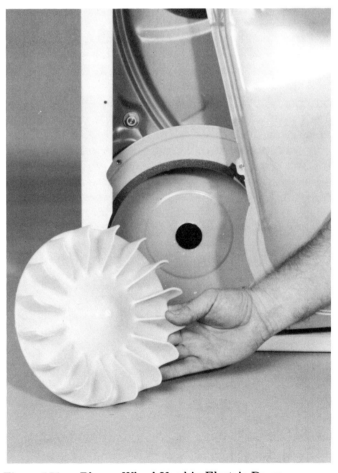

Figure 131 — Blower Wheel Used in Electric Dryer

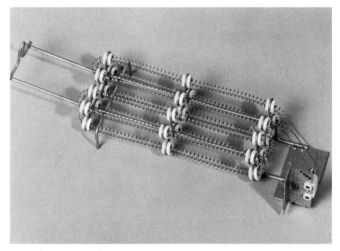

Figure 132 — Heating Element Used in Electric Dryer

## Dryer Vent Kit

The dryer vent kit is an auxiliary component designed to exhaust moisture-laden air to the outside. Without this device, the dryer would overheat the laundry room and would spread lint throughout the utility room or garage.

## DIAGNOSING PROBLEMS

The most common problems of dryers, and their symptoms are listed in the following discussion. Identifying symptoms and looking for faults should help in diagnosing and pinpointing exactly what is wrong with your clothes dryer. Also listed are repair procedures to correct the failure.

## DRYER DOES NOT HEAT

Specific failure symptoms include: 1) Clothes are not dry at end of cycle. 2) The dryer timer assembly is not advancing in the cycle properly.

Figure 133 — Door Switch Used in the Electric Dryer

61

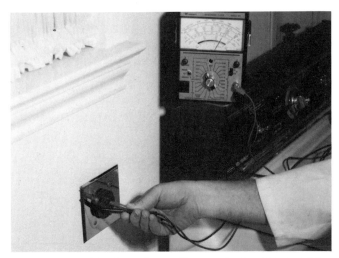

Figure 134 — Checking Dryer Receptacle for 220-240 Line Voltage

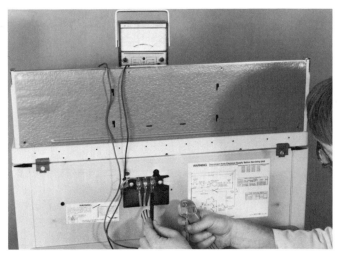

Figure 135 — Check Dryer Power Cord for Continuity with the Volt/Ohmmeter

To find the cause of the problem, first move the dryer out from the wall and remove the vent hose. With the dryer running, place your hand on the dryer exhaust duct to determine if there is any hot air being discharged. If the air is cold, you will have to make a line voltage check at the dryer receptacle to determine whether full 220-to-240-volt power is available.

## Using Test Equipment

To avoid any incorrect readings when using the volt/ohmmeter, always "zero" the ohmmeter before making continuity checks on components. See operating instructions that came with volt/ohmmeter.

Before making continuity checks with the volt/ohmmeter, always unplug the dryer power cord. Live voltage checks will damage the meter movement.

## Check Receptacle

To determine if electrical power is available at the dryer receptacle, first unplug the dryer power cord. Set the volt/ohmmeter on the 250-to 500-volt scale. Place one probe in one slot of the receptacle, and place the other probe in the remaining slot of the receptacle. If correct line voltage is available, a reading of 220-240 volts will be indicated. *Figure 134* shows a dryer receptacle being checked for voltage.

The gas dryer does not operate on 220-240 volts of electricity. For gas dryers, perform the same check as above except set the volt/ohmmeter on the 150-volt scale. If line voltage is available at the receptacle you will show a reading of 110-125 volts.

If no line voltage is indicated at the dryer receptacle, check the plug itself, house wiring, or the dryer circuit breaker as a cause of the problem. If you determine the dryer receptacle, electrical wiring, or circuit breaker to be faulty, call a licensed electrician to fix the problem.

## Check Dryer Cord

If you did get line voltage but the machine still doesn't work, check the dryer power cord. First, unplug the dryer from the wall receptacle. Set the volt/ohmmeter on the RX-1 scale. Place one probe of the volt/ohmmeter on one prong of the dryer cord, and place the other probe of the volt/ohmmeter on the other end of the power cord. If one side of the cord has no burned or broken wires within the cord, the volt/ohmmeter should show a continuity reading of 0 ohms resistance, or full-meter swing. Perform the same procedure as just described on the other side of the dryer cord and, again, the volt/ohmmeter should show a continuity reading of 0 ohms resistance. If you read continuity on both prongs of the dryer cord, the cord is not defective. No reading on the volt/ohmmeter means the cord is defective and must be replaced. *Figure 135* shows a dryer cord being checked with the volt/-ohmmeter.

The power cord on a gas dryer can be checked using the same procedure as discussed above.

## Check Timer Assembly

Check the dryer timer assembly as a possible cause of no heat. To check the dryer timer, unplug the dryer power cord and set the volt/ohmmeter on the RX-1 scale. Place one probe of the volt/ohmmeter on the heat terminal (see wiring diagram) of the dryer timer, and place the other probe to another terminal of the timer (see wiring diagram). As you turn the timer knob, the volt/ohmmeter should indicate continuity (which would mean the dryer contact points are closing). If the volt/ohmmeter does not indicate continuity or meter swing as you turn the timer knob, the contacts that supply voltage to electrical components within the dryer are faulty. You will have to replace the dryer timer to restore the dryer to proper operating order. *Figure 136* shows a dryer timer being checked.

NOTE: To locate the contacts that supply voltage to electrical components such as the heating element, you might have to refer to the wiring diagram of the dryer being serviced.

To check the timer assembly of a gas dryer, use the same procedures that were used to check the electric dryer timer.

## Check Selector Switch

Next, check the dryer selector switch as a possible cause of the dryer not heating. Set the volt/ohmmeter to the RX-1 scale. Place one probe on one switch terminal, and place the other probe on another terminal of the switch. With the selector switch knob turned to the heat selection corresponding to the terminals chosen, the volt/ohmmeter should indicate continuity or full-scale deflection. Repeat this terminal sequence for each setting on the selector switch. If you show no continuity at any switch setting, you will have to replace the selector switch to restore the dryer to proper operating order. *Figure 137* shows a temperature selector switch being checked with

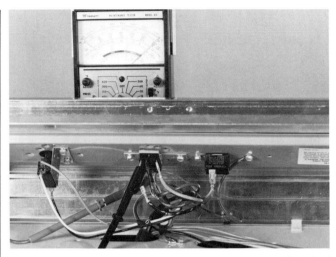

Figure 137 — Temperature Selector Switch Being Checked For Continuity

volt/ohmmeter.

NOTE: When making this check, also check the wiring from the switch to the timer assembly. Loose or broken wires in this area will cause the dryer to fail.

To check the selector switch on a gas dryer, use the same procedures that were used to check the electric dryer as described above.

## Check Heating Element (Electric Dryer)

When there is no heat, an obvious cause is the dryer heating element. To check the element, move the dryer out from the wall and remove the back panel of the dryer (see Repair Procedures). Locate the element and set the volt/ohmmeter on the RX-1 scale. Disconnect one lead from element and then place one probe of the volt/ohmmeter on one terminal of the

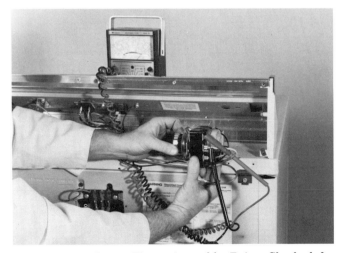

Figure 136 — Dryer Timer Assembly Being Checked for Continuity

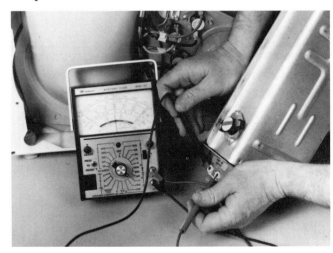

Figure 138 — Check the Dryer Heating Element for Continuity

63

element. Place the other probe of the volt/ohmmeter on the remaining terminal of the element. A continuity reading of the volt/ohmmeter of approximately 2-5 ohms is normal. *Figure 138* shows a heating element being checked with volt/ohmmeter. If there is no continuity reading, the heating element is defective (open) and should be replaced.

### Check Electrical Wiring

If the heating element tests OK, you should next check all the electrical wiring from the dryer timer assembly, thermostats, and drive motor. Electrical wiring in a dryer becomes brittle and burned because of the excessive heat. To locate defects in the wiring, use a volt/ohmmeter to make continuity checks on wires that you suspect are faulty.

### Check Wiring Harness (Gas Dryers)

The problem of no heat in the gas dryer is much the same as the electric dryer, except that instead of checking for a possible defective heating element, you must check the gas ignition circuit. A sure and simple test is check voltage to the gas burner wiring harness *(Figure 139)*. Set the volt/ohmmeter on the 150 A/C scale. Disconnect the electrical harness to the burner and place the probes of the volt/ohmmeter into the prongs of the harness. Close the dryer door, plug the dryer into a 110-to-125-volt A/C receptacle, and turn the dryer timer knob to a heat selection on the timer. If the meter indicates a reading of 110-125 volts, then power is available to the burner assembly. With proper voltage, the burner should operate normally. If it does not, it should be replaced or repaired.

If the meter check shows no voltage available to the burner wiring harness, the problem is not in the burner assembly. You will have to make further checks to the dryer wiring harness timer assembly and door switch to determine why the dryer does not heat.

### Check Thermocouple Assembly (Gas Dryer)

There are two sources of ignition that are used to ignite the gas main burner. The first is the thermocouple. As the dryer is turned ON and burner lever depressed, the power bulb of the thermocouple generates electricity (current) in sufficient quantities to eventually ignite the main gas burner. In time, this device will become defective and when it does, the dryer will not heat. You may temporarily relight the pilot and the dryer may dry a few loads of clothes, but it is a sure bet that the problem will return. When it does, you have no choice but to replace the thermocouple assembly.

To diagnose a faulty thermocouple assembly, a device known as a milli-volt meter is used to test the part. If you are in doubt as to whether the part is faulty, you should call a qualified technician for the dryer being serviced. *Figure 124* shows a typical thermocouple used in gas dryers.

### Check Electrical Ignitor (Gas Dryers)

The second source of ignition for the gas dryer is the gas burner electrical ignitor *(Figure 140)*. This device serves the same function as the gas flame ignitor and differs only in the fact that it uses a glow coil ignitor, *(Figure 125)* to ignite the main gas burner. A faulty glow coil is, for the

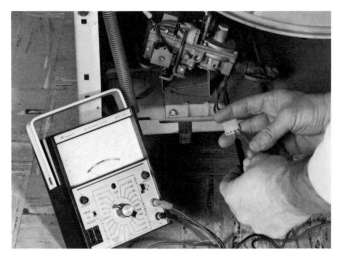

Figure 139 — Checking for Voltage to the Gas Dryer Wiring Harness with the Volt/Ohmmeter

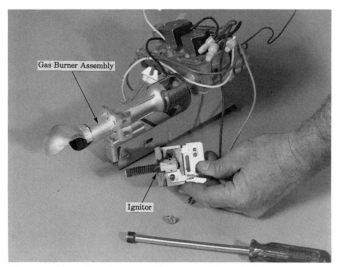

Figure 140 — Gas Burner Using an Electrical Ignitor

64

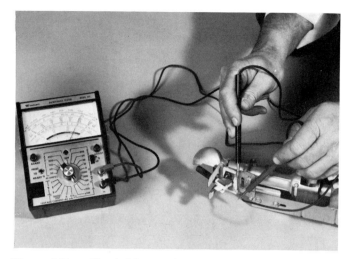

Figure 141 — Check Electrical Ignitor with Volt/Ohmmeter

most part, easier to diagnose than a faulty thermocouple. To check these devices, turn the gas supply to the burner valve to the OFF position and unplug the dryer power cord. Next, set the volt/ohmmeter on the RX-1 scale. Place a probe of the volt/ohmmeter on one terminal of the ignitor and place the other probe on the remaining terminal of the ignitor. The meter should show a continuity reading of approximately 20 ohms resistance on the scale *(Figure 141)*. No continuity reading on the volt/ohmmeter scale means you will have to replace the electrical ignitor.

*Figure 142* shows a faulty electrical ignitor used on a gas burner assembly being checked with the volt/ohmmeter. Note that there is no movement on the scale of the volt/ohmmeter.

## Check Coil Assembly (Gas Dryers)

A defective solenoid coil can cause the dryer

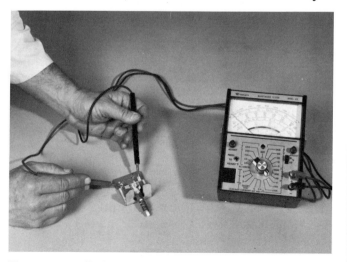

Figure 142 — Defective Electrical Ignitor Shows No Swing of the Meter (No Continuity)

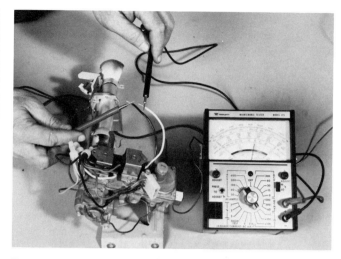

Figure 143 — Solenoid Coil Being Checked for Continuity With the Volt/Ohmmeter Mid-Scale Reading

not to heat. A defective solenoid will interrupt the flow of gas to the main burner valve, which will result in the dryer not heating. A check for a defective coil can easily be made with the volt/ohmmeter *(Figure 143)*. Set the volt/ohmmeter on the RX-1 scale. Place one probe of the volt/ohmmeter on one terminal of the solenoid coil. Place the other probe on the remaining terminal of the solenoid coil. You should show a continuity reading on the volt/ohmmeter scale of approximately mid scale. If you show no continuity reading, the solenoid coil is defective and you will have to replace it in order to restore the dryer to proper operating order.

## Check Drive Motor Centrifugal Switch

All dryers, whether they are electric or gas, use a motor switch that is referred to as the centrifugal switch. This switch is a safety device that will cause the dryer to stop heating and the drive motor to stop when the door is opened. The switch is also designed to complete a circuit to the heating element after the drive motor is running at full speed.

To test the switch, set the volt/ohmmeter on the 150-volt A/C scale. Place one probe on one terminal, usually red or blue, of the centrifugal switch, and place the other probe on the remaining terminal of the switch. With the drive motor running, a voltage reading on the volt/ohmmeter of 110-125 volts is normal. If you get no voltage reading, the centrifugal switch is faulty and must be replaced. In some cases, the complete drive motor would have to be replaced. If voltage is indicated on the volt/ohmmeter, then you must move on to the heating element and thermostats

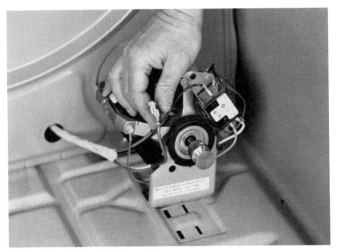

Figure 144 — Bypassing the Centrifugal Switch on an Electric Dryer.

to determine why the dryer does not heat.

When making the above check for a gas dryer, use the same procedures.

The drive motor can be checked without the volt/ohmmeter by bypassing the centrifugal switch *(Figure 144)*. Tie the motor switch wires (usually red) together with electrical tape. With the dryer power cord plugged in, check the heater element to see if it is heating. If so, you will have to replace the centrifugal switch or the drive motor to restore the dryer to operating order. NOTE: Bypassing the motor switch is for temporary checks only. Reinstall the wires in their original positions after all checks are completed.

## Check Cycling Thermostats

Next, check the dryer cycling thermostats as the possible cause for no heat in the dryer. The types of thermostats most commonly used in dryers (gas or electric), are the bi-metal fixed *(Figure 127)* and adjustable *(Figure 128)* thermostats. Their primary function is to break the circuit to the gas main burner or the heating element when a certain temperature has been attained in the dryer drum. You can easily check these thermostats by removing one lead from the suspected thermostat. Set the volt/ohmmeter on the RX-1 scale. Place one probe of the volt/ohmmeter on each terminal of the thermostat. You should see a continuity reading on the volt/ohmmeter scale of approximately 0 ohms, or full-meter deflection *(Figure 145)*. If the thermostat does not show continuity, replace the defective thermostat to restore the dryer to proper operating order.

You can also bypass the thermostat by tying

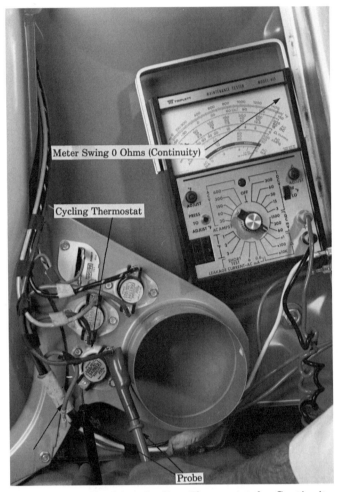

Figure 145 — Checking Cycling Thermostat for Continuity with the Volt/Ohmmeter

the terminal leads together to see if the dryer begins to heat *(Figure 146)*. If the element heats, this would indicate a faulty thermostat. NOTE: Under no circumstance should you operate the dryer for more than a few minutes when you bypass a thermostat.

Use the same procedures to check the cycling thermostats of a gas dryer.

## Check High-Limit Thermostat

Next, check the dryer high temperature, or high-limit thermostat, as the possible cause for no heat in the dryer. All dryers, whether electric or gas, use a high-limit thermostat in the heater box. This thermostat is a safety device used to break the circuit (by shutting OFF the heat source) if the dryer thermostat fails, or if other electrical or mechanical failures causes extreme high temperatures in the dryer.

To check the dryer high-limit thermostat, unplug the dryer power cord from the 220-to

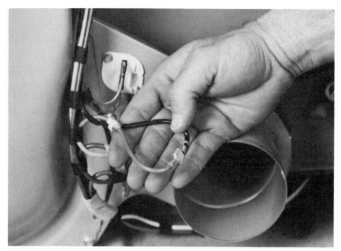

Figure 146 — Bypassing the Dryer Cycling Thermostat

240-volt receptacle. Set the volt/ohmmeter on the RX-1 scale. Place one probe of the volt/ohmmeter on each terminal of the thermostat. A continuity reading of 0 ohms, (full-meter deflection), means the thermostat is OK *(Figure 147)*. No continuity means the thermostat is defective, or open.

When making the above check, for gas dryers, use the same procedure.

## REPAIR PROCEDURES

Unplug the dryer power cord or gas supply before servicing the clothes dryer. Exercise care when moving the dryer from its original position, or the dryer legs could easily tear or scratch the floor.

### To Replace Dryer Cord

To replace the electric dryer cord, remove the access plate to the dryer terminal block *(Figure*

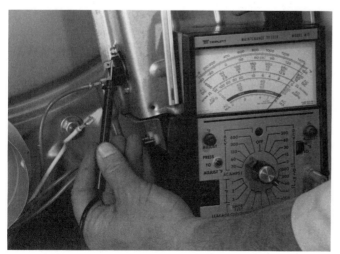

Figure 147 — Check Dryer High-Limit Thermostat for Continuity

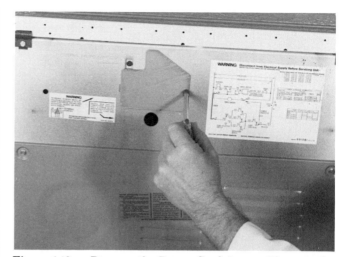

Figure 148 — Remove the Power Cord Access Plate on the Back of Dryer

*148)*. Remove the screws that secure the dryer cord to the terminal block *(Figure 149)*. Remove the defective power cord from the dryer and install the replacement part power cord *(Figure 149)*.

When replacing the power cord on the gas dryer, follow the same procedure as outlined above for the electric dryer.

### To Replace Dryer Timer Assembly

Unplug the dryer power cord and remove the dryer console back *(Figure 150)*. Remove the timer knob by pulling it forward *(Figure 151)*. Remove the screws that secure the timer assembly to the console and remove the timer assembly *(Figure 152)*.

Next, remove the electrical wires that are attached to the terminals of the timer assembly.

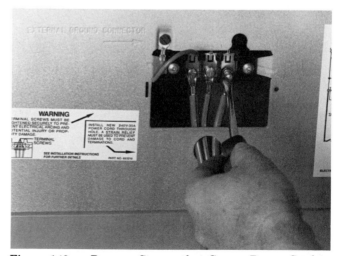

Figure 149 — Remove Screws that Secure Power Cord to Terminal Block

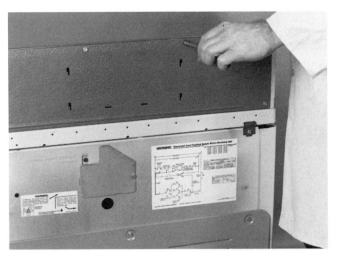

Figure 150 — Remove the Dryer Console Back Panel

They are to be reinstalled on the same terminals of the replacement part dryer timer assembly. Install the replacement timer by mounting in the same position as the failed part. Follow the instructions and procedures that are provided in the replacement timer assembly kit. If no installation steps are provided, reverse the above steps.

When replacing the timer assembly of a gas dryer, follow the procedures as outlined above for the electric dryer.

### To Replace Selector Switch

Unplug the dryer power cord, and with the dryer console back panel removed *(Figure 150)*, remove the screws that secure the switch to the console assembly *(Figure 153)*. Remove the selector switch knob *(Figure 154)* and remove the switch assembly from the dryer console *(Figure*

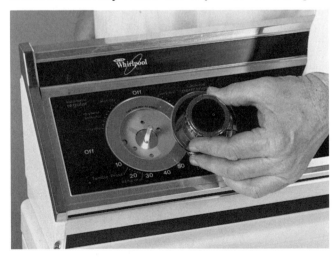

Figure 151 — Remove Timer Knob on an Electric Dryer by Pulling Forward

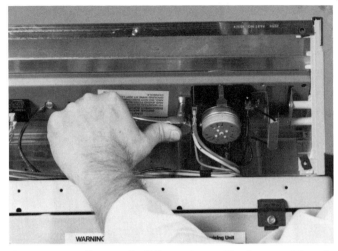

Figure 152 — Removal of Timer Assembly from an Electric Dryer

*155)*. When removing the electrical wires from the selector switch, note the sequence in which they were removed because you will have to reinstall them on the same terminals of the replacement switch.

Install the replacement selector switch by mounting in the same position as the failed part. Follow the instructions and procedures provided in the replacement part selector switch kit, or reverse the above steps.

Replacing the dryer selector switch on the gas dryer is basically the same procedure as outlined above for the electric dryer.

### To Replace Heating Element

Unplug the dryer power cord. Using small flatblade screwdriver, remove the screws that secure the fan scroll to the dryer top *(Figure 156)*.

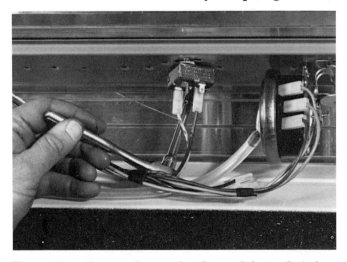

Figure 153 — Remove Screws that Secure Selector Switch to Dryer Console Assembly

Figure 154 — Remove Selector Switch Knob from Front of Electric Dryer

Figure 156 — Remove Screws that Secure Fan Scroll to Dryer Top

Next, wedge a small screwdriver between the dryer top and the dryer cabinet *(Figure 157)* and pry upward until top is released. Tilt top against a wall. Using hand tools, remove the screw that secures the heater box bracket to the bulkhead assembly and remove bracket *(Figure 158)*. Next, move dryer out and remove the screws that secure the back panel to the dryer cabinet *(Figure 159)*. Remove the wiring harness wires that are connected to the heating element and mark the wires as they are removed, because you will have to reinstall them on the same terminals of the replacement heating element *(Figure 160)*. Remove the heater box from the dryer *(Figure 161)*. Turn the heater box over and remove the screw that secures the heating element to the heater box *(Figure 162)*. Slide the heating element out of the heater box *(Figure 163)*.

Install the new heating element in the same

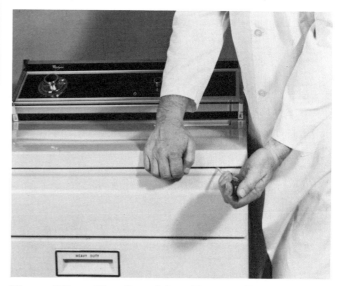

Figure 157 — Use Screwdriver Between Dryer Top and Cabinet to Release Top of Dryer

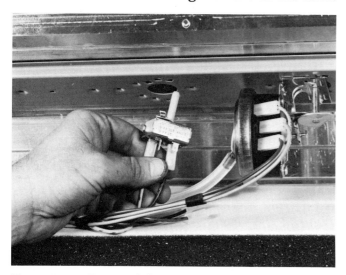

Figure 155 — Remove Selector Switch

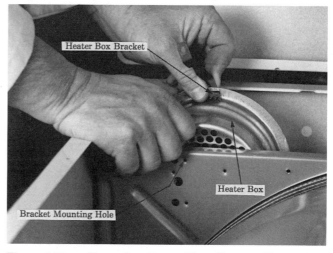

Figure 158 — Removing Screw That Secures Heater Box Bracket to The Dryer Bulkhead Assembly

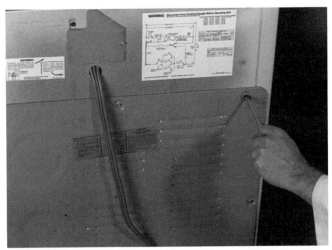

Figure 159 — Remove Screws that Secure Back Panel to Dryer Cabinet

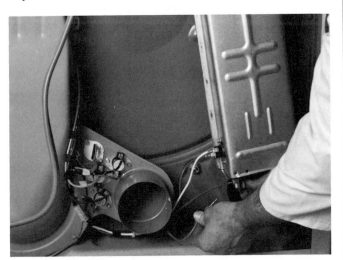

Figure 160 — Remove Wiring Harness Wires Connected to Dryer Heating Element

Figure 161 — Remove Heater Box that Houses the Heater Element

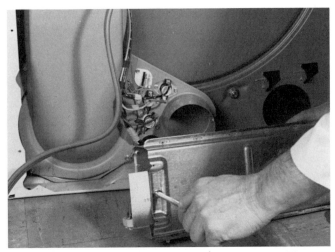

Figure 162 — Remove Screw that Secures Heating Element to Heater Box

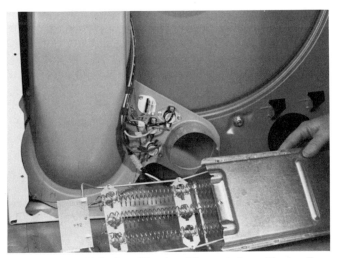

Figure 163 — Slide Out Heating Element from Heater Box

position as the failed unit that was removed. Follow instructions provided in the replacement heating element kit. If no installation steps are provided, reverse the above steps.

### To Replace Electrical Ignitor In Gas Dryer

To remove the ignitor, the gas burner must first be removed. Turn the burner gas valve to the OFF position *(Figure 164)*. Next, unplug the wiring harness that is connected to the gas burner assembly *(Figure 165)*. Remove the screws that secure the gas burner assembly to the dryer cabinet *(Figure 166)* with hand tools. Remove the gas burner assembly from the dryer cabinet *(Figure 167)*.

After removal of the gas burner, disconnect the electrical ignitor by removing the screws that secure the ignitor assembly to the gas burner *(Figure 168)*.

Figure 164 — Turn the Gas Dryer Gas Supply Valve to the OFF Position (Perpendicular to Gas Line)

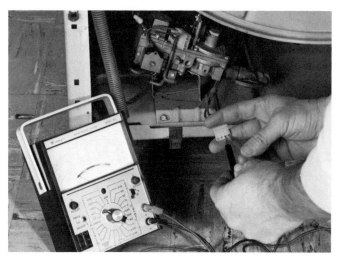

Figure 165 — Remove Wiring Harness from Gas Dryer Burner Assembly

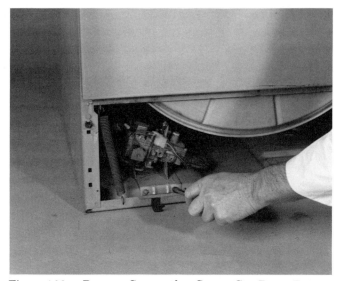

Figure 166 — Remove Screws that Secure Gas Dryer Burner Assembly to Cabinet

Figure 167 — Remove Gas Supply Line from Gas Burner Assembly Using Wrench; Remove Burner

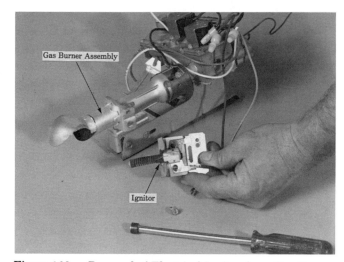

Gas Burner Assembly

Ignitor

Figure 168 — Removal of Electrical Ignitor from Gas Burner Assembly

When removing the electrical wires from the ignitor, note the sequence in which they are removed because you will have to reinstall them on the same terminals on the replacement part.

Install the replacement ignitor by mounting in the same position as the defective part. Follow instructions and procedures provided in the replacement ignitor kit. If no installation steps are provided, reverse the above steps.

## To Replace Solenoid Coil Assembly

Unplug the dryer power cord. Use hand tools to remove the dryer toe plate (Page 76). Unplug the wiring harness that connects to the gas burner (Figure 169). Remove the screws that secure the burner assembly to the dryer cabinet (Figure 166). The gas burner can now be removed from the dryer cabinet. Next, remove the wire

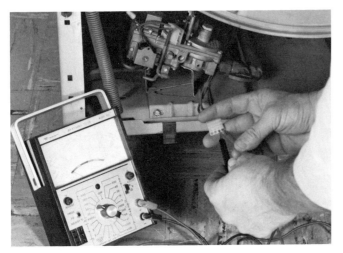

Figure 169 — Disconnect Wiring Harness that Connects to Gas Burner

connectors from the solenoid coil, and remove screws that hold the solenoid in place *(Figure 170)*. Remove the defective solenoid coil by pulling upward off the valve plunger *(Figure 171)*.

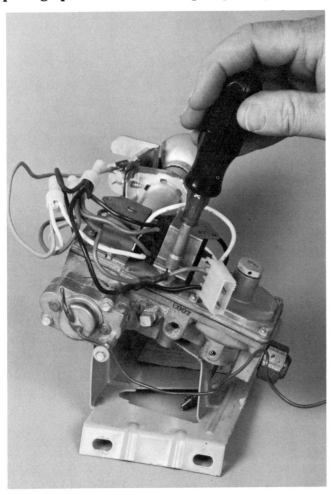

Figure 170 — After Removing Gas Burner From Dryer Cabinet Loosen Screws that Secure Solenoid Coil Assembly

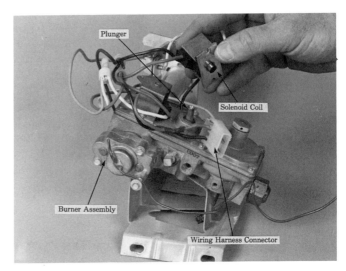

Figure 171 — Remove Solenoid Coil from Gas Burner

Install the replacement solenoid coil in the same position as the defective coil that was removed. Follow instructions provided by the manufacturer or reverse the above steps.

### To Replace Drive Motor Centrifugal Switch

To replace the dryer drive motor centrifugal switch, refer to "Dryer Does Not Start In Cycle" of this service guide, Page 73.

### To Replace Cycling Thermostats

To service the dryer cycling thermostats, unplug the dryer power cord, and with the back panel removed, locate the dryer cycling thermostats. These thermostats are usually located in the fan scroll area, and are about the size of a quarter. Remove the screws that secure the thermostats to the dryer bulkhead assembly *(Figure*

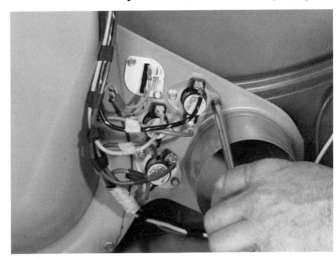

Figure 172 — Remove Screws that Secure Cycling Thermostat to Dryer Bulkhead Assembly

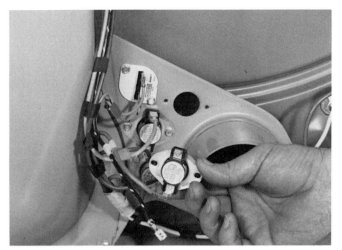

Figure 173 — Remove Defective Cycling Thermostat from Dryer

Figure 174 — Remove Harness Wires on High-Limit Thermostat

*172).* Remove the defective thermostats *(Figure 173).*

When removing electrical wires from a defective cycling thermostat, note the sequence in which they were removed, so they can be reinstalled on the same terminals of the replacement thermostat.

Install replacement thermostat(s) by mounting them in the same position as the thermostats that were removed.

When replacing the dryer cycling thermostat(s) on a gas dryer, follow the same procedure as outlined above for an electric dryer.

## To Replace High-Limit Thermostat

To replace the dryer high-limit thermostat follow the same procedure and installation steps described in replacement of the cycling thermostat. *Figure 174* shows harness wires on a high-limit thermostat being removed. *Figure 175* shows thermostat being removed.

## DRYER DOES NOT START IN CYCLE

An obvious failure symptom is when you select a drying cycle and attempt to start the dryer, but it does not run. To find the cause of the problem, move the dryer out from its position and unplug the power cord.

First check the dryer receptacle as the possible cause of failure. Refer to the "Dryer Does Not Heat" section of this service guide, Page 61.

If line voltage is indicated on the volt/ohmmeter, check the dryer power cord as possible cause of the problem. Refer to the "Dryer Does

Not Heat" section of this service guide, Page 61.

Next, check the dryer timer assembly as the possible reason why the dryer will not start in cycle. Again, refer to the "Dryer Does Not Heat" section on Page 61.

## Using Test Equipment

To avoid any incorrect readings when using the volt/ohmmeter, always "zero" the ohmmeter before making continuity checks on components. See operating instructions that came with volt/ohmmeter.

Before making continuity checks with the volt/ohmmeter, always unplug the dryer power cord. Live voltage checks will damage the meter movement.

Figure 175 — Removal of High-Limit Thermostat from Dryer

## Check For Burned Or Broken Wires

Next check inside the dryer cabinet for burned, corroded, loose, or broken wires to major components such as the wiring harness, timer assembly, switches, and drive motor assembly. A failure in the above components will cause the dryer to have erratic operation or the dryer will not start in the cycle.

## Check Dryer Door Switch

A faulty dryer door switch can prevent the dryer from starting. Start by making a visual inspection of the switch. You should hear a click as the striker is depressed against the switch, which would indicate that the striker and switch are good.

If you do hear a click you can assume that the door switch is mechanically OK. However, you still must check the door switch using a volt/-ohmmeter to test for continuity. First, unplug the dryer power cord and remove switch (see Repair Procedures). Remove screws that secure switch to cabinet. Set the volt/ohmmeter on the RX-1 scale. Place a probe of the volt/ohmmeter on each terminal of the door switch. With the switch depressed the volt/ohmmeter should indicate continuity, or 0 ohms *(Figure 176)*. No continuity means the switch is bad and will have to be replaced.

If a volt/ohmmeter is not available, you can bypass the switch (with power cord unplugged) by inserting a paper clip, wire, solder, or other round metal object between the two terminals of the switch *(Figure 177)*. If the dryer starts when plugged in, this would indicate that the dryer door switch is faulty.

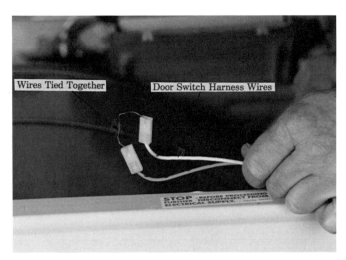

Figure 177 — Bypassing the Dryer Door Switch

Proper operation of the door switch can also be determined by a voltage check using a volt/-ohmmeter. If line voltage is available to the door switch terminals, the volt/ohmmeter will show a reading of 110-125 volts.

To check the door switch of a gas dryer, use the same procedures as discussed above for the electric dryer.

## Check Drive Motor

The drive motor must be suspected when the dryer will not start in the operate cycle. An easy check, which involves no test equipment, is to listen for a low-pitched hum when the dryer timer is turned ON or the push-to-start switch is pushed to the ON position. If there is a low-pitched hum when the dryer tries to start, there is a good possibility the drive motor starting switch or motor windings are defective. To restore the

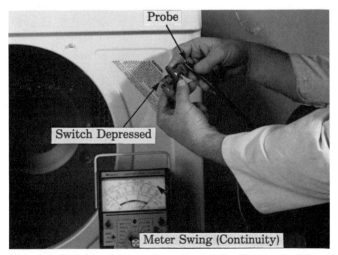

Figure 176 — Check Dryer Door Switch for Continuity Using a Volt/Ohmmeter

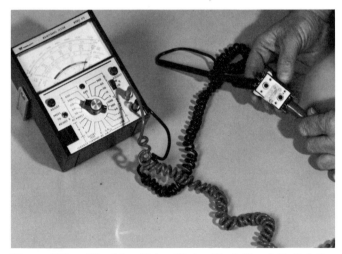

Figure 178 — Checking Drive Motor Centrifugal Switch for Continuity with the Volt/Ohmmeter

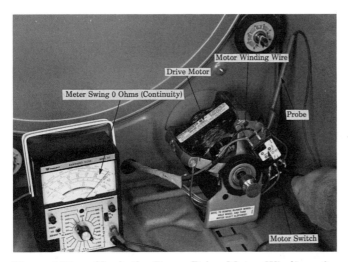

Figure 179 — Check the Dryer Drive Motor Windings for Continuity With the Volt/Ohmmeter

dryer to proper operating order, you will have to replace the drive motor or motor centrifugal switch.

### Check Drive Motor Centrifugal Switch

An easy check that can be made is to test the condition of the switch with a volt/ohmmeter. Set the meter on the RX-1 scale and place one probe on terminal 6 (black wire). The other probe is attached to either the yellow or blue terminal. With the switch depressed, there should be continuity (full-meter swing) *(Figure 178)*. If continuity is not indicated, replace the switch.

### Check Drive Motor Windings

The volt/ohmmeter can be used to check the condition of the drive motor windings. Set the scale of the volt/ohmmeter to the RX-1 scale and place one of the probes of the volt/ohmmeter on the BK or black wire from the motor. Place the other probe on the white wire. A continuity reading of near 0 ohms should be indicated on meter. A second winding can be checked by moving the probe of the volt/ohmmeter from the white to the blue wire on the drive motor. Again, continuity should be indicated *(Figure 179)*. An open winding will give a high resistance reading or no reading on the volt/ohmmeter. It can then be assumed that the drive motor is faulty and you will have to replace it to return the dryer to proper operation.

NOTE: To locate the proper motor windings of the drive motor, it might be necessary to refer to the wiring diagram of the dryer that you are servicing.

### Check Drive Motor Bearings

If you hear a humming sound and the drive motor does not start, it could safely be assumed that line voltage is available to start the drive motor. The next step is a mechanical check to see if the drive motor shaft is frozen. With the dryer front panel and idler pulley removed, turn the motor shaft in a clockwise or counterclockwise rotation. The motor shaft should turn freely *(Figure 180)*. If there is binding or the shaft is frozen or hard to turn, the drive motor would have to be replaced.

### Check Idler Pulley

With the idler pulley removed *(Figure 181)*, turn the pulley to see if the roller turns freely. If not, replace it.

### REPAIR PROCEDURES

Unplug the power cord or gas supply before

Figure 180 — Checking Dryer Motor Shaft for Frozen Bearings

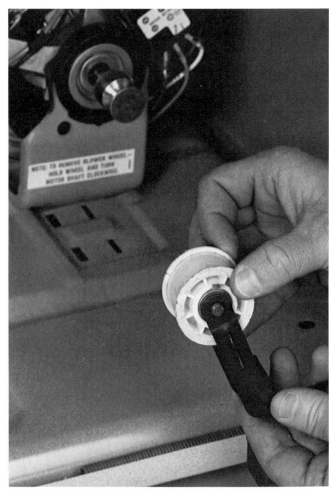

Figure 181 — Check Idler Pulley for a Bind

servicing the clothes dryer. Move clothes dryer out from the wall. Exercise care when moving the dryer from its original position because the dryer legs can easily tear holes in your floor.

## To Replace Door Switch

Remove screws to dryer top *(Figure 156)*. Lift the top of the dryer by inserting a flat-blade screwdriver between the cabinet and the top of the dryer *(Figure 182)*. Remove the screws that secure door switch to dryer front panel *(Figure 183)* and discard the door switch *(Figure 184)*.

Install the replacement part door switch by securing the striker to the replacement part switch and mounting it in the same position as the defective door switch that was removed. Replace wires on same terminals of new switch. Follow other instructions provided in the replacement part door switch kit. If no installation steps are provided, reverse the above steps.

Replacing the door switch of a gas dryer, involves basically the same procedures as discussed above for the electric dryer.

## To Replace Drive Motor

To remove the drive motor, unplug the dryer power cord and move the dryer out from the wall. Remove screws that secure the dryer top to the fan scroll *(Figure 156)*. Use a small flat-blade screwdriver to wedge it between the top and the dryer cabinet to lift top *(Figure 182)*. Raise the dryer top and lean it against a wall. Remove the screws on the left-hand and right-hand sides that secure the dryer front panel to the cabinet *(Figure 185)*. Remove the dryer toe plate by using a small screwdriver and wedging between the toeplate and holding clip *(Figure 186)*. Remove the harness wires from the door switch and note the terminals from which they were removed as they are to be re-installed on the same terminals. Next, ap-

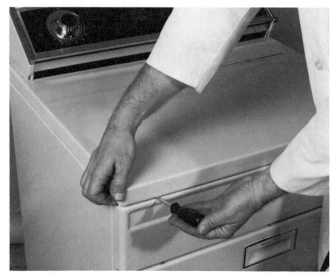

Figure 182 — Use Flat Screwdriver to Open Top of Dryer

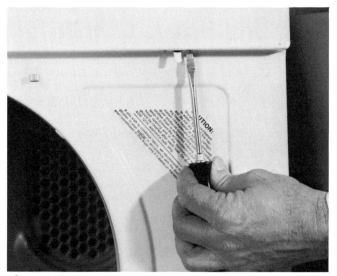

Figure 183 — Use Screwdriver to Remove Door Switch.

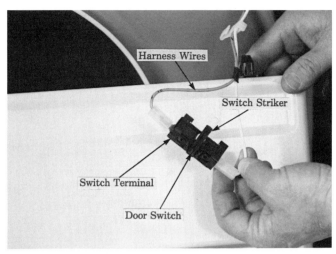

Figure 184 — With Dryer Top Up Door Switch Can be Removed

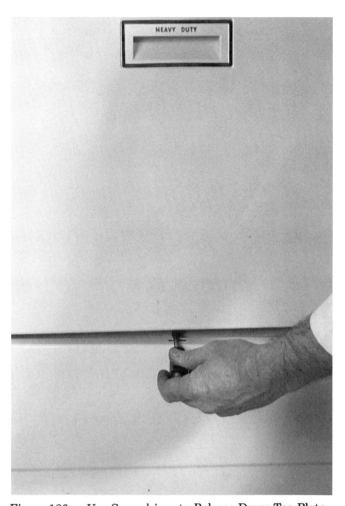

Figure 186 — Use Screwdriver to Release Dryer Toe Plate

ply pressure downward with fingers and remove door springs *(Figure 187)*, loosen screws at the bottom of front panel *(Figure 188)*, and remove the front panel from the dryer *(Figure 189)*. Remove the wiring harness wires from the drive motor *(Figure 190)* and mark the wires as they are removed, since they are to be reinstalled on the same terminals of the replacement drive motor. Remove the dryer idler pulley *(Figure 191)* and remove belt and drum *(Figure 192)*. Place one wrench on the blower wheel hub (back of motor) and another wrench on the motor shaft that secures the belt pulley. While holding one wrench, turn the other in a clockwise direction so that the blower wheel can be removed *(Figure 193)*. Locate the drive motor clips and with a screwdriver inserted in slot, press downward and remove the drive motor clip *(Figure 194)*. Next, make an

alignment mark of the position of the drive motor as it sits in the motor cradle and lift out the drive motor *(Figure 195)*. NOTE: The replacement drive motor is to be reinstalled in the motor cradle in

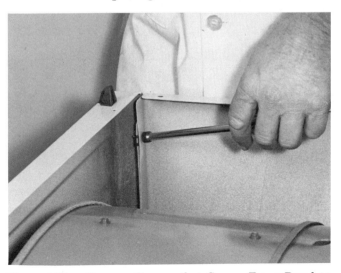

Figure 185 — Remove Screws that Secure Front Panel to Cabinet

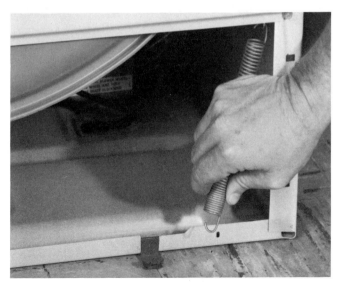

Figure 187 — Remove Door Springs

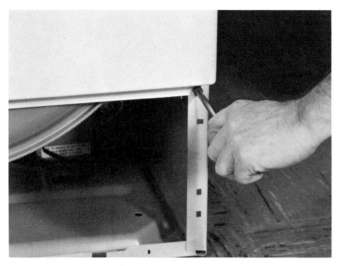

Figure 188 — Loosen Screws at Bottom of Dryer Front Panel

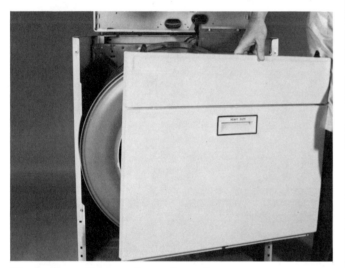

Figure 189 — Remove Dryer Front Panel

Figure 190 — Remove Drive Motor Wiring Harness

Figure 191 — Remove Idler Pulley from the Dryer

Figure 192 — Remove Dryer Drum

the same position as the defective drive motor that was removed. Failure to do so would result in misalignment of the drive motor and might allow it to rub against the dryer drum as the drum is turning.

Install the replacement drive motor by mounting in the same position as the defective drive motor that was removed. Follow instructions and procedures provided with the replacement motor. If no installation steps are provided, reverse the above steps.

Replacing the drive motor on the gas dryer requires basically the same procedures as outlined above for an electric dryer.

Figure 193 — Remove the Blower Wheel from Back of Drive Motor

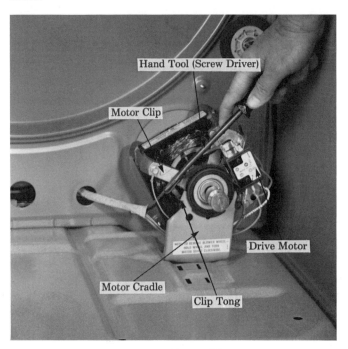

Hand Tool (Screw Driver)

Motor Clip

Drive Motor

Motor Cradle

Clip Tong

Figure 194 — Remove Drive Motor Clips

Figure 195 — Lift Out the Drive Motor

## To Replace Drive Motor Centrifugal Switch

To gain access to the drive motor centrifugal switch, refer to "Replacement Of Drive Motor" in this section of this service guide. After removal of the drive motor, use a flat-blade screwdriver to remove the screws that secure the centrifugal switch to the drive motor housing *(Figure 196)*. Remove the wiring harness wires from their terminals and note the sequence that the wires were removed. The wires are to be reinstalled on the terminals of the replacement switch exactly as they were removed from the defective centrifugal switch. The switch can now be removed from the drive motor.

Install the replacement switch by mounting in the same position as the drive motor centrifugal switch that was removed. Follow the instructions and procedures that are provided by

Figure 196 — Remove Screws that Secure Centrifugal Switch to Drive Motor Housing

the manufacturer. If no installation steps are provided, reverse the above steps.

When replacing the drive motor centrifugal switch on the gas dryer, follow the same procedures as outlined above for the electric dryer.

## DRYER STOPS IN CYCLE

This failure is normally attributed to a loss of electrical power or an electrical overload.

To find the cause of the problem, move the dryer out from the wall and unplug the dryer power cord from dryer wall receptacle. Make a voltage check with the volt/ohmmeter to determine if there is electrical power available to the dryer receptacle or to the dryer power cord. To check the dryer receptacle and the dryer power cord, refer to the "Dryer Does Not Heat" section of this service guide, Page 61.

### Using Test Equipment

To avoid incorrect readings when using the volt/ohmmeter, always "zero" the ohmmeter before making continuity checks. See operating instructions that came with your volt/ohmmeter.

When making continuity checks on components, always unplug the dryer power cord from the receptacle because live voltage checks will damage the meter movement.

### Check For Drive Motor Overheating

If the dryer works OK for two or three loads before it stops, attempt to restart the dryer after waiting for approximately thirty to forty-five minutes. If the drive motor restarts after cool-down, it is safe to assume that the motor is overheating, causing the dryer to stop in mid-cycle. Probably the drive motor has been damaged permanently, and will have to be replaced *(Figures 185 through 195)*.

Before replacing the dryer drive motor, it would be worth the effort to remove the dryer toe-plate, unplug the dryer power cord, locate the drive motor and brush or clean it thoroughly with a vacuum cleaner. Remove all traces of lint, dirt and debris from the drive motor housing. **NOTE: You should perform this cleaning at least once a** year to prevent the buildup of debris in the drive motor housing. After cleaning the motor housing, turn the dryer timer to the ON position, and recheck the dryer operation. Sometimes, cleaning the drive motor is all that is necessary to fix the intermittent operation.

If this check fails, check inside the dryer cabinet for burned, corroded, loose, or broken wires to the dryer's major components. Problems in the wiring harness, timer assembly, switches, and drive motor can result in the dryer stopping in the cycle.

### Check Dryer Power Cord

To check the dryer power cord, refer to "Dryer Does Not Heat In Cycle" in this section of this service guide, Page 61.

### Check Dryer Timer Assembly

To check the dryer timer assembly, refer to "Dryer Does Not Heat In Cycle" in this section of this service guide, Page 61.

### Check Door Switch

To check the dryer door switch, refer to "Dryer Does Not Start" in this section of this service guide, Page 73.

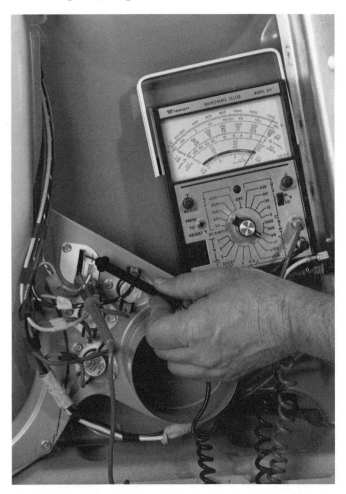

Figure 197 — Check Safety Thermostat for Continuity with the Volt/Ohmmeter

### Check Safety Thermostat

There are some late-model dryers that have a protective device type thermostat, which is really no more than a fuse that melts when the dryer reaches high temperatures. As the dryer approaches dangerously high temperatures, the safety thermostat will melt, interrupting power to the drive motor.

You can easily check the safety thermostat or fuse with a volt/ohmmeter. First remove it from the dryer (see Repair Procedures). With the volt/ohmmeter set on the RX-1 scale, place one probe of the volt/ohmmeter on each terminal of the thermostat. If the thermostat is good, look for a reading of 0 ohms, or full-meter swing, on the volt/ohmmeter *(Figure 197)*. No continuity means the safety thermostat is faulty. To restore the dryer to working order, you will have to replace the operating thermostat that caused the dryer to overheat, in addition to the safety thermostat.

## REPAIR PROCEDURES

Unplug the dryer power cord or gas supply before servicing the clothes dryer. Exercise care when removing the dryer from its original position as the dryer legs can easily tear or scratch the floor.

To service the clothes dryer, remove the dryer back panel so that you can make a voltage check with the volt/ohmmeter at the dryer terminal block and dryer receptacle *(see Figure 134)*.

### Replace Dryer Power Cord

To replace the dryer power cord, refer to the "Dryer Does Not Heat" section of this service guide, Page 61.

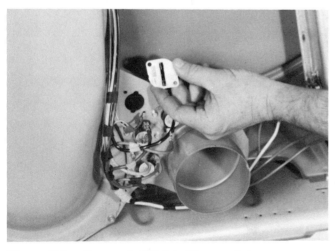

Figure 198 — Removal of Safety Thermostat

### Replace Timer Assembly

To replace the dryer timer assembly, refer to "Dryer Does Not Heat" section of this service guide, Page 61.

### Replace Door Switch

To replace the dryer door switch, refer to the "Dryer Does Not Start In Cycle" section of this service guide, Page 73.

### To Replace Safety Thermostat

To replace the safety thermostat, unplug the dryer power cord. Remove the screws that secure the thermostat to the dryer cabinet and remove the defective thermostat *(Figure 198)*.

Install the replacement safety thermostat by mounting in the same position as the defective part that was removed. Follow instructions and procedures provided with the replacement part or reverse the above steps.

When removing and replacing the safety thermostat of the gas dryer, the repair procedures are the same as was discussed for the electric dryer.

## DRYER GETS TOO HOT

Specific failure symptoms include: 1) An unusual smell in the laundry room. 2) The top of the dryer is very hot to the touch. 3) The clothes are extremely hot and wrinkled at the end of the cycle.

### Check Cycling Thermostats

When a dryer is overheating, the first concern should be whether the heater element is cycling (turning ON and OFF). An easy check is to set the heat selector to a heat position and turn the timer to the ON position. With the dryer running, turn the overhead lights OFF. Check the back of the dryer (with the back panel removed). On left-hand side of cabinet there should be a visible glow from the heater box. This glow would indicate that the dryer is heating and has the required voltage. After a period of four to six minutes, the heater should cycle off and the glow should fade. If not, then probably the dryer cycling thermostats or adjustable thermostat is not functioning properly. You will have to replace the defective thermostat(s) in order for the dryer to operate properly.

To check the cycling thermostats, refer to "Dryer Does Not Heat" in this section of this service guide, Page 61.

## Check High-Limit Thermostat

To check the dryer high-limit thermostat refer to "Dryer Does Not Heat" in this section of this service guide, Page 61.

## Check Adjustable Thermostat

Some clothes dryers use an adjustable thermostat, which is similar to a cycling thermostat. But while the cycling thermostat employs a bi-metal disc to open the circuit to the heating element when a certain temperature has been attained, the adjustable thermostat employs a sensing bulb that senses the temperature outside the dryer drum before the heating element is cut OFF *(Figure 128)*.

The adjustable thermostat is easily checked by using the volt/ohmmeter. Unplug the dryer power cord and set the scale of the volt/ohmmeter on RX-1. Place a probe of the volt/ohmmeter on each terminal of the thermostat. Slowly turn the knob of the switch in a clockwise direction and look for a reading of 0 ohms on the volt/ohmmeter *(Figure 199)*. As the knob is turned to the left (counterclockwise) the volt/ohmmeter needle should return to the left of the scale (infinity). This would mean that the dryer is no longer calling for heat. Abnormal readings would suggest that the switch is defective and should be replaced.

## REPAIR PROCEDURES

Unplug the dryer power cord or gas supply before servicing the clothes dryer.

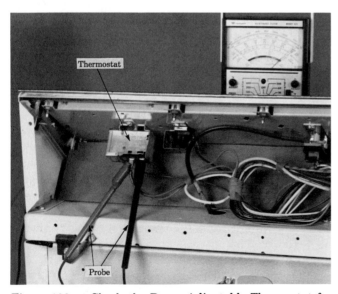

Figure 199 — Check the Dryer Adjustable Thermostat for Continuity with a Volt/Ohmmeter

## To Replace Cycling Thermostat(s)

To replace the dryer cycling thermostat(s), refer to the "Dryer Does Not Heat" in this section of this service guide, Page 61.

When removing and replacing the cycling thermostat(s) on the gas dryer, the repair procedures are the same as was discussed for the electric dryer.

## To Replace High-Limit Thermostat

To replace the dryer high-limit thermostat, refer to the "Dryer Does Not Heat" in this section of this service guide, Page 61.

When removing and replacing the high-limit thermostat on the gas dryer, the repair procedures are the same as was discussed for the electric dryer.

## To Replace Adjustable Thermostat

To replace an adjustable thermostat in a typical clothes dryer, unplug the dryer, move it out from the wall and remove the screws that secure the console back panel to the dryer top *(Figure 150)*. Remove the screws that attach the thermostat to the dryer console *(Figure 200)*. Remove the thermostat control selector knob *(Figure 201)* by gently pulling off the control shaft and remove thermostat *(Figure 202)*.

Remove the wires from the defective thermostat and remove the thermostat from the dryer console assembly. NOTE: When removing the thermostat wires, note the sequence in which

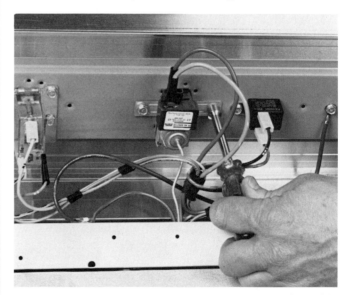

Figure 200 — Remove Screws that Secure Adjustable Thermostat to Dryer Console Panel

Figure 201 — Remove Dryer Adjustable Thermostat Control Knob

they were removed because they are to be reinstalled on the same terminals of the replacement thermostat. Remove the two screws that secure the thermostat sensing bulb to the dryer fan exhaust *(Figure 203)*. *Figure 204* shows an adjustable thermostat sensing bulb being removed from dryer.

NOTE: When replacing the adjustable thermostat control, you must mount the replacement thermostat capillary tube with no kinks or binds in the same position as the defective thermostat that was removed. Failure to install the thermostat capillary tube properly would cause the dryer to operate improperly.

Install the replacement adjustable thermo-

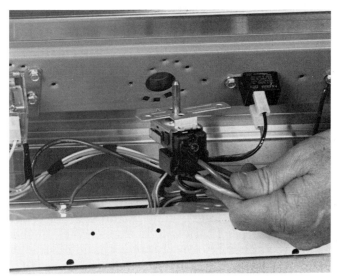

Figure 202 — Removing the Adjustable Thermostat from a Dryer

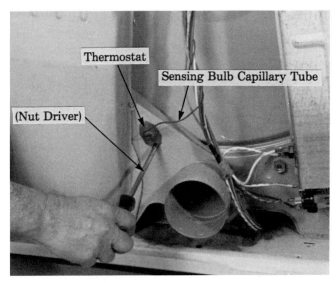

Figure 203 — Remove Screws that Secure Adjustable Thermostat Sensing Bulb to Dryer Cabinet

stat control by mounting in the same position as the defective thermostat that was removed. Follow instructions supplied by the manufacturer. If no installation steps are provided, reverse the above steps.

To replace the adjustable thermostat of the gas dryer, follow the same procedures outlined above for the electric dryer.

## CLOTHES DRYER TAKES TOO LONG TO DRY CLOTHES

Specific failure symptoms include: 1) The clothes dryer is running longer than normal. 2) The clothes are extremely damp at the end of the drying cycle.

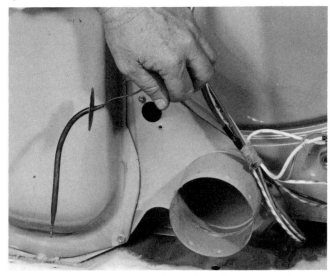

Figure 204 — Removing Adjustable Thermostat Sensing Bulb From Dryer

Although the problem could be that the automatic washer is not spinning your clothes properly, in most cases the problem is inadequate air movement in the dryer.

Before blaming the dryer, you should check the automatic washer. At the end of the spin cycle, open the washer lid and check to see if there is excess water left in the washer basket. If so, (1) check for a bind or kink in the washer drain hose, (2) open the washer top and see if discharge hose from pump assembly has kinked, (3) check the washer water pump for a possible hose kink or restriction within pump assembly, (4) check for a restriction within washer self-cleaning filter, (5) check to make sure the washer is spinning correctly (if any trace of excess soap remains in the clothes, the washer is not spinning in the cycle or not spinning properly).

## Check Ventilation

If the washer is OK, move the dryer out from the wall and look behind the dryer to see if the exhaust duct tubing has developed a kink or restriction. If so, remove the old duct material and replace.

After replacing the dryer exhaust duct, never move the dryer all the way against the wall. Leave about 6 to 8 inches from the wall.

Lastly, check the dryer for other restrictions that would result in improper air flow. Locate the outside dryer exhaust duct, usually on an outer wall or on the roof. Place one hand over the exhaust deflector flap and check for air flow. If there appears to be little or no air flow at all, there probably is a lint restriction somewhere in the exhaust duct that you must clear for the clothes dryer to operate properly.

NOTE: If a clothes dryer has been vented through an inside wall and onto the roof, it would be normal for the dryer to take longer to dry the clothes, because the exhaust air is being pushed through the vent upstream to distances of up to 10 to 12 feet.

When checking an exhaust vent outside the wall of the house, make sure that the exhaust deflector flap or door is opening and closing properly. This door is spring-loaded and it should stay closed when the dryer is in the OFF position. When the dryer is ON, the exhaust air flow will open the door. If the vent door is not operating properly, water, insects, and rodents can enter the vent and cause an air-flow restriction.

## Check Drum Belt

Another possible cause of slow heating is a slipping or broken drum belt. This belt is used to move the dryer drum. With the dryer running, open the door and quickly check to see if the drum is revolving. If the drum appears to be sitting still, you can assume that (1) the dryer drum belt is slipping or broken, (2) idler pulley is frozen.

The next possible cause for the dryer taking too long to dry is a defective adjustable thermostat. The dryer heating element may be cutting OFF too soon, due to incorrect signals from the thermostat. To check the adjustable thermostat, refer to the "Dryer Gets Too Hot" section of this service guide, Page 81.

## Check Idler Pulley

To check the clothes dryer idler pulley, refer to "Dryer Does Not Start In Cycle" in this section of this service guide, Page 73.

## REPAIR PROCEDURES

Unplug the dryer power cord or gas supply before servicing the clothes dryer. Move dryer out from wall.

### To Replace Drum Belt

To replace a slipping or broken drum belt, remove the screws that secure the dryer top to the fan scroll (Figure 156). Raise the dryer top by wedging a small screwdriver between the top and the dryer cabinet (Figure 157) and lean it against the wall. Using hand tools, remove the screws on the left- and right-hand sides of dryer cabinet (Figure 185). Loosen the screws that secure the dryer front panel to the cabinet (Figure 188). Remove the wiring harness wires that are connected to the door switch. Remove toe plate (Figure 186) and remove the door springs by disconnecting them from the cabinet and the door (Figure 187). Next, remove the dryer front panel (Figure 189).

If the drum belt is broken, remove it from the drum and install the replacement drum belt (with grooves down) in the same position on the drum as the broken belt that was removed (Figure 205). Next, install the idler pulley in the slots next to the drive motor. There will be excess slack in the belt that should be run through the idler pulley and over the drive motor front pulley (Figure 206). NOTE: It is important to position a replacement belt correctly on the dryer drum. Installing a belt

Figure 205 — Positioning the Replacement Drum Belt Around Drum

improperly could result in belt slipping on the drive motor pulley.

After installing the drum belt, reassemble all parts in the reverse order from which they were removed. Connect the dryer power cord to a 220-240 volt receptacle, and turn the dryer timer dial to the ON position. Check the new drum belt by starting and stopping the dryer for a few minutes. This procedure will allow the belt to properly align itself on the idler pulley.

To replace the drum belt on the gas dryer, follow the same procedures outlined above for the electric dryer.

### To Replace Idler Pulley

To replace the idler pulley, refer to "Dryer Does Not Start In Cycle" in this section of this service guide, Page 73.

When replacing the idler pulley on the gas dryer, follow the same procedures as outlined for the electric dryer.

## CLOTHES DRYER IS NOISY

Specific problems include: 1) The clothes dryer has excessive noise while running. 2) The clothes dryer stops in cycle. 3) The clothes are extremely damp when removed from the dryer drum at end of cycle.

All of the above symptoms are related to mechanical problems which develop from years of use.

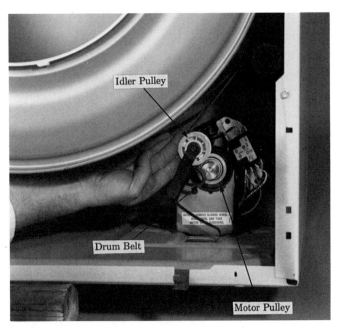

Figure 206 — Installing the Dryer Drum Belt Around Drive Motor Pulley

### Check Drum Belt

Check the clothes dryer drum belt for excessive play or a stretched condition. A drum belt that is excessively stretched will cause the idler pulley to bang against the drum, resulting in excessive noise. In order to restore the dryer to proper operating order, you will have to replace the drive belt.

### Check Idler Pulley

To check the idler pulley, refer to "Dryer Does Not Start In Cycle" in this section of this service guide, Page 73.

### Check Drum Supports

The drum support is a roller that guides the dryer drum and eliminates wobble while the drum is turning. To check for a defective drum support, unplug the dryer power cord and remove screws to the dryer top *(Figure 156)*. Next, remove the dryer drum (see Repair Procedures). Underneath the drum, locate the drum supports and check for excessive wear. If the supports are badly worn, you will have to replace them.

### Check Drive Motor

Worn bearings in the drive motor can cause constant noise while the dryer is running. To check the drive motor, unplug the dryer power cord. and remove screws to the dryer top *(Figure 156)*. Next, remove the dryer drum (see Repair Procedures). After removal of the dryer drum, locate the drive motor and check for excessive play in the drive motor shaft *(Figure 180)*. If excessive wear is evident, you will have to replace the drive motor in order to restore the clothes dryer to proper operating order.

## REPAIR PROCEDURES

Unplug the clothes dryer power cord or gas supply before servicing the clothes dryer.

### To Replace Drum Belt

To replace the clothes dryer drum belt refer to "Dryer Takes Too Long To Dry Clothes" in this section of this service guide, Page 83.

When replacing the drum belt on the gas dryer, follow the same procedures as outlined for the electric dryer.

### To Replace Idler Pulley

To replace the idler pulley, refer to "Dryer

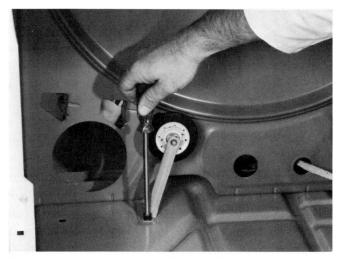

Figure 207 — Remove Drum Support Braces

Figure 208 — Remove Clip from Drum Support

Does Not Start In Cycle" in this section *(Figure 191)*.

When replacing the idler pulley on the gas dryer, follow the same procedures as outlined for the electric dryer.

## To Replace Drum Supports

Unplug the clothes dryer power cord and move the dryer out from the wall. Remove the screws that secure the dryer top to cabinet *(Figure 156)*. Wedge a screwdriver between the top and the dryer cabinet and lift top *(Figure 157)*. Next, remove the dryer drum *(Figure 192)*. To remove drum support, remove the screws that secure the support brace to dryer cabinet *(Figure 207)*. Next, remove the clip that secures the support to the support shaft *(Figure 208)*. The support can now be removed from the support shaft.

Install the replacement part drum support by mounting in the same position as the defective support that was removed. Follow the instructions and procedures provided with the replacement part.

When replacing the drum supports on the gas dryer, follow the same procedure as outlined for the electric dryer.

# 4

# The Household Refrigerator

We felt that the simplest way to organize this guide to help the do-it-yourselfer solve a problem was to organize it in the following manner:

- Show pictures of and describe all the components that make up the system.
- List specific problems (or failures) and suggest other symptoms that will help isolate the problem.
- List components to be checked in the proper sequence to isolate the faulty part.
- Give step-by-step replacement instructions for removing and replacing the faulty part.

The home repairmen should be very cautious when it comes to repair of the household refrigerator. They should be aware of the fact that they are dealing with a very expensive product, and one that contains a very delicately balanced cooling system. One small error could damage the system beyond repair.

There are some repairs that readers should never attempt. Replacing a faulty compressor requires special vacuum and freon filling equipment that only professional technicians can handle.

The refrigerator cooling system is not like the family automobile air conditioner. You can't simply attach a hose and add a little freon when it isn't cooling properly. The refrigerator is a carefully balanced, sealed system, and normally should not have a freon-loss problem. If the unit is not cooling properly, and you have determined that the compressor is running, then there are several electrical components in the system that could be at fault.

These are parts that the homeowner can test and replace with relative ease by following the instructions in this guide.

Often the problem is found in the defrost circuit. Most homeowners are not aware of the fact that the so-called "frost-free" refrigerator is really just an old-style refrigerator with a new twist. For many years we lived with frost buildup in the freezer compartment of the old-style units until

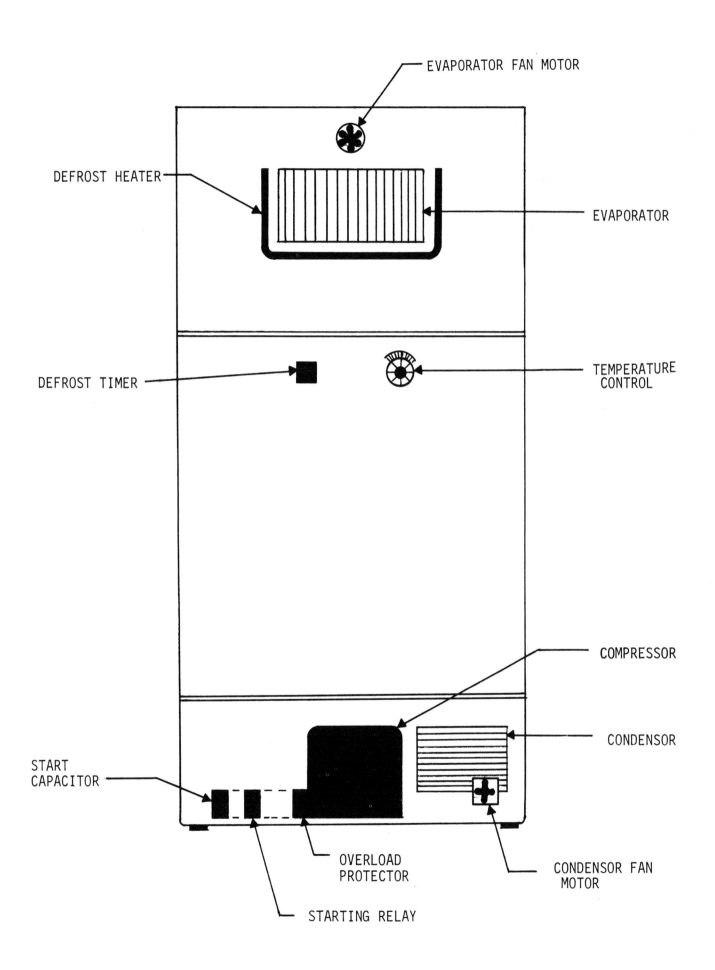

EVAPORATOR FAN MOTOR

DEFROST HEATER

EVAPORATOR

DEFROST TIMER

TEMPERATURE CONTROL

COMPRESSOR

CONDENSOR

START CAPACITOR

OVERLOAD PROTECTOR

CONDENSOR FAN MOTOR

STARTING RELAY

finally we shut the machine off, opened the freezer, door and let the frost melt and drain to the bottom of the machine.

The new frost-free refrigerator does basically the same thing, but it does it automatically on a timed sequence. The defrost timer shuts OFF the compressor/cooling circuit and activates a metal rod that quickly heats the freezer compartment to approximately 70 degrees F. Frost on the hidden evaporator coil melts and drains into a pan at the bottom of the refrigerator. (You never have to empty the pan, however, because the water evaporates between defrost cycles.) The frost is removed and the machine is back on before your frozen lamb chops even start to thaw.

When the defrost timer fails, you can actually have the compressor trying to cool the freezer compartment at the same time that the defrost heater is almost glowing red. Later in this chapter we describe all the steps necessary to examine the defrost cycle components and to isolate and repair faulty parts.

One final word of caution in working on the household refrigerator: do not use a hair dryer to remove frost build-up in a freezer compartment. Use a pan of hot water to speed up the process if desired.

## THE REFRIGERATOR - HOW IT WORKS

All household refrigerators require 110-to-125-volt electricity. The refrigerator compressor receives refrigerant vapor from the suction line in the low side of the unit where it is compressed and then sent through the discharge line into the condenser. The condenser is located either under the refrigerator cabinet or on the back of the cabinet. As the vapor enters the condenser, it contains heat. The condenser removes the heat, either by convection or forced air. As the refrigerant vapor passes through the condenser and is cooled, it condenses to a liquid.

The refrigerant, which is now a liquid, passes from the condenser into the liquid line, where it flows back into the refrigerator cabinet. The liquid refrigerant then enters a restrictor tube, which is a length of tubing of very small diameter. A small flow of refrigerant is allowed to enter the evaporator, which has tubing of much larger diameter. This allows the refrigerant to expand.

As the refrigerant travels through the evaporator, it absorbs heat through evaporation and super cools the coils. Toward the end of the evaporator tubing, the refrigerant turns to gas and warms again. This warm refrigerant vapor then passes into the suction line and into the compressor, where the refrigeration cycle starts all over again.

As the refrigerant circulates throughout the system, it eventually cools the refrigerator and freezer sections to the desired temperature. If the refrigerator compressor operated continuously, the temperature inside the refrigerator cabinet would soon freeze everything. Therefore, the refrigerator cycles ON and OFF through signals from a thermostat. *Figure 209* shows the refrigerant flow pattern during the complete cooling cycle of a typical household refrigerator.

### Refrigerator/Freezer Combination

Most refrigerators being sold and serviced today are refrigerator/freezer combinations. These models usually contain two separate compartments fully insulated using urethane foam or fiberglass. Each compartment operates at a different temperature. The refrigerator section is maintained at a temperature selected by control and ranging from 38 to 42 degrees F. The temperature in the freezer section is normally fixed at or near 0 degrees F.

While it may appear that a refrigerator/freezer combination has two evaporators, it actually has only one set of cooling coils. The evaporator coil is located in the freezer section, and it is here that the refrigerant enters the evaporator, chills the coils, and drops the temperature to 0 degrees. Cold air is circulated over the coils and throughout the freezer by the evaporator fan motor.

Temperature in the refrigerator section of the appliance is controlled by a mechanical baffle that allows cold air from the freezer section to enter an air duct, which forces cold air into the refrigerator section. Adjustment of the air control varies the desired temperature from 38 to 42 degrees.

### Household Freezers

The household freezer works on the same principle as the refrigerator, with the exception that the temperatures in a freezer are approximately 40 degrees lower than those of a refrigerator. Because the mechanical systems are so similar, the household freezer will not be discussed in this service guide.

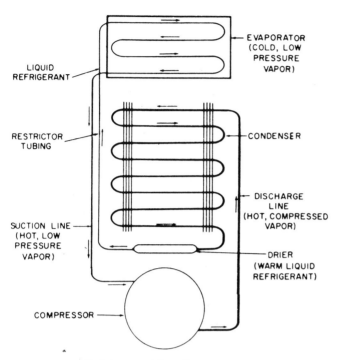

Figure 209 — Refrigerant Flow Pattern

## REFRIGERATOR COMPONENTS

The components of a typical household refrigerator are described below:

### Compressor

The heart of the refrigerator system is the compressor *(Figure 210)*. It is made up of a pump and an electric motor and is contained in a sealed dome through which the refrigerant travels.

### Starting Relay

The starting relay *(Figure 211)* is an

Figure 211 — Start Relay for Refrigerator

electro-mechanical switch used to start the compressor motor. As electricity flows, the starting relay energizes the start winding of the refrigerator compressor motor until the motor is almost up to speed. At this point, the relay breaks the electrical circuit to the start winding and the compressor motor continues to run on its run (or motor) winding.

### Starting Capacitor

Some refrigerator compressor motors must have excessive starting torque in order to start under high load conditions. To deliver this high starting torque, a starting capacitor *(Figure 212)* is placed in series with the start winding of the compressor motor. When the start winding is energized, the start capacitor builds up voltage and then discharges, causing a power surge to the

Figure 210 — Compressor Motor used in a Refrigerator

Figure 212 — Start Capacitor for Refrigerator

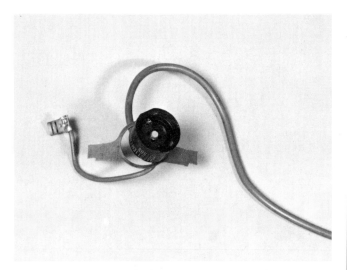

Figure 213 — Overload Protector used in a Refrigerator

start winding. This power surge, in turn, gives the compressor motor more momentum, enabling the compressor to start easier.

## Overload Protector

The compressor overload protector *(Figure 213)* is an electrical device attached to the compressor motor housing that senses any unusual temperature rise. Excess temperature causes the overload bi-metal disc to break the circuit to the compressor motor.

## Evaporator Fan Motor

The function of the evaporator fan motor *(Figure 214)* located in the freezer section is to move cold air from the freezer compartment to the refrigerator compartment.

Figure 214 — Evaporator Fan Motor used in a Refrigerator

Figure 215 — Condenser Fan Motor used in Refrigerator

## Condenser Fan Motor

The condenser fan motor *(Figure 215)* serves two functions: to keep the compressor cool and to remove heat from the condenser coil.

## Defrost Termination Switch

The function of the defrost termination switch *(Figure 216)* is to open the circuit to the defrost heater when the refrigerator cabinet reaches a pre-selected temperature.

## Thermostat

A thermostat *(Figure 217)* controls the temperature of the refrigerator by cycling

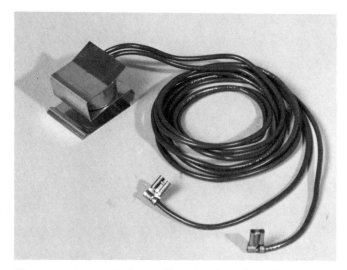

Figure 216 — Defrost Termination Switch used in Refrigerator

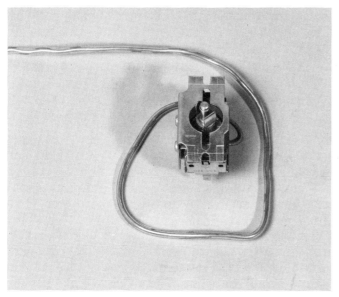

Figure 217 — Thermostat used in Refrigerator

the compressor ON and OFF when it senses changes of temperature in the refrigerator cabinet.

### Defrost Heater

The function of the defrost heater *(Figure 218)* is to melt the frost buildup that accumulates on the evaporator coils between the defrost cycles. The water then runs into the condensation drain pan.

### Defrost Timer

The function of the defrost timer *(Figure 219)* is to energize the defrost heater at certain intervals, usually once every twelve hours.

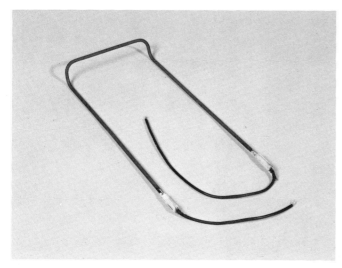

Figure 218 — Defrost Heater

Figure 219 — Defrost Timer

## DIAGNOSING PROBLEMS

The most common complaint about refrigerators is that they are not cooling properly. But this information in itself is not enough for you to begin the process of checking the refrigerator components to find the cause of the problem. To avoid the trouble of checking components that do not need checking, you must first identify other related symptoms.

If the food is not cold enough, the first thing to look for is the interior light. If the light does not come ON, electric power to the refrigerator may be OFF.

If the food is not cold enough, but the interior light does come ON, the next thing to check for is whether the compressor is cycling ON and OFF. To check the compressor, listen at the front of the refrigerator grill for the humming sound of the motor. Also, if the compressor is running, there will be a draft of warm air at the front of the grill. If the compressor DOES NOT cycle ON, there are several components that could be causing the failure. We will be discussing each one in this section. If the compressor DOES cycle ON (and possibly never even cycles OFF in a futile attempt to keep the cabinet cold), you will have to check another set of components.

Finally, if the food is not cold enough, the interior light is ON, and the compressor seems to be cycling ON and OFF properly, you will have to look further for related symptoms. Are the walls of the refrigerator possibly saturated with water? Is there an excessive frost build-up in the freezer? Is the refrigerator "spot cooling" — cooling properly at times and then not cooling at other times? After you have looked for the related symptoms, the following section will be helpful to you in diagnosing and pinpointing exactly what is wrong with your refrigerator.

## REFRIGERATOR DOES NOT RUN, NO INTERIOR LIGHT

Other specific failure symptoms include: 1) Food not remaining at the desired temperature. 2) Icemaker not making ice. 3) Compressor does not cycle ON.

The obvious cause of this problem is that the refrigerator is not receiving electricity. To find out exactly why, move the refrigerator out and check to see if the refrigerator power cord has fallen from the receptacle or whether there has been damage to the refrigerator power cord. If the power cord seems OK, check the components in the order that they are listed below:

### Check Receptacle

To determine if electrical power is available to the receptacle, first unplug the refrigerator power cord. Set a volt/ohmmeter on the 150-volt scale. Place one probe in one slot of the receptacle, and the other probe in the remaining slot. If line voltage is available, you will get a reading of 110 to 125 volts. *Figure 220* shows a receptacle being checked for voltage with the volt/ohmmeter.

If there is no line voltage at the refrigerator receptacle, the electrical wiring or circuit breaker must be checked. NOTE: You should call a licensed electrician to repair the problem.

### Check Refrigerator Power Cord

If line voltage is available at the receptacle,

check the refrigerator power cord. Unplug the refrigerator power cord and remove refrigerator back (see Repair Procedures). Set the volt/ohmmeter on RX-1 scale. Check continuity by placing one probe of the volt/ohmmeter on one prong of the cord, and the other probe on the other end of the power cord. If the cord has no burned or broken wires, the volt/ohmmeter should show 0 ohms resistance, or full meter deflection *(Figure 221)*. Check both sides of the power cord and replace it if there is no continuity in either wire.

You can also check the refrigerator power cord by measuring voltage with the power cord plugged into a 110-125 volt outlet. Set the volt/ohmmeter to the 150-volt scale, and place the probes across the terminals of the refrigerator terminal block and refrigerator power cord. If the cord is good, you will notice a reading of 110-125 volts. *Figure 222* shows a refrigerator power cord being checked with the volt/ohmmeter.

### Check Circuit Breaker

Check to see if the circuit breaker has "tripped." If it is tripped, reset the breaker and plug in the refrigerator power cord. If the breaker again trips after two or three seconds, the problem is a short in the electrical system of the refrigerator. However, if after plugging in the refrigerator, it runs for approximately thirty to forty minutes and the breaker trips, the problem is a breaker that is getting too hot. You will have to replace the breaker to return the refrigerator to proper operating order.

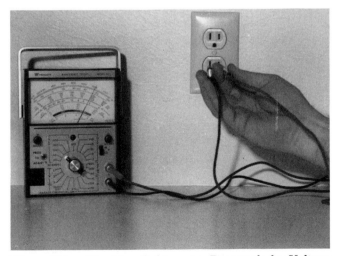

Figure 220 — Checking Refrigerator Receptacle for Voltage with Volt/Ohmmeter

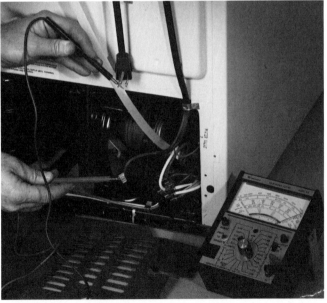

Figure 221 — Checking the Refrigerator Power Cord for Continuity with the Volt/Ohmmeter

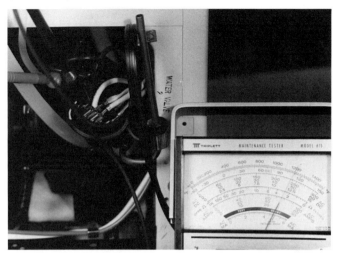

Figure 222 — Checking the Refrigerator Power Cord for Voltage at the Terminal Block with the Volt/Ohmmeter

NOTE: Circuit breakers should be replaced or repaired only by a licensed electrician. See Chapter 1, "General Information" section, "Electrical Testing," of this service guide for more information on circuit breakers.

## REPAIR PROCEDURES

Unplug the refrigerator power cord before

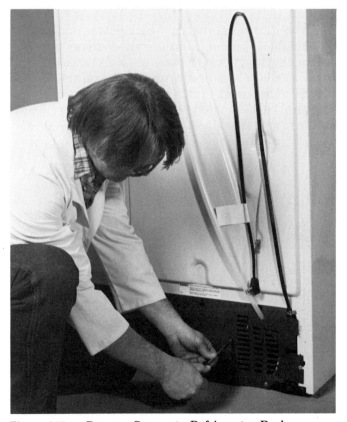

Figure 223 — Remove Screws to Refrigerator Back

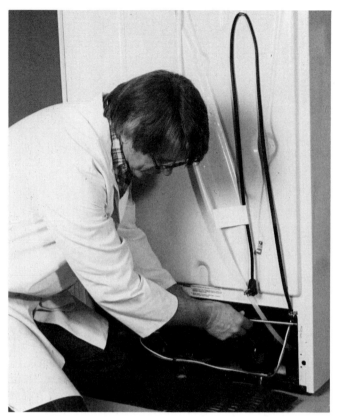

Figure 224 — Remove Screws that Secure Refrigerator Power Cord to Terminal Block

servicing the refrigerator. **Exercise care when moving the refrigerator from its original** position, or the refrigerator legs might tear or damage the floor.

### To Replace The Refrigerator Power Cord

Using hand tools, remove screws on the back panel of refrigerator *(Figure 223)*. Remove screws that secure power cord to terminal block *(Figure 224)*. Remove the defective power cord from the refrigerator and install the replacement power cord *(Figure 225)*.

### To Replace Circuit Breaker

It is recommended that a qualified electrician perform this repair.

## REFRIGERATOR DOES NOT RUN, INTERIOR LIGHT COMES ON

Other specific symptoms include: 1) Food not remaining at desired temperature. 2) Compressor does not cycle ON.

Because the interior light is ON, the refrigerator has the required electric power to operate.

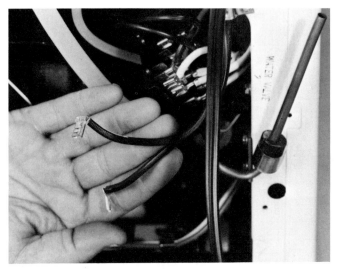

Figure 225 — Remove Refrigerator Power Cord

Something is causing the compressor not to cycle ON. Check the components in the order that they are listed below. The most likely component at fault is the defrost timer, which could be stuck in the defrost cycle. The refrigerator is then in a permanent state of defrost and does not cycle ON. However, if the compressor tries to start and the interior light dims, the problem is probably not the defrost timer or the thermostat; therefore, check the components of the compressor assembly starting with the starting relay.

Check Defrost Timer

You can easily determine if the defrost timer is defective without the use of test equipment. Remove the bottom grill or open door of refrigerator and locate the defrost timer. (Refrigerator defrost timers are located either in the refrigerator section compartment in the front or on the back of the refrigerator). With the refrigerator plugged in, insert a flat-blade screwdriver or table knife in the slot on the front of the timer. Turn the screwdriver slowly clockwise until you hear a click *(Figure 226)*. If the refrigerator starts to run, the defrost timer is defective internally. For the refrigerator to operate properly, you will have to replace the timer.

Also, if there is a slight resistance while turning the screwdriver, the timer ratchet mechanism is binding or frozen and must be replaced. Defrost timer failures occur as moisture and water enter the timer and corrode the internal parts. This can be verified by water stains on the timer terminals and timer case. If the timer turns freely with the screwdriver, this is an indication that the timer is mechanically OK.

Figure 226 — Use Screwdriver to Check Refrigerator Defrost Timer

You can also check the defrost timer motor by removing the timer from the refrigerator cabinet and inspecting the small window on the back of the timer. With the refrigerator plugged in and the timer motor running, the sprocket and gears will be moving inside the window *(Figure 227)*. If the gears are stalled inside the window, the timer motor is defective and must be replaced.

The defrost timer can be checked internally by the use of the volt/ohmmeter. With the refrigerator unplugged, set the volt/ohmmeter on the RX-1 scale. Place one probe on terminal "1" of the defrost timer and the remaining probe on terminal "2". With a screwdriver or knife inserted in the slot of the defrost timer, slowly turn in a clockwise direction until you hear a

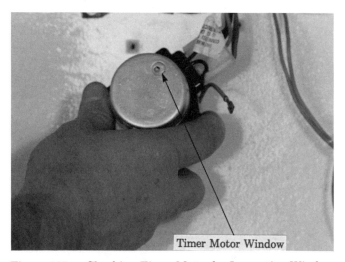

Timer Motor Window

Figure 227 — Checking Timer Motor by Inspection Window on Timer

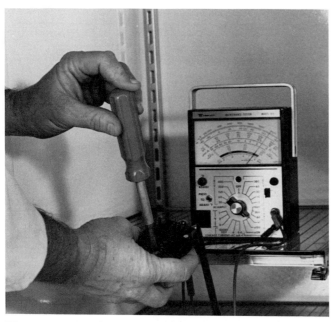

Figure 228 — Check Defrost Timer for Continuity in Refrigeration and Defrost Cycles

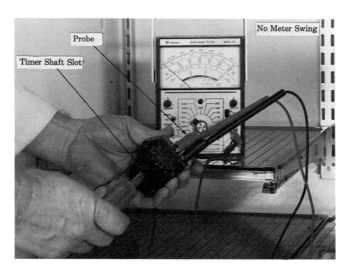

Figure 229 — Check for Continuity in Defrost Timer Compressor Contacts

click. At this point, you should see full-scale deflection *(Figure 228)*. This reading would indicate that the refrigerator has entered the defrost cycle and the defrost timer switches internally are not defective. If, however, there is no meter movement on the scale of the volt/ohmmeter, the defrost timer is defective internally and must be replaced.

The contact switches in the defrost timer that operate the compressor circuit can easily be checked with the volt/ohmmeter. Again, the volt/ohmmeter is set on the RX-1 scale. Place one probe on terminal "1" of the defrost timer and the other on terminal "3". With a screwdriver or knife inserted in the slot of the defrost timer, slowly turn in a clockwise direction until you hear a click. At this point there may or may not be full-scale deflection (0 ohms) on the volt/ohmmeter. Continue to turn the screwdriver until a second click is heard. The meter should now show full-scale deflection *(Figure 229)*, or 0 ohms. A continuity reading would mean that the switches are not defective internally and the defrost timer is OK.

To check for line voltage to the defrost timer, plug in the refrigerator to a 110-to-125-volt receptacle. Set the scale of the volt/ohmmeter on the 150 A/C scale. Locate the defrost timer and place one of the probes on terminal "1" and the remaining probe on terminal "3." If line voltage is available to the defrost timer, the

meter should indicate 110-125 volts *(Figure 230)*. If no voltage is indicated, check for defective wiring to the defrost timer or a defect in the terminal block.

### Check Thermostat

If the defrost timer is OK, check the thermostat next. You can easily check the thermostat with the volt/ohmmeter. First, unplug the refrigerator power cord, and remove the thermostat from the control console (see Repair Procedures). Set the volt/ohmmeter on the RX-1 scale, and place the probes of the volt/ohmmeter to each one of the thermostat terminals. With the thermostat control knob in the OFF position, there should be no continuity—no

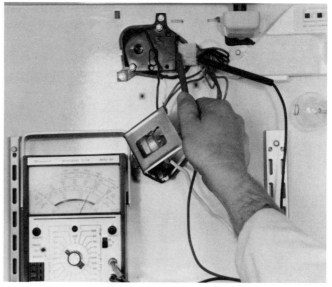

Figure 230 — Check for Voltage to Refrigerator Defrost Timer with Volt/Ohmmeter

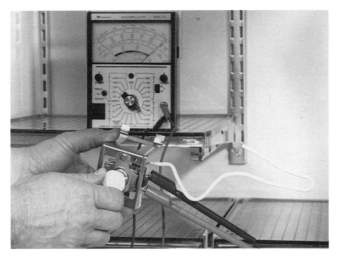

Figure 231 — Check Refrigerator Thermostat for Continuity

meter movement. With the control knob in the ON position, or a number on the dial, there should be continuity (full-scale deflection) on the meter. If not, you will have to replace it. *Figure 231* shows a thermostat continuity check being made with a volt/ohmmeter.

If the above test shows that the thermostat is defective, you can double-check it by bypassing the thermostat (wires jumped) *(Figure 232)*. Plug in the refrigerator power cord, and if the refrigerator compressor motor starts, the thermostat obviously is the cause of the failure. Replacing the thermostat is described in the repair procedure section.

## Check Start Relay

With the refrigerator door open and the power cord plugged in, observe the interior light for an intermittent dimming as the compressor motor tries to start. If the interior light shows

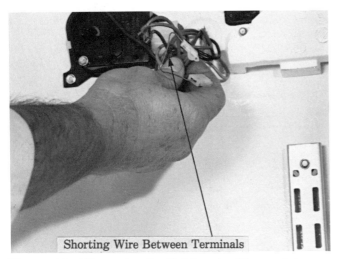

Shorting Wire Between Terminals

Figure 232 — Bypassing the Refrigerator Thermostat

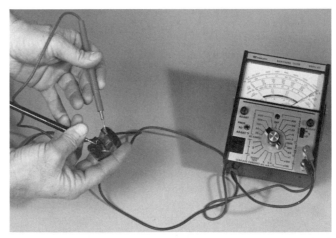

Figure 233 — Check the Refrigerator Relay for an Open Coil

signs of dimming in approximately fifteen second intervals, this means that the compressor motor is trying to start. Two possible causes of the problem are the start relay or the start capacitor. Listen at the bottom front grill for a buzzing or clicking sound in six to fifteen second intervals. If the buzzing or clicking sounds are evident, this is an indication that electricity is available to the start relay and start capacitor. If the compressor finally starts, the problem is a "struggling" relay. If the compressor does not start after repeated attempts, the problem is the start capacitor or possibly the compressor motor.

To check the starting relay for an open coil, remove the relay from the compressor starting package (See Repair Procedures in this section). Set the volt/ohmmeter to the RX-1 scale. Place one probe on each terminal of the starting relay. A continuity (0 ohm) reading would mean the relay coil is not defective *(Figure 233)*. If no reading is shown on the volt/ohmmeter, the relay is defective and will have to be replaced.

The volt/ohmmeter can also be used to check the start relay contacts. Set the volt/ohmmeter on the RX-1 scale. Place a probe on each terminal of the relay. When making this check, you must turn the relay upside down to check the contacts for continuity. The meter should show continuity or full-scale deflection if the relay contacts are closing properly. This would enable the refrigerator to electrically start the compressor motor. No reading would mean the start relay is bad, and must be replaced.

## Check Start Capacitor

There are three types of failures that are associated with the refrigerator start capacitor. These failures are a defective capacitor. an open

98

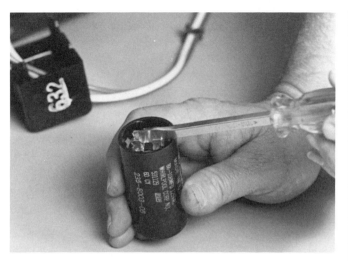

Figure 234 — Discharge Capacitor with Screwdriver Before Testing

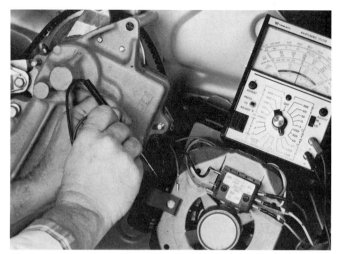

Figure 235 — Check Start Capacitor for an Open Filament

filament capacitor, and a grounded capacitor. You can check each of the above failures with the volt/ohmmeter. First, unplug the refrigerator power cord. Using hand tools, remove the screws that secure the refrigerator back and remove the starting capacitor from the compressor starting package (see Repair Procedures). Look for traces of oil on or around the capacitor. If oil is present, the capacitor is defective.

CAUTION: A charged capacitor is extremely dangerous. A capacitor that has been removed from the compressor starting package will hold a charge indefinitely, even when not in use. If you touch the terminals of a charged capacitor, the built-up voltage could give a high-voltage shock that could be fatal. A flat-blade screwdriver across the terminals should be used to discharge a capacitor. *(Figure 234)*.

To check the capacitor for an open filament, set the volt/ohmmeter on the RX-100 scale. Place one probe on each terminal of the capacitor. The volt/ohmmeter scale should immediately show continuity or full-scale deflection, and then return to infinity or to the start of the volt/ohmmeter scale *(Figure 235)*. Reverse the probes of the volt/-ohmmeter, and again the needle of the volt/-ohmmeter should immediately go to full-scale deflection (0 ohms), and return to infinity. If so, the capacitor is normal. No deflection of the meter means the capacitor is defective.

To check the starting capacitor for internal ground, set the volt/ohmmeter on the RX-10 scale. Touch one probe to capacitor terminal and other probe to case of capacitor. NOTE: This test is only applicable to starting capacitors that have metal

cases. Capacitors that have plastic cases cannot be accurately checked using this method. If the capacitor is grounded internally, the volt/ohmmeter scale will show continuity (full-scale meter deflection). You will have to replace the capacitor to restore the refrigerator to proper operating order. If the volt/ohmmeter showed no meter movement, the capacitor is good, and you will have to check the compressor motor or overload protector to find the cause of the problem. *Figure 236* shows a starting capacitor being checked for ground.

### Check Overload Protector

Unplug the refrigerator power cord, remove the screws that secure the back cover, and check for possible burned or broken wires that are attached to the overload protector. If there are burned or frayed wires, you can assume that the

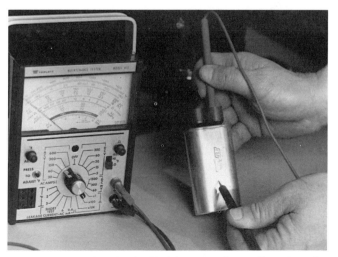

Figure 236 — Check the Refrigerator Start Capacitor for Ground

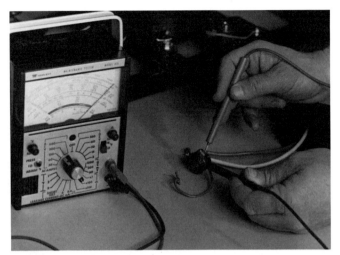

Figure 237 — Check the Refrigerator Overload Protector with the Volt/Ohmmeter

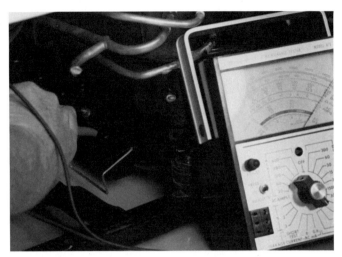

Figure 238 — Check the Start Winding of a Compressor Motor for Continuity with the Volt/Ohmmeter

failure is caused by a defect in the compressor motor circuit.

To check the overload protector, set the volt/-ohmmeter on the RX-1 scale, and attach one probe of the volt/ohmmeter to each terminal. If the overload protector is good, the meter should show continuity or full scale deflection, *(Figure 237)*. If the above check showed no continuity across the overload protector terminals, the component is defective and needs to be replaced.

### Check Refrigerator Compressor

Two failures will cause the refrigerator compressor motor to malfunction: the compressor motor is defective internally, or it is grounded internally. You can check for these failures with the volt/ohmmeter and the refrigerator test cord. The test cord is described in "Electrical Testing" section of the "General Information" Chapter 1.

All refrigerator compressor motors have terminal pins on the compressor housing that are marked "C", which represents the common side of the line, "S", which represents the start winding of the compressor motor, and "R" or "M", which represents the run winding of the compressor motor. To manually start the refrigerator compressor motor with the test cord, place one lead to terminal "C" on the compressor housing. Place the remaining lead to terminal "R". Place a screwdriver with a plastic-insulated handle from "R" terminal to "S" terminal. (This is called bridging.) Plug the test cord into a 110-to-125-volt receptacle. With the screwdriver bridged across terminals "S" and "R", the compressor should start. Remove the screwdriver

after a period of two to three seconds. If the compressor motor continues to run, you can assume that the compressor motor is fully operational.

There will be cases where you cannot use a test cord to manually start a compressor motor. Compressor motors that include a start capacitor in the starting package cannot be manually started using a test cord. For applications of this type, a test cord used by professional appliance technicians must be used to manually start the compressor motor.

In situations where a wiring diagram is not available, you can use the volt/ohmmeter to identify the windings of the compressor motor terminals in order to manually start the compressor. To locate the "S" and the "R" windings, place one probe on the compressor top terminal, which will be labeled "C" or common. Place the remaining probe of the volt/ohmmeter on one of the remaining terminals of the compressor motor. Set the dial of the volt/ohmmeter on the RX-1 scale. A reading of approximately 10 to 12 ohms indicates that the start winding terminal of the compressor has been located *(Figure 238)*.

Move the volt/ohmmeter probe from the terminal that has been identified as the start winding of the compressor, and place it on the remaining compressor terminal. The meter should indicate a reading of approximately two to four ohms. The terminal that shows the lowest reading will always be the run winding of the compressor motor *(Figure 239)*.

Also, use the volt/ohmmeter to determine if a compressor motor is internally grounded (wires

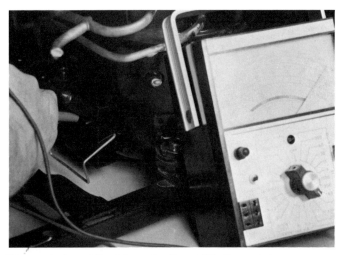

Figure 239 — Checking the Run Winding of Compressor Motor for Continuity

touching the compressor case). Set the dial on the RX-10 scale on the volt/ohmmeter. Place one probe on the compressor mounting bolt or other outside metal part, and attach the remaining probe to the compressor terminal pin(s) *(Figure 240)*. If there is meter deflection of any type, the compressor motor is internally grounded. You will have to replace the compressor motor in order to restore the refrigerator to proper working order.

## REPAIR PROCEDURES

Unplug the refrigerator power cord before servicing the refrigerator. Move the refrigerator out from the wall. Use extreme care when moving the refrigerator, because the refrigerator legs can easily damage the floor.

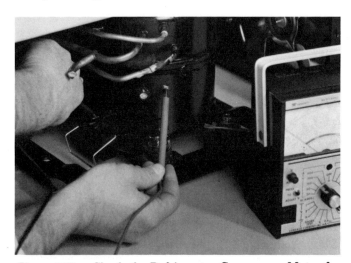

Figure 240 — Check the Refrigerator Compressor Motor for Internal Ground

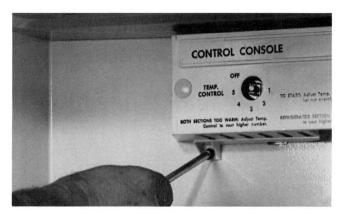

Figure 241 — Remove Screws that Secure Console Cover to Refrigerator Cabinet.

## To Replace Defrost Timer

Open the refrigerator door and locate the control console in the back of the refrigerator cabinet. Remove the screws that secure the console cover *(Figure 241)*. Remove the thermostat bracket *(Figure 242)*. NOTE: Before removing the defrost timer from the refrigerator cabinet, mark the wires, so they can be replaced correctly on the replacement part. Next, remove the screws that secure the defrost timer to the refrigerator cabinet *(Figure 243)*. Next, remove wiring harness and remove defrost timer *(Figure 244)*.

NOTE: In some units the defrost timer will not be in the refrigerator cabinet area. Sometimes the defrost timer will be on the left- or right-hand side at front of refrigerator cabinet. To gain access to these defrost timers, it is usually necessary to remove the refrigerator front grill.

Install the replacement timer by mounting it in the same position as the defective part. Follow the instruction steps and procedures that are pro-

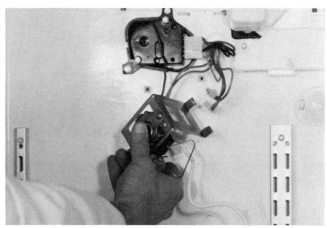

Figure 242 — Removing Thermostat Bracket from the Refrigerator Cabinet

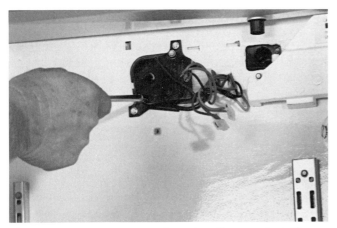

Figure 243 — Removing Mounting Screws that Secure Defrost Timer to Refrigerator Cabinet

vided in the replacement refrigerator defrost timer kit. If no installation procedure is provided, reverse the above steps.

## To Replace Thermostat

Open the refrigerator door and locate the control console in the back of the refrigerator cabinet. Remove the screws that secure the control console cover *(see Figure 241)*. Remove the thermostat bracket screws from the refrigerator cabinet. Remove and discard the defective thermostat *(Figure 245)*. NOTE: Notice the position of the thermostat sensing bulb as it is mounted into the air diffuser. The replacement thermostat sensing bulb will have to be formed to fit the air diffuser the same as the defective part that was removed. Most thermostat replacement parts are of a universal design. The replacement part will usually be different from the original thermostat, because the replacement part has been engineered to fit several models in a manufacturer's line.

Install the replacement thermostat by

Figure 244 — Disconnect Defrost Timer Wiring Harness and Remove Defrost Timer

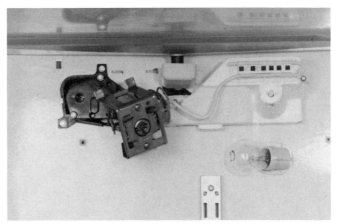

Figure 245 — Removing Defective Refrigerator Thermostat

mounting in the same position as the defective part that was removed. Follow instructions provided by the manufacturer or reverse the above steps.

## To Replace Compressor Start Relay

Move the refrigerator out from the wall and remove the screws that attach the back cover *(Figure 223)*.

Using a flat-blade screwdriver, remove the clip and cover that secures the starting components to the compressor *(Figures 246, 247)*. Remove and discard the defective relay *(Figure 248)*. NOTE: Record the wiring sequence of the defective relay so replacement relay can be wired in the same sequence as the old relay.

Install the replacement relay by mounting in the same positon as the defective relay that was removed. Follow installing steps provided in the replacement relay kit, or reverse the above steps.

## To Replace Compressor Start Capacitor

Remove the cabinet back cover *(Figure 223)*. and locate the compressor motor and starting

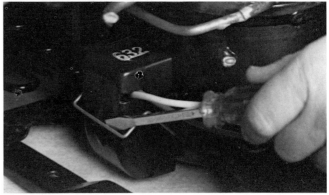

Figure 246 — Remove Clip that Secures the Compressor Starting Components

Figure 247 — Remove Component Cover of Compressor Starting Components

package components.

Use a flat-blade screwdriver to remove the clip and cover that secures the starting components to the compressor *(Figure 246-247)*. Remove the defective starting capacitor and discard the capacitor. The replacement capacitor must be wired in the same sequence as removed from the defective capacitor.

Install the replacement capacitor by mounting in the same position as the defective capacitor that was removed.

## To Replace Overload Protector

Remove the cabinet back cover *(Figure 223)*. and locate the compressor motor and the starting package components.

Using a flat-blade screwdriver, remove the clip and cover that secures the compressor starting components *(Figure 246-247)*. Remove and discard the defective protector *(Figure 249)*. Replace according to manufacturer's instructions.

## To Replace The Compressor

If you have diagnosed the compressor as being defective, you should call a qualified factory technician that is familiar with sealed system procedures. You should not attempt this repair, because a thorough knowledge of refrigeration procedures and special tools are required.

## REFRIGERATOR RUNS CONTINUOUSLY, CABINET WARM

Other specific failure symptoms include: 1) Food not remaining at the desired temperature. 2) Refrigerator compressor does not cycle OFF.

If the compressor motor runs continuously in an attempt to keep the refrigerator cool but the cabinet is still not cool enough, you will have to find the component or failure that is restricting the cooling capacity of the refrigerator. Check the components in the order that they are listed below.

### Check Refrigerator Condenser Coils

Remove the refrigerator front grill, and check the condenser for obstructions such as lint or dirt. To remove lint, use a good strong suction vacuum cleaner. An alternate method is to use a portable air tank to blow the lint away from the refrigerator condenser coil.

### Check Refrigerator Door Gasket

Most no-frost refrigerators manufactured today use magnetic door gaskets to seal or bond the refrigerator or freezer door against the refrigerator cabinet. The gaskets keep outside air from entering the freezer or refrigerator sections of the appliance. Constant opening and closing of a refrigerator door can eventually result in a gap, tearing, or door misalignment.

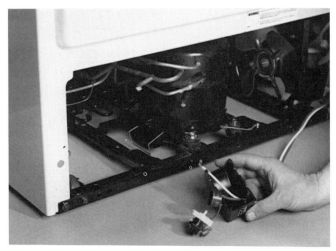

Figure 248 — Remove the Start Relay

Figure 249 — Remove the Overload Protector

Visually check the refrigerator and freezer doors for the proper mating or bonding of door seals to the refrigerator cabinet. If the refrigerator or freezer doors show any gap or misalignment, adjust or re-align the doors using the procedure discussed in the "Proper Care And Use Of Refrigerators" *(Page* 12*)*. If the door gasket is torn, replace it.

## Check Interior Light Switch

Open the refrigerator section door and locate the interior light switch *(Figure 250)*. It is usually located on the side or the top of the refrigerator section cabinet. Push the switch plunger in, and confirm that the interior light goes out. If the interior light is inoperative, check the bulb. A visual check will usually determine if a filament in the bulb is broken. If so, replace the bulb with an "appliance bulb" from your local grocery store or hardware.

If the interior light now comes ON with the door open, close the refrigerator section door, and place a small knife or screwdriver gently through the door seal to see if the interior light is ON. (Turn off room lights to see better.) If the interior light is ON, then the light switch is not operating properly. This is a common problem, and the result is higher-than-normal temperatures in the refrigerator section. A small appliance bulb can, surprisingly, raise cabinet temperatures approximately 20 degrees above the normal 38- to 42-degree temperature.

If the switch is not operating properly, open the refrigerator door to see if the switch plunger strikes the door liner as the door is being closed. Sometimes misalignment is caused by a sagging door liner.

Also, check to see if the refrigerator door is closing properly against the refrigerator cabinet. If the door is out of line, check the alignment

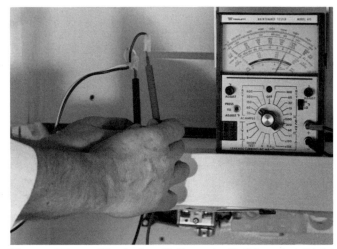

Figure 251 — Check for Voltage to Refrigerator Light Switch

procedures fully discussed in the "Proper Care And Use Of Refrigerators" section (Page 12).

A check for voltage to the interior light switch can easily be made with the volt/ohmmeter. Set the volt/ohmmeter on the 150-volt scale. Plug the refrigerator power cord into a 110-125 volt receptacle. Place the probes of the volt/ohmmeter across the switch terminals. A reading on the volt/ohmmeter scale of 110-125 volts should be indicated *(Figure 251)*. If voltage is available to the light switch, check for a defective switch.

Unplug the power cord, set the volt/ohmmeter on the RX-1 scale. Place the probes of the volt/ohmmeter across the switch terminals. With the switch plunger out, the volt/ohmmeter should show continuity, 0 ohms *(Figure 252)*. If there is no meter movement, the switch is defective, and will have to be replaced for the refrigerator to operate properly.

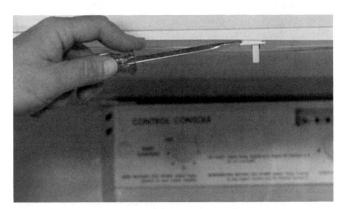

Figure 250 — Interior Light Switch Used on a Refrigerator

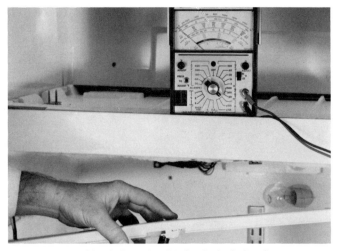

Figure 252 — Check Interior Light Switch for Continuity

## Check Evaporator Fan Motor

You can check the evaporator fan motor by removing the plastic breaker strips on the left- and right-hand sides of the freezer section of the refrigerator. See "Refrigerator Runs Continuously, Cabinet Warm," Repair Procedures Section, (Page 103).

NOTE: When removing the plastic breaker strips, it is recommended that they be pre-heated using a 40-to-60-watt light bulb. The light bulb is applied to each breaker strip for 5 to 7 minutes, to warm the pieces and make them more pliable and less subject to breakage.

NOTE: On refrigerators that are equipped with factory-installed icemakers, the icemaker will have to be removed before servicing the evaporator fan motor.

With above parts removed and the refrigerator plugged in, open the freezer door, and listen for a whirling sound of the fan. If there is no sound, visually check (if visible) the motor and fan blade to see if it is turning. If you cannot see the fan blade turning, check to see if there is an obstructin such as meat wrappers or ice blocking the movement of the fan. Remove the obstruction if detected. (See Repair Procedures)

If there is no obstruction, it is possible that the evaporator fan motor is defective. Some refrigerators have a light inside the freezer that is controlled by a switch that makes or breaks an electrical circuit when the door is opened or closed . Manually push this switch in or out to see now if the evaporator fan motor begins to run. If the motor still does not work, the problem is probably a defective evaporator fan motor.

Before removing the evaporator fan motor, turn the thermostat to the ON position. With the refrigerator power cord plugged in, make a voltage check with the volt/ohmmeter to determine if electricity is available to the evaporator fan motor. With the volt/ohmmeter set on the 150-volt scale, place the probes of the volt/ohmmeter across the evaporator fan motor terminals. If the required voltage is available, a reading of 110-125 volts will be indicated. If voltage is available, the fan motor should be checked next.

To check the evaporator fan motor with the electrical test cord, remove the unit from the refrigerator cabinet (See Repair Procedures). Attach leads of the test cord to each terminal of the fan motor. With the test cord plugged into a 110-to-125-volt receptacle, the fan motor should run *(Figure 253)*. If the motor does not run, it must be replaced.

Rather than use the power test cord, you can check the condition of fan motor windings by using the volt/ohmmeter. On the RX-1 scale, place one probe of the volt/ohmmeter on one terminal of the fan motor and the remaining probe of the volt/ohmmeter on the other terminal of the fan motor. The volt/ohmmeter should show a reading of approximately 100 ohms resistance *(Figure 254)*. A higher reading would indicate that the fan motor is defective and will have to be replaced in order for the refrigerator to operate properly.

## Check Condenser Fan Motor

With the refrigerator power cord plugged in a 110-to-125-volt receptacle and the refrigerator running, remove the front grill. With your hand, feel

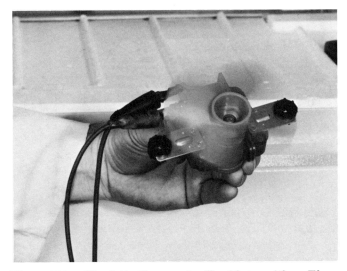

Figure 253 — Check the Evaporator Fan Motor with an Electrical Test Cord

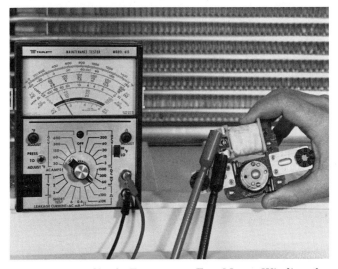

Figure 254 — Check Evaporator Fan Motor Winding for Continuity

Figure 255 — Check the Condenser Fan Motor for a Bind

for warm air that is being discharged from the condenser fan motor. If there is no air discharge, either the condenser fan motor blade is stuck, there is no voltage to fan motor, or the motor is defective internally.

Unplug the refrigerator and remove the screws in back of the refrigerator with hand tools *(Figure 223)* and check for obstruction; insulation, paper wrappers, debris, etc., that could clog the motor fan blade and cause it to stall. If there is an obstruction, unplug the refrigerator power cord and remove the debris. If there is no obstruction, turn the motor fan blade by hand *(Figure 255)*. If you feel a slight resistance, the fan motor shaft bearings are frozen. You will have to install a new condenser fan motor for the refrigerator to operate properly.

To check the condenser fan motor with the electrical test cord, remove the unit from the

Figure 256 — Check Condenser Fan Motor with Electrical Test Cord

Figure 257 — Check Condenser Fan Motor Winding with Volt/Ohmmeter

refrigerator cabinet (See Repair Procedures). Attach leads of the test cord to the two terminals of the fan motor. With the test cord plugged into a 110-to-125-volt receptacle, the fan motor should run *(Figure 256)*. If the fan motor does not start, then the condenser fan motor is defective, and must be replaced.

A static test of the fan motor winding can be made by using the volt/ohmmeter. Set the volt/ohmmeter on the RX-1 scale and place one probe of the volt/ohmmeter on one terminal of the fan motor and the remaining probe of the volt/ohmmeter on the other terminal of the fan motor. The scale of the volt/ohmmeter should show 1 to 10 ohms resistance *(Figure 257)*. A high resistance reading, or no reading at all, would indicate that the fan motor is defective and will have to be replaced.

## REPAIR PROCEDURES

Unplug the refrigerator power cord before servicing the refrigerator. Move the refrigerator out from the wall. Use extreme care when moving the refrigerator, because the refrigerator legs can tear or damage the floor.

### To Replace Door Gasket

Using hand tools, remove the screws on all four sides of the refrigerator or freezer doors so that you can remove and discard the defective gasket(s) *(Figure 258)*. Before removing the old gasket, note carefully how the gasket is installed, because the replacement gasket has to be installed in the same position as the defective gasket that is removed. Before installing the replacement

Figure 259 — Forming the Replacement Door Gasket with Hair Dryer

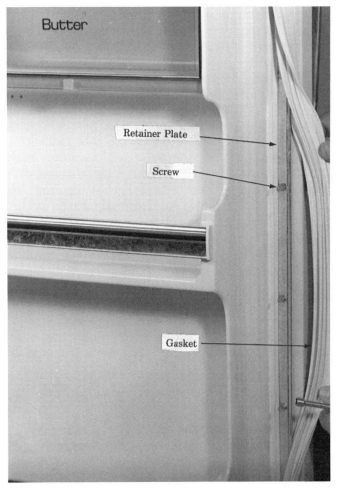

**Butter**

Retainer Plate

Screw

Gasket

Figure 258 — Replace Door Gasket by Removing Several Screws

gasket, heat the rubber with a home hair dryer set on low heat *(Figure 259)*. This will make the rubber more flexible, and easier to install on the refrigerator or freezer door. Install the replacement door gasket by mounting the lip of the gasket under the retainer plate *(Figure 260)*.

NOTE: After a replacement gasket has been installed, it might be necessary to realign the door so that it closes properly. The alignment procedures have been fully covered in the "Proper Care And Use Of Refrigerators" section of Chapter 1.

### To Replace Interior Light Switch

Unplug the refrigerator power cord from receptacle and remove the plastic breaker strips on the left and right-hand side of the refrigerator *(Figure 261)*. NOTE: When removing the plastic breaker strips, heat them with a small 40-to-60 watt light bulb for a minimum of 5 to 7 minutes. This will make the plastic more pliable and less susceptable to breakage. Never use high heat appliances

such as the home hair dryer to remove ice and frost build-up from the plastic breaker strips. Excessive heat could damage the plastic breaker strips.

NOTE: When removing the plastic breaker strips, be especially careful when removing the one to which the light switch is attached. The cabinet wires that lead to the light switch can be jarred loose from the light switch and result in incorrect wiring.

Using a flat-blade screwdriver, pry out the defective light switch *(Figure 262)*. Remove the cabinet wires from the defective light switch terminals and discard the old switch.

Install the new replacement light switch by mounting it in the same position as the defective switch. Follow closely the instructions that are provided in the replacement light switch kit. If no

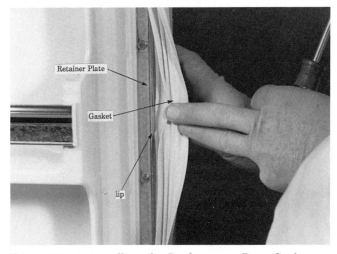

Retainer Plate

Gasket

lip

Figure 260 — Installing the Replacement Door Gasket on Refrigerator Door

Figure 261 — Remove Breaker Strips in Refrigerator Section of Refrigerator

installation procedure is provided, reverse the above steps.

## To Replace Evaporator Fan Motor

Remove the plastic breaker strips on either the left-hand or right-hand side in freezer section of the refrigerator cabinet *(Figure 263)*. Using hand tools, remove the icemaker from the refriger-

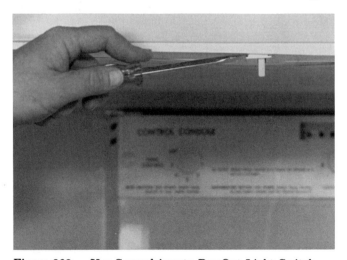

Figure 262 — Use Screwdriver to Pry Out Light Switch

ator (if equipped) *(Figure 264)*. Remove screws that secure the evaporator food pan to refrigerator cabinet and remove food pan *(Figure 265)*. Remove screws that secure the evaporator back plate to the evaporator and remove back plate *(Figure 266)*. Finally, remove screws that secure the evaporator fan motor air diffuser and remove diffuser *(Figure 267)*. Remove the harness wires that are connected to the evaporator fan motor and note the sequence as they were removed from the defective fan motor *(Figure 268)*. Next, remove the screws that secure the evaporator fan motor to the refrigerator cabinet *(Figure 269)*. Remove the defective evaporator fan motor and fan blade *(Figure 270)*. NOTE: When removing the fan motor note its position carefully as it is removed because it is possible to install the part motor in the upside-down position. This error would cause inadequate air flow within the freezer and refrigerator compartments.

NOTE: When removing the evaporator fan motor, it is advisable to wear work gloves while

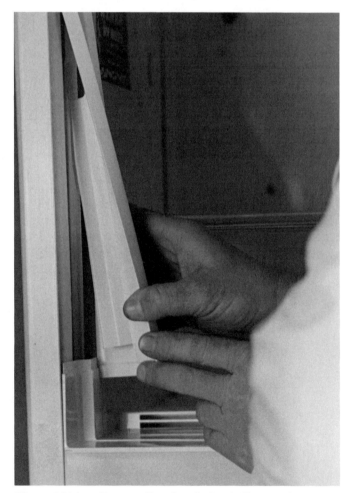

Figure 263A — Remove Breaker Strips in Freezer Section of the Refrigerator

working around the evaporator coil. The fins of the coil are razor-sharp and could cause cuts and abrasions to the hands.

After removing the evaporator fan motor, visually check the fan blade for warping, broken pieces, and cracks. If there are any defects which would affect the movement of air to the freezer and refrigerator sections, replace the fan blade. With a small screwdriver, remove the screws that secure the fan blade to the fan motor shaft and remove the fan blade.

Install the replacement evaporator fan motor or fan blade by following the installation steps provided by the manufacturer. If no installation instructions are provided, reverse the above steps.

## To Replace Condenser Fan Motor

Remove the screws that attach refrigerator back *(Figure 223)*. Locate the condenser fan motor on either the left- or right-hand side of refriger-

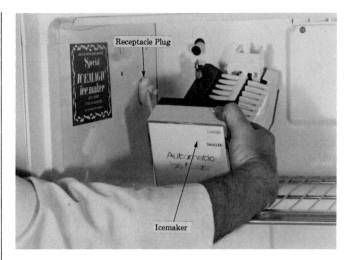

Figure 264 — Remove Icemaker from the Refrigerator Cabinet

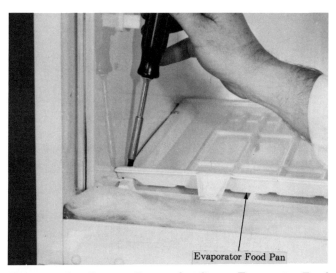

Figure 265A — Remove Screws that Secure Evaporator Food Pan to Refrigerator Cabinet

Figure 263B — Remove Bottom Breaker Strips in Freezer Section of Refrigerator

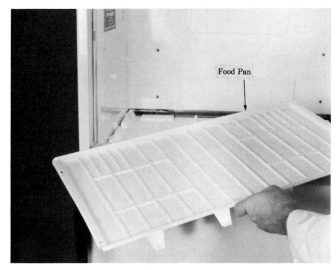

Figure 265B — Remove Evaporator Food Pan from Refrigerator

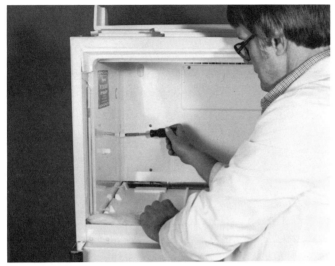

Figure 266A — Remove Screws that Secure Evaporator Back Plate

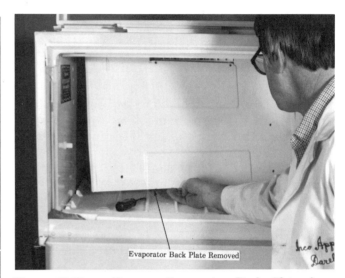

Figure 266B — Remove Evaporator Back Plate from Refrigerator

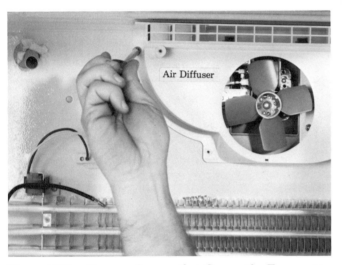

Figure 267A— Remove Screws that Secure the Evaporator Fan Motor Air Diffuser

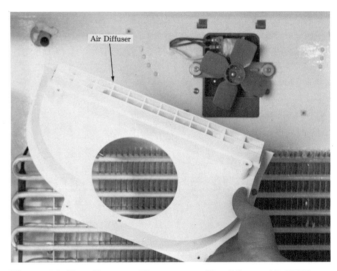

Figure 267B — Remove Evaporator Fan Motor Air Diffuser from Refrigerator

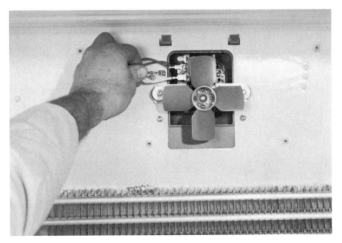

Figure 268 — Remove Wires from Evaporator Fan Motor

Figure 269 — Remove Screws that Secure Evaporator Fan Motor to Refrigerator Cabinet

Figure 270A — Remove Evaporator Fan Motor

Figure 270B — Remove the Evaporator Fan Motor and Fan Blade

ator. Using hand tools remove screws that secure the refrigerator wiring terminal block to cabinet *(Figure 271)*. Locate the wires that run from the condenser fan motor to the terminal block. Disconnect the fan motor wires. NOTE: It is important that the wires of the replacement fan motor be installed on the same terminals as the defective condenser fan motor.

Remove screws that secure the condenser fan motor to the fan motor bracket *(Figure 272)*. Next, remove the condenser fan motor and bracket from the refrigerator cabinet and remove fan blade *(Figure 273)*. NOTE: After removing the condenser fan motor, use a knife or screwdriver to mark the position on the fan motor bracket so that the replacement fan motor can be properly aligned. Improper alignment of the replacement fan motor could cause the fan blade to hit the fan motor bracket when the refrigerator is running.

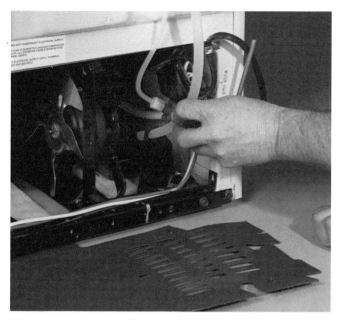

Figure 271 — Remove Screws that Secure Refrigerator Wiring Terminal Block to Cabinet

Remove screws that secure the condenser fan motor to the fan motor bracket and remove condenser fan motor *(Figure 274)*.

Install the replacement part condenser fan motor by mounting in the same position as the defective condenser fan motor that was removed. Follow instructions provided in the replacement condenser fan motor kit. If no installation steps or procedures are provided, reverse the above steps. NOTE: When reinstalling the replacement condenser fan motor, always make sure that the fan blade is not installed backwards.

## REFRIGERATOR SPOT COOLING

Specific symptoms include: 1) Food not remaining at the desired temperature. 2) Refrigerator cools intermittently. 3) Food in freezer section thaws out and then refreezes or is only partially frozen.

When a refrigerator has intermittent cooling, it is known as "spot cooling." Spot cooling is a situation where the refrigerator does not cool the food adequately for a period of time and then mysteriously returns to proper operating order. The erratic behavior in the refrigerator is caused by one of two things: a defective defrost timer, or a moisture restriction. First, check the defrost timer.

### Check Defrost Timer

First, you must determine if the defrost timer is causing the refrigerator to heat and cool at the

111

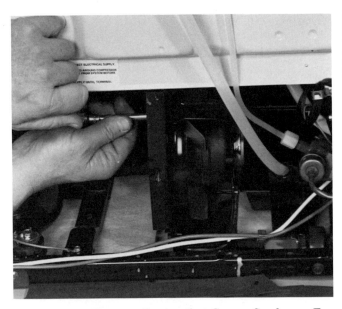

Figure 272 — Remove Screws that Secure Condenser Fan Motor to Fan Motor Bracket

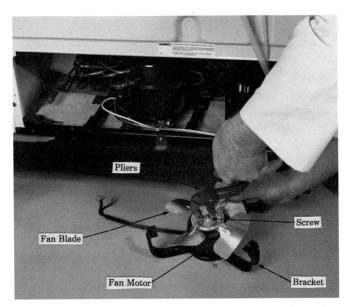

Figure 273A — Remove Condenser Fan Motor and Bracket from the Refrigerator Cabinet

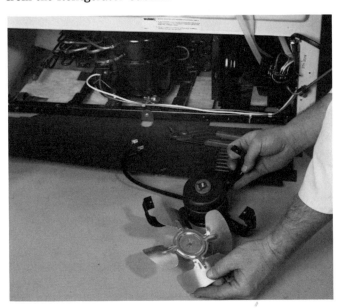

Figure 273B — Remove Fan Blade from Condenser Fan Motor

same time. It is not uncommon for a refrigerator to develop this problem. It simply means that while the refrigerator is running and cooling, the defrost timer is activating the defrost heater at the same time. This causes the food to thaw out in the freezer section and develop high refrigerator cabinet temperatures.

To check the defrost timer, refer to the "Refrigerator Does Not Run, Interior Light ON" section of this chapter (Page 95). You can also use a volt/ohmmeter to check the defrost timer. Unplug the refrigerator power cord. Set the volt/ohmmeter on the RX-1 scale. Place one probe of the volt/ohmmeter on the timer terminal that supplies voltage to the defrost timer. Place the remaining probe of the volt/ohmmeter to the timer terminal that supplies voltage to the defrost heater (see your refrigerator wiring diagram). In most cases, you will use the #2 and #4 terminal of the defrost timer for this check. With probes connected *(Figure 275)* use a knife or screwdriver to slowly turn tne defrost timer knob in a clockwise direction a complete revolution (360 degrees). While turning the screwdriver, look for any meter movement or deflection on the volt/ohmmeter scale. If there is any meter movement, repeat the check again. If meter movement is repeated, the defrost timer is defective internally. The defective defrost timer is the reason that the refrigerator is cooling intermittently in the cycle. To return the refrigerator to proper operating order, you will have to replace the faulty part. *Figure 276* shows a defrost timer that has been diagnosed as being defective with the volt/ohmmeter.

## Check For Moisture Restriction

Although a refrigerator system is supposedly a permanently sealed unit, it can be contaminated by water. This is called a "moisture restriction." When moisture gets into the system it can cause intermittent cooling. There is no set pattern as to when this failure will occur. In some cases, refrigerators have been in service for seven to ten years and then have demonstrated this symptom.

How does moisture get into the sealed refrigeration system? At the manufacturer's assembly plant, all refrigeration systems are charged with

112

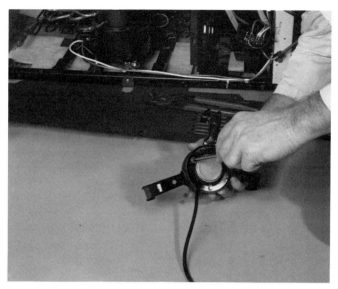

Figure 274 — Remove Condenser Fan Motor from Bracket

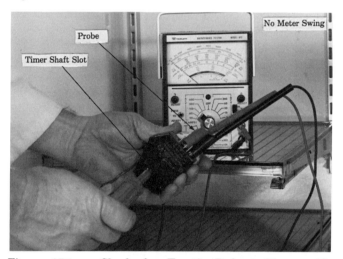

Figure 275 — Check for Erratic Defrost Timer with Volt/Ohmmeter

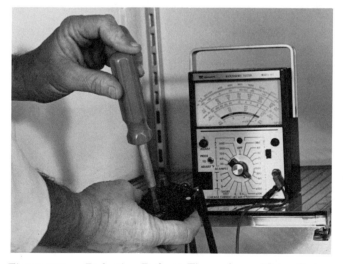

Figure 276 — Defective Defrost Timer shows Meter Swing as Timer is Rotated

refrigerant in a contamination-free environment. In time, however, moisture has a way of entering the refrigeration sealed system no matter how careful the manufacturer is. This moisture mixes with the refrigeration oil and eventually finds it way to the bottom of the compressor case. The moisture in the oil may lie there undisturbed for days, weeks, and sometimes years before a problem develops. As the refrigeration oil is mixed with the refrigerant, the moisture works its way into the refrigerant lines on both the high side (condenser) and the low side (evaporator) of the refrigeration system.

The closed refrigeration system uses a device known as a dryer that is designed to trap water particles that enter the refrigeration sealed system. The dryer will absorb most of this moisture, but eventually it will become saturated. Water particles then find their way into the restrictor or capillary tube before entering the evaporator, the coldest point of the system. If the earlier check of the defrost timer as the possible cause of "spot cooling" proved negative, the problem is probably a moisture restriction.

To determine further if there is a moisture restriction, unplug the refrigerator power cord or turn the thermostat to the OFF position and leave it OFF for at least an hour with both the freezer and refrigerator doors open. If ice crystals have formed in the capillary tube and are restricting coolant flow, they will dissolve.

After an hour, plug the refrigerator power cord in and turn the thermostat to the ON position. Let the refrigerator run for about two hours. If the refrigerator begins to cool properly, you can be sure that there is a moisture restriction in the sealed system.

Do not assume that the refrigerator repaired itself if it starts to cool. Once the ice crystals have formed in the system, they will return in time. There is no way to predict when these ice crystals will reform in the refrigerator sealed system and again cause intermittent cooling problems.

## REPAIR PROCEDURES

### To Replace The Defrost Timer

To replace the defrost timer, refer to the "Refrigerator Does Not Run, Interior Light ON" section of this service guide. Page 95.

### To Repair Moisture Restriction

If you have diagnosed a moisture restriction

as the cause of the refrigerator "spot cooling," call a qualified factory technician who is familiar with the sealed system of your refrigerator. Do not attempt this repair yourself, because it requires a thorough knowledge of a refrigeration sealed systems diagnosis and expensive special tools.

## REFRIGERATOR FROST BUILD-UP IN FREEZER SECTION

Specific failure symptoms include: 1) Frost build-up on back wall in freezer section of refrigerator. 2) refrigerator ice maker not making ice. 3) Food not remaining at the desired temperature in both the refrigerator and freezer sections.

When the refrigerator starts to build up frost in the freezer section, you can assume that something is preventing the refrigerator from going into the defrost cycle. You will have to check the components of the defrost circuit. Move the refrigerator out from the wall and unplug the refrigerator power cord. Check the components in the order listed below.

### Check Defrost Timer

First, check the defrost timer as the most likely component to cause a frost build up. Refer to the "Refrigerator Does Not Run, Interior Light ON" section for the correct procedure in checking the refrigerator defrost timer.

If you have checked the defrost timer and found it to be operating properly, insert a flat-blade screwdriver or table knife in the slot in front of the timer. Turn the screwdriver slowly clockwise until you hear a click or until all fan motors (condenser and evaporator) and the compressor motor have stopped running. Open the freezer door, and after five to seven minutes, listen for a popping and cracking sound. This sound indicates that the defrost heater is operating properly—it is doing the job by electrically heating and melting the frost accumulation on the evaporator coil. If you do not hear a popping sound in the above check, the defrost heater or the defrost termination switch should next be checked.

### Check Defrost Heater

You can check the defrost heater by removing the plastic breaker strips on the left- and right-hand sides of the freezer section (*Figure 263*). See "Refrigerator Runs Continuously, Cabinet Warm," section of this service guide, Page 103. Locate the defrost heater (see

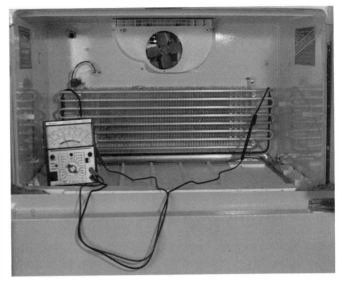

Figure 277 — Check the Defrost Heater for Continuity with Volt/Ohmmeter

Repair Procedures). Visually check for burned or broken wiring to the defrost heater. If no defect in the cabinet wiring is evident, remove one wire from the defrost heater and attach a probe of the volt/ohmmeter to the heater wire.

Set the selector switch of the volt/ohmmeter on the RX-1 scale. Place the other probe of the volt/ohmmeter to the remaining terminal of the defrost heater. If the heater is good, a continuity reading of approximately 2 to 12 ohms should be indicated (*Figure 277*). If there is no continuity or meter deflection in the above check, you will have to replace the defrost heater in order for the refrigerator to operate properly.

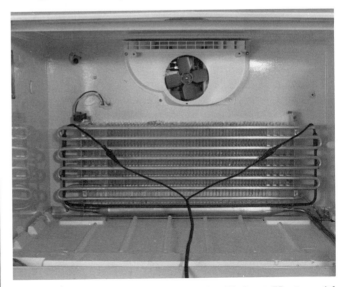

Figure 278 — Check the Refrigerator Defrost Heater with Electrical Test Cord

114

NOTE: You should remove one wire from the defrost heater before making a volt/ohmmeter check. This step will eliminate the possibility of any electrical feedback and false reading from the various electrical circuits.

If a volt/ohmmeter is not available, you can check the defrost heater with an electrical test cord. As voltage is applied across the terminals of the defrost heater, the heater should show a slight glow or heat in the lower area of the defrost heater if it is good *(Figure 278)*. If you see no glow or feel heat, the defrost heater is defective. You will have to replace it to restore the refrigerator to proper operating order. If you do see a glow on the defrost heater, check the defrost termination switch.

## Check Defrost Termination Switch

After removing above parts, locate the defrost timer termination switch (see Repair Procedures) and check for burned or broken wires. If you see no noticeable defect in the wiring, unplug the refrigerator power cord to check the defrost termination switch with the volt/ohmmeter. Set the selector switch of the volt/ohmmeter to the RX-1 scale. Place one probe of the volt/ohmmeter to one terminal of the defrost termination switch. Place the other probe to the remaining terminal. A continuity reading on the volt/ohmmeter of 0 ohms (full-scale meter deflection) indicates that the termination switch is closed or an electrical circuit exists through the termination switch. No continuity reading means the switch is defective and you will have to replace the switch in order for the refrigerator to operate properly.

NOTE: For the above volt/ohmmeter check of the defrost termination switch, the refrigerator must be at 0 degrees temperature in the freezer section. The defrost termination switch will open and the compressor will start when the evaporator has reached a temperature of 50-70 degrees.

NOTE: You should remove one wire from the defrost termination switch before making volt/-ohmmeter checks. This will eliminate the possibility of any electrical feedback from the various circuits that would show a false reading.

You can also check the defrost termination switch without the volt/ohmmeter. Simply remove the two wires to the defrost termination switch from the wiring harness, and tie these wires together (bypass the switch) to energize the defrost heater *(Figure 279)*. First, plug the refrigerator power cord into an 110-to-125-volt recep-

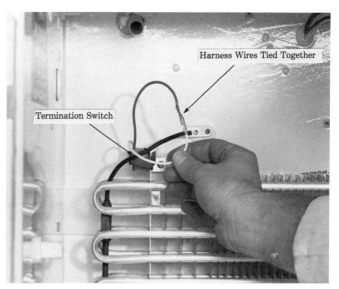

Figure 279 — Check Refrigerator Termination Switch by Bypassing the Switch

tacle. With the defrost timer advanced to the defrost cycle *(Figure 228)*, the defrost heater should be energized. With the heater energized, there should be a red glow in the lower area of the defrost heater. If a red glow is visible, this is evidence that the defrost termination switch is defective. You will have to replace it in order to restore the refrigerator to proper operating order.

NOTE: **Never leave the termination switch out of the defrost circuit, because in a short time** a severe buildup of frost would appear on the evaporator coil. Install the tied wires in their original positions on the defrost termination switch.

## Check Drain Trough Orifice

*Figure 280* shows a drain trough that is used in a typical no-frost refrigerator. As the evaporator frost is melted by the defrost heater, the water drips into the drain trough. It then flows into the drain orifice tube and then trickles into the defrost drain cup *(Figure 281)*. If an obstruction such as ice or frozen food wrappers has lodged over the drain orifice, it will only be a short time before the evaporator will become clogged with ice and the refrigerator will not cool properly. Remove the obstruction in order for the refrigerator to operate correctly.

## REPAIR PROCEDURES

Unplug the refrigerator power cord before servicing the refrigerator. Move the refrigerator out from the wall. Use care when moving the

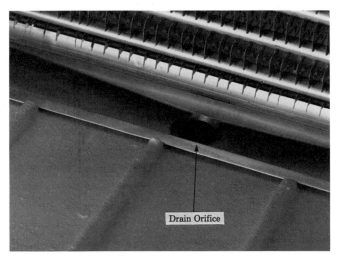

Figure 280 — Typical Defrost Drain Trough in a No-Frost Refrigerator

refrigerator, because the metal feet can tear or damage the floor.

### To Replace Defrost Timer

Refer to the "Refrigerator Does Not Run, Interior Light ON" section, Page 95, for the replacement of the refrigerator defrost timer.

### To Replace Defrost Heater

Open the freezer door and remove the plastic breaker strips at the front of freezer section (see "Refrigerator Runs Continuously, Cabinet Warm," section of this service guide). NOTE: When

Figure 281 — Drain Trough Orifice Tube on a Typical Refrigerator

Figure 282 — Remove Defrost Heater Wires from Wiring Harness

removing plastic breaker strips, heat them with a low-wattage (40-60) light bulb for 5 to 7 minutes. Heat will make the plastic more pliable and less susceptible to breakage.

NOTE: You should never use high heat appliances such as the home hair dryer to remove the plastic breaker strips. Heat from the hair dryer will destroy the plastic.

Remove screws that secure the food pan and remove the food pan (*Figure 265*). Remove screws that secure the evaporator back plate and remove the plate (*Figure 266*). NOTE: On refrigerators that have compact ice makers that are attached in the freezer section, you must remove the icemaker before you can remove the evaporator back plate and replace the defrost heater (*Figure 264*).

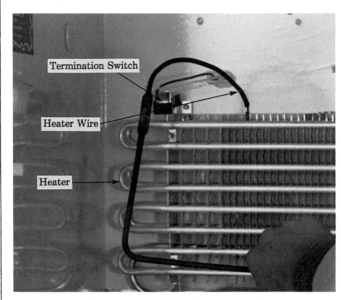

Figure 283 — Remove Defrost Heater from the Refrigerator

Locate the wires in the cabinet that are attached to the defrost heater terminals *(Figure 282)*. Remove the wires from the heater terminals by pulling out with fingers. Remove the screws and clamps that secure the defective heater to the evaporator coil. Next, remove the defrost heater *(Figure 283)*.

NOTE: Exercise care when working around the evaporator coil and removing the defective defrost heater. The fins are very sharp and can cause cuts and abrasions to the fingers and hands. Wear light-duty work gloves when working around the evaporator coil.

Install the replacement defrost heater by following the installation steps provided in the replacement part defrost heater kit. If no installation procedure is provided, reverse the above steps.

### To Replace Defrost Termination Switch

Refer to the previous section, "To Replace the Defrost Heater," for the procedure to remove the breaker strips and evaporator back plate. Then, locate the two wires in the cabinet wiring that are attached to the defrost termination switch. Remove the wires from the termination switch. Next, remove the clamp and lift out the termination switch.

Install the replacement defrost termination switch by mounting it in the same position as the defective part that was removed. Follow instruction provided with the replacement defrost termination switch. If no installation steps or procedures are provided with the replacement defrost termination switch kit, reverse the above steps.

## REFRIGERATOR COLLECTS WATER IN REFRIGERATOR SECTION

Specific failure symptoms include: 1) Water collecting on shelves and food, and under crisper pans in the refrigerator section. 2) Water running down back wall of refrigerator. To find the cause of the problem, which is probably a defrost drain obstruction, unplug the refrigerator power cord and open the refrigerator door.

### Check Defrost Drain

As a no-frost refrigerator enters the defrost cycle, a defrost heater is energized and melts the frost and ice that has accumulated on the evaporator coil between defrost cycles. Water from the melted frost then runs down the defrost drain

Figure 284 — Check the Refrigerator Condensation Pan

cup, through the drain tubing, and finally down to the condensation drain pan. This is the normal flow of water when the defrost system is working properly. Sometimes, however, the water meets obstructions, which causes the refrigerator to collect water in the refrigerator section.

To determine if there is a drain obstruction, remove the refrigerator bottom grill to check for water droplets in the condensation drain pan. If there is no water in the pan *(Figure 284)*, there is probably a drain obstruction in the defrost drain cup or the defrost drain tube.

### Check Defrost Drain Cup

To check for an obstruction in the defrost drain cup, remove the refrigerator control knob and console *(Figures 285 and 286)*. Next, check the drain cup *(Figure 287)* for obstructions such as algae and foreign objects. All municipal water supplies have chemicals added to the water for sanitation purposes. In time, these chemicals form an algae buildup in the water line or tube, which in turn chokes off the drain opening and causes an obstruction.

If you find an obstruction, gently pull on the drain cup and remove it. Clean the cup in hot water, removing all chemicals and debris. Reinstall the drain cup. Next, slowly pour water from a long-necked bottle into the drain cup *(Figure 288)*. The purpose of this check is to determine if there is a restriction in the drain tube to the condensation drain pan. After pouring water in the drain cup, wait for a period of approximately thirty seconds. Then place your ear to the front grill and listen for water trickling into the condensation drain pan. If you hear no

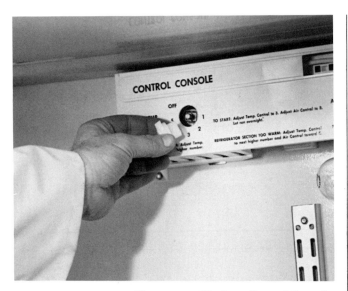

Figure 285 — Remove Thermostat Knob on Control Console

sound, remove the condensation drain pan and check for traces of water in the pan *(Figure 289)*. If there is a small amount of water, this verifies that there is no restriction in the drain tube. If, however, no water collected in the drain pan, you will have to make a further check for a restriction in the drain tube.

### Check Defrost Drain Tube

To check the drain tube, which is a round plastic tube of approximately ½ inch in diameter, move the refrigerator out from the wall and unplug the refrigerator power cord. Locate the defrost drain tube on the back of the refrigerator. Remove this tube by pulling it out with your fingers *(see Figure 290)*. Refer to the "Repair Pro-

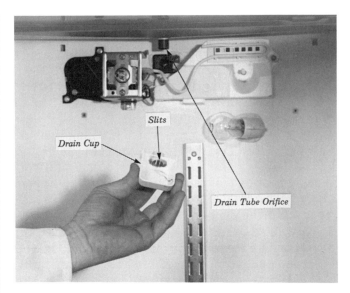

Figure 287 — Remove Refrigerator Drain Cup and Check for an Obstruction

cedures" section for the correct procedure to clean the drain tube.

After cleaning, thoroughly inspect the drain tube for cracks that could cause water to leak onto your floor. If you notice any cracks, replace the defrost drain tube.

Then using a drop light or flashlight, look for a small grommet that is attached to the end of the drain tube. This grommet is commonly referred to as a duck-bill grommet *(see Figure 291)*. It serves to retard the sound of the defrost water as it enters the condensation pan. Without this grommet, the water would make an annoying sound. Remove this grommet from the drain tube and check it for debris that could cause an obstruction in the opening of the grommet. Clean

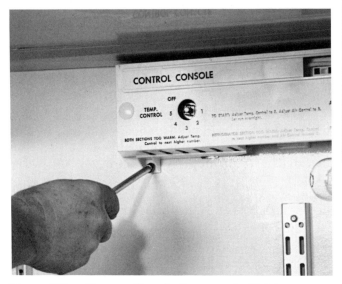

Figure 286 — Remove Console Cover on the Refrigerator

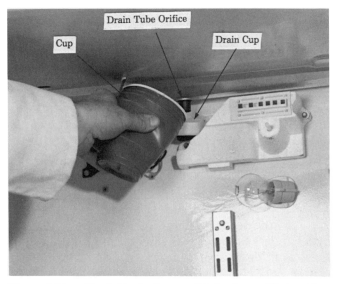

Figure 288 — Check Drain Cup and Tube for an Obstruction

118

Figure 289 — Water Droplets in a Refrigerator Condensation Pan

the grommet in warm water and detergent and reinstall in the drain tube.

## REPAIR PROCEDURES

Unplug the refrigerator power cord before servicing the refrigerator. Move the refrigerator out from the wall. Use extreme care when moving the refrigerator, because the refrigerator legs can easily tear or damage the floor.

### To Clean Defrost Drain Cup

To clean the defrost drain cup, remove the refrigerator console cover. Next, locate the drain cup. The drain cup is usually not secured by

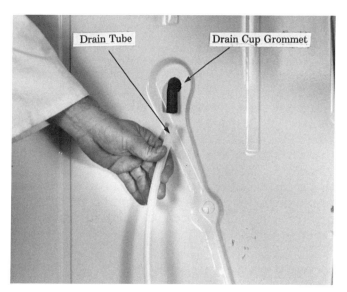

Figure 290 — Drain Tube on No-Frost Refrigerator

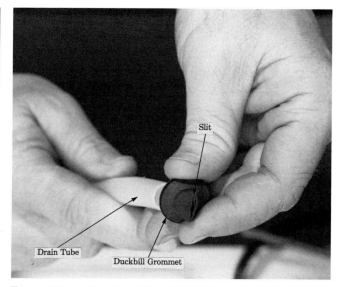

Figure 291 — Checking "Duckbill" Grommet on Drain Tube for an Obstruction

screws, so by placing fingers on cup, pull straight out and remove cup. The drain cup is next cleaned by washing in a solution of detergent and warm water to remove all debris. Reinstall the defrost cup. Using a long-necked bottle filled with water, slowly pour water into the cup to see if the water is slowly running into the drain condensation pan *(Figure 288)*. If the water slowly flows into the drain condensation pan, then you can assume that the drain obstruction problem has been corrected and the refrigerator is restored to proper operating order.

### To Clean Defrost Drain Tube

To clean the drain tube, you will need a can of R-12 refrigerant, a charging hose, and a can tap valve. You can purchase these materials at any hardware or auto parts stores. With the drain cup removed, place one end of charging hose into the drain grommet opening. With the R-12 refrigerant can in an upright position, slowly open the can tap valve, and the refrigerant under pressure will enter the drain tube. Remove the algae and debris from the drain grommet and the drain tube. CAUTION: Never invert or turn the refrigerant can upside down when cleaning the grommet and drain tube. Under no circumstances should you apply a heat source such as propane torch or acetylene torch to the refrigerant container. The liquid is under pressure and could burst the can or container, and cause severe bodily injury. If the refrigerant pressure from the can is low, you can safely place the container in a bucket of hot water. This enables the

119

refrigerant to be removed from the can or container at a greater pressure.

## REFRIGERATOR RUNS CONTINUOUSLY, CABINET TOO COLD

Specific symptoms include: 1) Compressor motor runs all the time and does not cycle regularly. 2) Food freezing in the refrigerator section of the refrigerator. To find the cause of this problem, which is usually caused by a faulty thermostat, move the refrigerator out from the wall and unplug the refrigerator power cord.

### Check Refrigerator Thermostat

To check the refrigerator thermostat, refer to "Refrigerator Does Not Run, Interior Light Comes ON" section of this service guide, Page 95.

### REPAIR PROCEDURES

Unplug the refrigerator power cord before servicing the refrigerator. Move the refrigerator out from the wall. Use extreme care when moving the refrigerator because the refrigerator feet can damage the floor.

### To Replace Refrigerator Thermostat

To replace the refrigerator thermostat, refer to the "Refrigerator Does Not Run, Interior Light ON" section of this service guide, Page 95.

## REFRIGERATOR IS NOISY IN OPERATION

Specific failure symptoms include: 1) Refrigerator makes unusual noises in refrigerator cabinet. 2) Refrigerator makes unusual noises when the refrigerator shuts OFF. 3) Refrigerator has vibrating sounds in the unit.

Refrigerators, through their duty cycle and day-to-day use, will eventually develop squeaks, rattles, vibrations, and unusual noises. Since the refrigerator is one large mass of metal, there are a number of areas where the refrigerator can start to make noise. For example, most no-frost refrigerators have at least two auxiliary motors and others have more than four auxiliary motors. These motors (condenser fan motor, evaporator fan motor, and ice maker motors) will eventually show signs of wear and fatigue. Wear will cause the motors to make unusual noises while they are running. As the motors start to fail, they will have to be serviced or possibly replaced in order to quiet the refrigerator.

To find the cause and check for these problems, move the refrigerator out and unplug the refrigerator power cord.

### Check Refrigerator Tubing

Look behind refrigerator to see if the tubing of the ice maker is hitting or rubbing against the refrigerator cabinet. If the tubing is rubbing, it can usually be corrected by repositioning the tubing. In cases where repositioning the tubing will not eliminate the rattle or noises, it can be wrapped with newspapers or plastic wrappers. This noise in the icemaker tubing is caused by the hammering or chattering of the tubing as the water inlet valve releases water into the icemaker mold.

Remove the back of the refrigerator and look for refrigerator tubing that might have vibrated against the compressor housing or the refrigerator cabinet. Check the tubing around the condenser that might be responsible for vibrations.

### Check Fan Motors

Check condenser fan motor housing for loose screws that could be responsible for unusual noise or vibration. Check housing area for objects such as candy wrappers or metal objects that strike the condenser fan motor fan blade as it is running.

Check evaporator fan motor for unusual noises or rattles. Check fan motor housing for ice obstructions and meat wrappers that could be responsible for noises in the evaporator fan motor.

### Check For Vibrations Inside Refrigerator Cabinet

Open door of the refrigerator section of the refrigerator and listen for vibrations and rattles around the shelves. Tighten the screws to the brackets that secure the adjustable or fixed shelves. Reposition all food on the shelves where vibrations could occur. Open the freezer door of the refrigerator and listen for unusual noises and vibrations. If the noises appear to be coming from the evaporator or ice maker motor areas, you would have to replace the motor(s) in order to restore the refrigerator to normal operating order.

### REPAIR PROCEDURES

Unplug the refrigerator power cord before

servicing the refrigerator. Move the refrigerator out. Use extreme care when moving the refrigerator, because the refrigerator legs can easily tear or damage the floor.

To Replace The Condenser Fan Motor

Refer to "Refrigerator Runs Continuously, Cabinet Warm" section Page 103 of this service guide for the replacement of the refrigerator condenser fan motor.

To Replace The Evaporator Fan Motor

Refer to "Refrigerator Runs Continuously, Cabinet Warm" section Page 103 of this service guide for the replacement of the refrigerator evaporator fan motor.

# 5

# *The Refrigerator Compact Icemaker*

We felt that the simplest way to organize this guide to help the do-it-yourselfer solve a problem was to organize it in the following manner:

- Show pictures of and describe all the components that make up the system.
- List specific problems (or failures) and suggest other symptoms that will help isolate the problem.
- List components to be checked in the proper sequence to isolate the faulty part.
- Give step-by-step replacement instructions for removing and replacing the faulty part.

As with the automatic washer, the icemaker is often treated with fear and reverence by the home repairman, because he is afraid he might flood the refrigerator with water by taking out the icemaker. Or even worse, he might damage the sealed freon system.

Actually, the icemaker is the simplest unit to remove, and very easy to work on. On the demonstration refrigerator we are showing in this guide, the icemaker can be removed in about two minutes. Simply remove two screws beneath the unit and unplug its electrical connection. It's out.

Most of the tests that need to be run to determine the cause of faulty operation will be made with the icemaker installed in the refrigerator. Probably the most common problem with icemakers doesn't involve the icemaker unit itself. A faulty water inlet valve doesn't allow the proper supply of water to reach the icemaker. This solenoid-operated valve is located at the back of the refrigerator near the bottom (look for the copper line that supplies water to the machine).

Sometimes the problem is even before the water inlet valve. Often the lack of sufficient water can be traced to the water cutoff valve that is located at the back of refrigerator.

By following the testing procedures outlined in this guide, the home repairman should be able to diagnose any problem with his icemaker, and in most instances, return it to good working order for little or no cost.

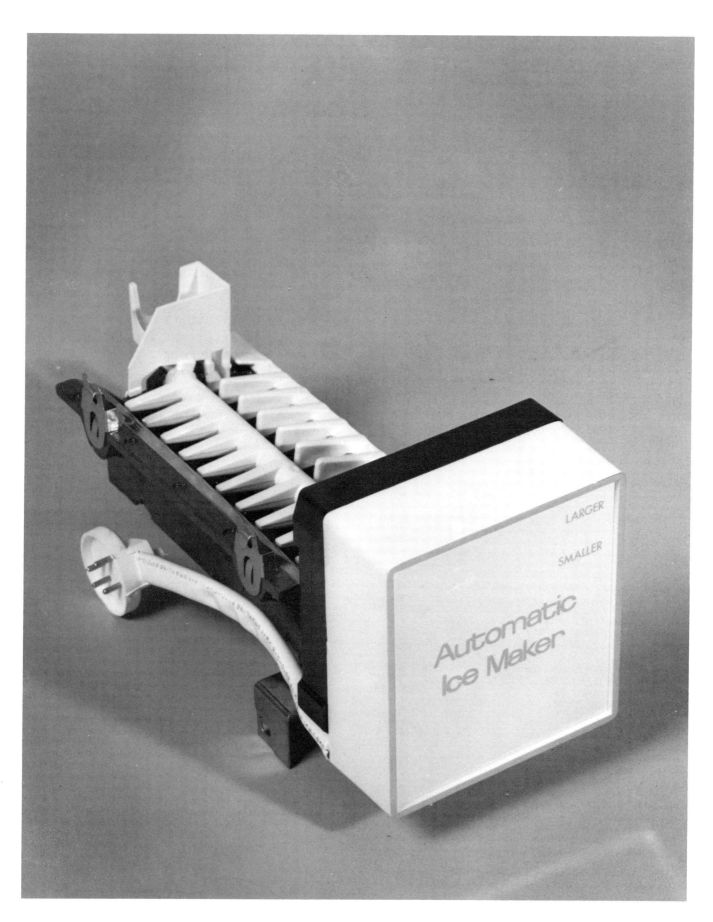

# THE ICEMAKER-HOW IT WORKS

The water supply that is controlled by a water inlet valve enters the mold cavity of the compact icemaker. The water then freezes in the icemaker mold. An electric heater thaws the frozen ice crescents so that they can be ejected from the mold. An electric motor then drives an ejector blade through a cam assembly, which frees the released crescents. The crescents revolve in a clockwise rotation and tumble into the ice storage bin.

## COMPACT ICEMAKER COMPONENTS

The electrical components of a typical refrigerator compact icemaker are described below:

### Water Inlet Valve

The water inlet valve is a solenoid-operated switch located at the bottom of the refrigerator. When it is energized by electrical power, water is released from the supply line through the water valve and into the compact icemaker mold. *Figure 292* shows a typical icemaker water inlet valve.

### Ice Mold

The ice mold is made of an aluminum or plastic material with separations that mold either six, eight, or twelve ice crescents *(Figure 293)*.

### Mold Heater

The mold heater is an electrical device that thaws the ice quickly so it can be released from the icemaker mold *(Figure 294)*.

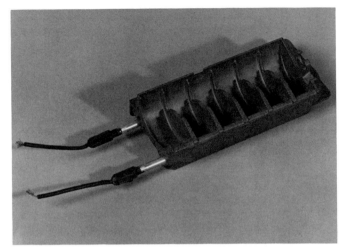

Figure 293 — Ice Mold for Six Crescents

### Cycling Thermostat

The cycling thermostat is a bi-metal device that controls the activation of the icemaker ejection cycle *(Figure 295)*.

### Shut-Off Arm

The shut-off arm is a component that operates a switch to control icemaker ON/OFF *(Figure 296)*.

### Ice Ejector Blade

The ice ejector is a molded plastic component. The blade sweeps the ice from the mold cavities during the ejection cycle *(Figure 297)*.

### Water Supply Valve

The water supply valve supplies water from the supply line to the inlet valve *(Figure 298)*.

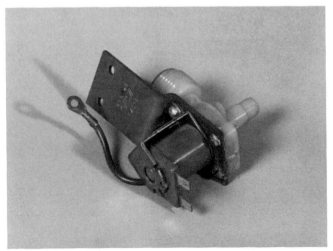

Figure 292 — Water Inlet Valve Used In Refrigerator

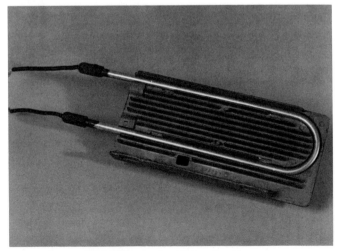

Figure 294 — Mold Heater for Releasing Ice

124

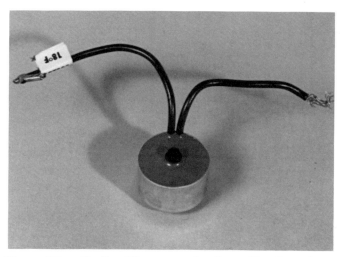

Figure 295 — Cycling Thermostat for Controlling Icemaker

## Timing Switches

Two or three switches are most commonly used in refrigerator compact icemakers. Their functions are listed below:

- The HOLDING SWITCH assures the completion of a cycle once the icemaker has started ejecting the ice *(Figure 299)*.
- The WATER VALVE SWITCH opens the water inlet valve during the icemaker fill cycle *(Figure 299)*.
- The SHUT-OF SWITCH stops ice maker operation when the storage bin is full *(Figure 299)*.

## Timing Cam Assembly

In the compact icemaker there are separate cams that are molded as one part to control the timing sequences of the icemaker.

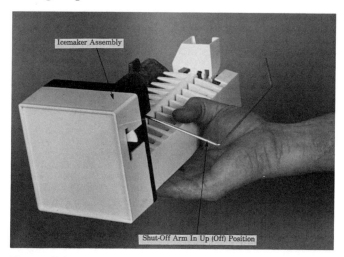

Figure 296 — Shut-Off Arm Stops Operation of Icemaker When Bin is Full

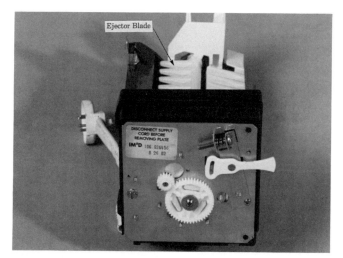

Figure 297 — Ejector Blade Forces Frozen Ice Out of Mold

## Icemaker Drive Motor

The drive motor is a single-shaft, low-wattage type motor, that powers the refrigerator icemaker. This motor turns the timing cams and the ejector blade *(Figure 300)*.

## DIAGNOSING PROBLEMS

Unlike the other major appliances discussed in this service guide, either the icemaker works completely (makes ice) or it doesn't work at all. Therefore, there is only one problem listed for the icemaker: the icemaker doesn't make ice. The most obvious failing sequence of this problem is listed in the following discussion. This discussion should aid you in diagnosing and pinpointing exactly why the refrigerator compact icemaker doesn't make ice. Also listed are repair procedures to fix the unit.

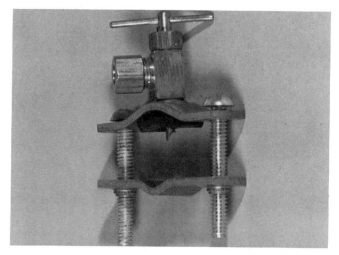

Figure 298 — Water Supply Valve Used to Tap into Copper Water Line

Figure 299 — Timing Switches Used in Refrigerator Icemaker

## REFRIGERATOR IS RUNNING - ICEMAKER NOT MAKING ICE

Specific failure symptoms include either: 1) Refrigerator temperature too warm to make ice. 2) No water getting to icemaker mold. 3) Icemaker not ejecting the frozen ice.

### Check Refrigerator

For a compact icemaker to operate properly, the refrigerator freezer compartment must be maintained at 10 degrees F or lower. The design of the icemaker is such that the icemaker will not eject the ice until it is frozen hard.

Check freezer temperature by placing an inexpensive thermometer in the freezer compartment. Close the door and wait thirty minutes before making a temperature check. If the thermometer check indicates that the freezer compartment is above 10 degrees, then you can assume

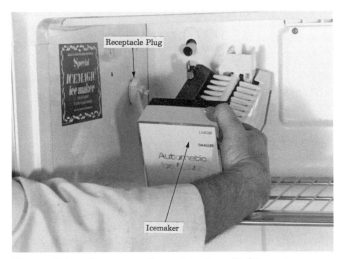

Figure 301 — Removing Icemaker from Refrigerator

that the refrigerator has a problem that will have to be repaired in order for the refrigerator to make ice. Refer to the "Household Refrigerators" chapter, Page 88. However, if the thermometer check shows that the freezer compartment temperature is 10 degrees F or lower, then you can assume that the icemaker has a problem and will need repair.

### Check Electrical Power To Icemaker

Using standard hand tools, remove the compact icemaker from the freezer section of the refrigerator (Figure 301). Keep the refrigerator power cord plugged into receptacle. Set volt/-ohmmeter on the 150-volt scale. Place one probe of the volt/ohmmeter on each side of the icemaker receptacle. The volt/ohmmeter should read 110-125 volts, which verifies that voltage is available to the wiring harness (Figure 302). If

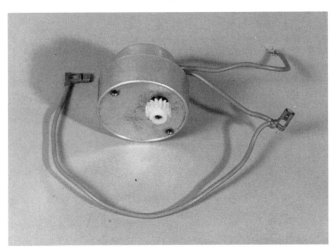

Figure 300 — Icemaker Drive Motor

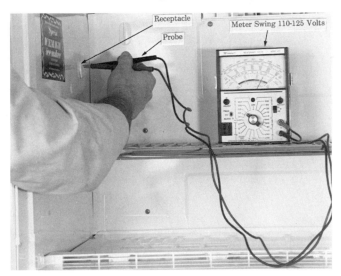

Figure 302 — Check Icemaker Receptacle for 110-125 Volts

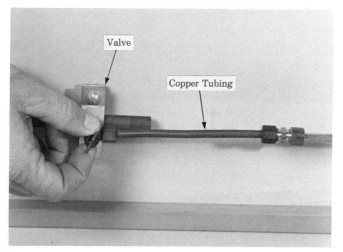

Figure 303 — Water Supply Valve Used to Supply Water to Icemaker

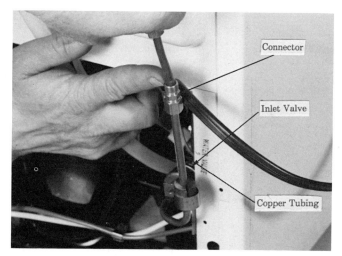

Figure 304 — Remove Icemaker Tubing Connected to Water Inlet Valve

voltage is not available to the icemaker, an electrical problem such as a broken wire to the water inlet valve, broken wire to icemaker receptacle, or burned or broken wire at the refrigerator electrical terminal block would have to be suspected, diagnosed, and repaired.

## Check Water Supply Valve

After determining that the refrigerator is cold enough to make ice and that electrical power is available to the icemaker, next check to see if supply water is available to the icemaker. If no water flows into the icemaker mold, the first suspect is the water supply valve.

Locate the water supply valve (see Repair Procedures). This valve supplies water to the icemaker from the water supply line. The valve usually can be opened and closed, so that you can turn the water to the icemaker OFF if the unit develops a water leak.

Some typical locations for the water supply valve are under the kitchen sink, under cabinets, wet bar sinks, and on water heater lines. A typical icemaker water supply valve is shown in *Figure 303*. After locating the valve, turn the supply water to the icemaker OFF by turning the valve stem clockwise.

By using hand tools, remove the icemaker tubing from the connection to the water supply valve *(Figure 304)*. Hold a small container or bucket over the disconnected water line, and turn the water supply ON by turning valve stem in a counterclockwise direction. If the valve is in good working order, water will be forced through the valve very quickly. However, if small amounts or only a trickle of water is being forced through the valve, the

water supply valve is defective. You will have to replace it for the icemaker to operate properly.

## Check Water Inlet Valve

Next in line after the water supply valve is the water inlet valve, usually located at the back of the machine near the bottom. The role of the water inlet valve is to release supply water from the supply line so that it can enter the icemaker mold cavity. However, the valve's internal components can eventually become worn out from the corrosive properties and algae in the water, and fail to supply water to the mold cavity. Check the water inlet valve to see if it is electrically releasing the water on command to the mold cavity.

The easiest way to check this valve is to check the water level in the mold cavity itself. First, make sure that the icemaker shut-off arm is in the down (ON) position. Also, note the position of the ejector blade — it should be in the horizontal position (start of the cycle) *(Figure 305)*. Providing that electricity is available, this indicates that the icemaker has made a revolution (360 degrees) and the icemaker should have filled with water.

If water is reaching the mold and the icemaker is filling with water properly, there should be a water level of at least 1/2 inch in the mold. This would indicate that the water inlet valve is operating properly. However, if you see no water or only a small amount of water in the mold, it can be assumed that the water inlet valve is defective and should be replaced. You should also check the water inlet tube on the back of the refrigerator for possible ice obstruction

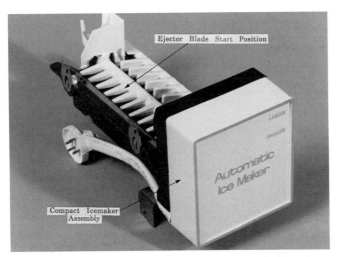

Figure 305 — Refrigerator Icemaker Ejector Blade in Start Position

*(Figure 306).*

Remove two screws and pull the tube out gently. An ice formation in the water inlet tube is caused by a defective water inlet valve. If you find this condition, you will have to replace the inlet valve in order for the icemaker to make ice.

If there is no ice formation in the water inlet tube and no water has entered the mold cavity, you should next test the water inlet valve electrically to verify its operation. Move the refrigerator out from the wall. Unplug the power cord and open the freezer door. Slowly turn the icemaker ejector blade by hand in a counter clock-

wise direction until it reaches the 6 o'clock position. NOTE: Do not manually turn the icemaker ejector blade too fast. You can easily strip the drive motor gears and ruin the motor.

**The reason for manually turning the ejector blade counterclockwise is to get the icemaker in a position so that electrical checks can be made to the water inlet valve.** Next, remove screws in the back of the refrigerator *(Figure 223).* Remove the screws that secure the water inlet valve to the refrigerator cabinet, and remove the water inlet valve (see Repair Procedures).

Set the volt/ohmmeter to the 150-volt scale and connect the probes to the refrigerator wiring harness that was disconnected from the water inlet valve. Plug the refrigerator power cord into the receptacle.

With power to the unit, the icemaker will begin to revolve clockwise until it reaches the 8 o'clock position, at which time the fill switch in the icemaker will complete a circuit to the water inlet valve. As the ejector blade of the icemaker approaches the 8 o'clock position, you should show a reading on the volt-meter scale of 110-125 volts *(Figure 307).* This indicates that electricity is being supplied from the icemaker to the water inlet valve.

Correct voltage reading means power has been verified to the water inlet valve wiring harness. The problem has now been isolated to a defective water inlet valve.

If, however, there is no reading on the volt/ohmmeter, this would indicate that voltage required to operate the icemaker is not available. A check for the following should be made:

Figure 306 — Check Refrigerator Icemaker Inlet Tube for Obstruction

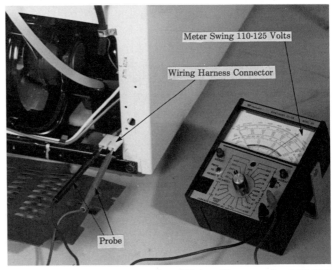

Figure 307 — Check Icemaker Wiring Harness for 110-125 Volts

128

- Defective wires to icemaker wiring harness receptacle.
- Broken wires in compact icemaker assembly.
- Defective timing switch in icemaker assembly.
- Defective wires from terminal block to icemaker assembly.

A check for a defective water inlet valve can also be made with the electrical test cord. With the water inlet valve removed (see Repair Procedures) and water supply valve turned ON, place one lead of the test cord on each terminal of the water inlet valve. Place a container over water inlet tube in freezer. Next, plug the test cord into a 110-to-125-volt receptacle. The valve should now force water through the tubing and into the icemaker inlet tube or container *(Figure 308)*. If no water enters the inlet tube, then it is a good indication that the water inlet valve is defective and will have to be replaced in order for the icemaker to work.

## Check Icemaker Cycling Thermostat

A simple check for a possible defective cycling thermostat is to place the icemaker shut-off arm in the up (OFF) position and leave for a period of approximately 2 hours. After an extended OFF period, place the shut-off arm in the down (ON) position. The icemaker ejector blade should

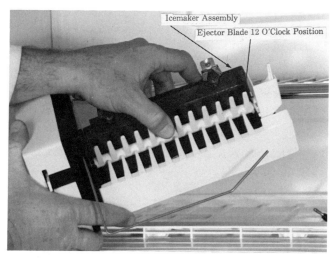

Figure 309 — Icemaker Advanced to Twelve O'Clock Position

revolve in a clockwise rotation toward the 12 o'clock position *(Figure 309)*. If, however, the ejector blade remains in the start position, check for electrical power to the icemaker receptacle *(Figure 302)*. If power is available, then some component in the icemaker or the cycling thermostat is defective.

A visual check can also be made to diagnose a defective cycling thermostat. Open the refrigerator freezer door and note the position of the icemaker ejector blade. If, for example, the ejector blade is stalled in the 12, 2, or 4 o'clock positions, it could mean that there is a defective component

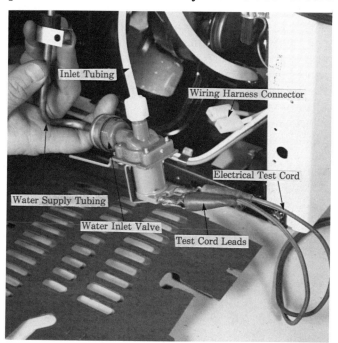

Figure 308 — Check Icemaker Water Inlet Valve With Electrical Test Cord

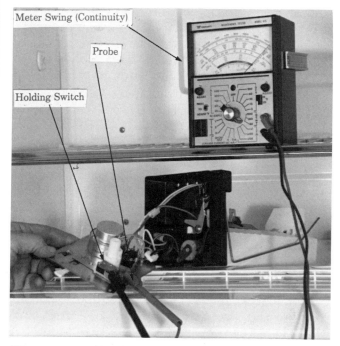

Figure 310 — Check Icemaker Holding Switch with Volt/-Ohmmeter

129

inside the icemaker. If, however, the ejector blade is stalled in the "start" or horizontal position, and it stays in this position for two to three days, then it could be diagnosed that the icemaker cycling thermostat is defective and should be replaced.

### Check Icemaker Holding Switch

Unplug refrigerator power cord, open the refrigerator freezer door, locate the compact icemaker and place your hand on the ejector blade. Turn it slowly in a clockwise direction. If the icemaker ejector blade continues to turn unaided, the problem is a defective icemaker holding switch. The icemaker holding switch can be checked with the volt/ohmmeter. First, set the ohmmeter to the RX-1 scale. Next, place the probes of the volt/ohmmeter on the terminals of the holding switch. With the switch button depressed, you should see full-scale deflection (continuity), on the scale of the volt/ohmmeter *(Figure 310)*. No reading on the ohmmeter means the holding switch is open and must be replaced.

### Check Icemaker Drive Motor

Locate the compact icemaker, place your hand on the ejector blade and turn it slowly in a clockwise direction. While the blade is turning, and the motor is running, try to hold the blade with the fingers. If the blade stalls, the drive motor gears are faulty internally. You will have to replace the drive motor in order for the icemaker to operate. If, however, the blade continued to turn, this is an indication that the icemaker drive motor is in working order.

The icemaker drive motor can also be checked with the electrical test cord by removing from the icemaker component plate. With the icemaker motor removed, the test cord is attached to the motor leads and plugged into a 110-to-125-volt receptacle. Now observe the motor gear, which should turn slowly in a clockwise direction. If no gear movement is noticed, it could be assumed that the icemaker drive motor is defective internally and it will have to be replaced in order for the icemaker to make ice.

### To Check Support Housing

A check for a defective support housing *(Figure 311)* can be made by removing front cover and the screws with hand tools that secure the component plate to the icemaker support housing.

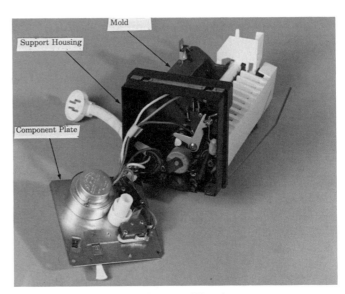

Figure 311 — Icemaker Support Housing

With the component plate removed, inspect the support housing, which is normally made of a plastic material, for worn or broken parts. Any parts that are broken in the housing will cause the icemaker to fail. To restore the icemaker to normal operation, the housing will have to be replaced.

### To Check Mold Heater

To check the icemaker mold heater, the icemaker is first removed from the refrigerator *(Figure 301)*. The component plate screws are removed with hand tools (see Repair Procedures). The leads from the mold heater are removed from the wiring harness. The mold heater is next checked for continuity by using the volt/ohmmeter. Set the scale of the volt/ohmmeter on the RX-100 scale. Place one of the probes of the volt/ohmmeter on one terminal of the mold heater. Place the other probe of the volt/ohmmeter on the remaining terminal of the mold heater. If continuity is present within the element of the heater, a reading of approximately 20 ohms resistance should be indicated on the volt/ohmmeter *(Figure 312)*. If no reading is noticed on the volt/ohmmeter scale, the mold heater is defective and it will have to be replaced in order for the icemaker to make ice.

### To Check Shut-Off Arm

Check the icemaker shut-off arm *(Figure 296)* for a bind (clogged with ice or bent) that would result in the icemaker not making ice properly or not making any ice. If it has been determined that the shut-off arm is bent or defective, the ice

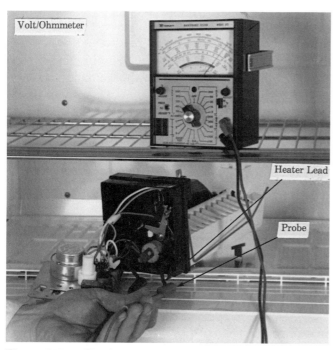

Figure 312 — Check Icemaker Mold Heater for Continuity with Volt/ohmmeter

maker will have slow ice production or the icemaker will not make any ice. The shut-off arm will have to be replaced (see Repair Procedures).

## REPAIR PROCEDURES

Move the refrigerator out from the wall. Unplug the refrigerator power cord, and turn OFF the water supply to the icemaker.

### To Replace Water Supply Valve

Using hand tools, remove screws and discard the defective water supply valve *(Figure 313)*. When installing a water supply valve on the

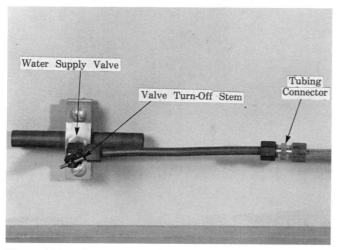

Figure 313 — Removing Icemaker Water Supply Valve

water heater, install only on the cold-water side of the water heater.

When installing a new self-tapping valve on an icemaker water supply line, only install on standard 3/8-inch or 1/2-inch copper tubing. Never install these valves on plastic pipes. Some icemaker installations have chrome or "shiny" tubing under the sink. This tubing is stainless steel, and under no circumstances should you install a self-tapping valve on this type tubing.

Install the new replacement water supply valve by mounting it in the same position as the defective water supply valve that was removed. Follow closely the installation steps that are provided in the replacement valve kit. NOTE: When installing a replacement water supply valve, it is sometimes better to use two neoprene hose washers to bridge between the valve body and the copper tubing. This will assure that the stinger will pierce the tubing and not distort the tubing, resulting in a possible water leak.

### To Replace Water Inlet Valve

Unplug refrigerator power cord and remove screws to refrigerator back *(Figure 223)*. Using hand tools, unscrew the fitting attached to the water inlet valve threads and remove the tubing. Remove the refrigerator wiring harness and defective water inlet valve from the refrigerator cabinet and discard the old valve *(Figure 314)*. Install the replacement water inlet valve by mounting it in the same position as the defective valve that was removed. Follow installation steps that are provided in the replacement valve kit.

After you have installed a replacement water inlet valve, you should test cycle the icemaker and make adjustments to achieve the proper water fill in the icemaker mold. These adjustments are usually necessary because of pressure variations throughout the country.

To test cycle an icemaker, first remove the icemaker from the freezer section of the refrigerator *(Figure 301)*. Unplug the wiring harness slowly and turn the icemaker ejector blade counterclockwise to the 8 o'clock position. Connect the wiring harness to the cabinet wiring or receptacle. Place a measuring cup that is graduated in ounces under the icemaker water inlet tube. As the icemaker revolves in a clockwise rotation to the 10 o'clock position, the icemaker will call for water and approximately 6 ounces of water should enter the measuring cup.

If the water fill adjustment is not correct, the icemaker will produce undersized or oversized

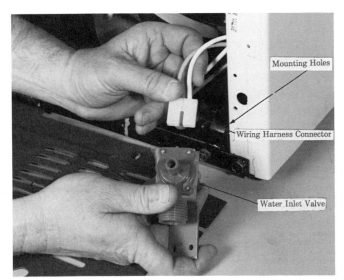

Figure 314 — Remove the Water Inlet Valve from Refrigerator Cabinet

crescents. It might be necessary, if the water calibration is out of adjustment, to test cycle the icemaker several times to achieve proper water fill.

Use the adjustment screw on the icemaker to calibrate the water fill *(Figure 315)*. When you turn this screw clockwise, less water will enter the mold cavity. When you turn the screw counterclockwise, more water will enter the mold cavity.

It is usually advisable to test cycle the icemaker two or three times after you have replaced a water inlet valve. The purpose is to remove any discolored water, algae, contaminents, and possible air that might have entered the water line.

After you have made a proper water fill

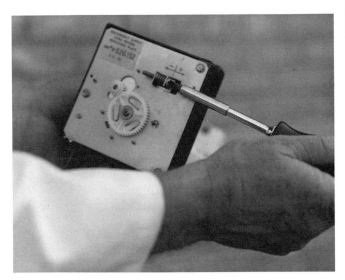

Figure 315 — Using Screwdriver to Adjust Screw to Calibrate Water Fill

adjustment, turn the ejector blade counterclockwise to the 8 o'clock position. Connect the wiring harness to the cabinet wiring or receptacle. Secure the icemaker to the freezer section of the refrigerator. Now check for proper water fill after the icemaker has completed a cycle.

### To Replace Cycling Thermostat

Unplug refrigerator power cord. Using hand tools, remove the icemaker from the freezer section of the refrigerator *(Figure 301)*. Remove the front cover from the icemaker. Remove the front component plate that is secured to the ice maker support housing. Remove the screws that secure the cycling thermostat to the icemaker support *(Figure 316)*.

Remove electrical wires from the terminals on the support housing, and carefully remove the thermostat *(Figure 317)*. The cycling thermostat is secured to the support by an adhesive, which is used to provide good thermal contact. NOTE:

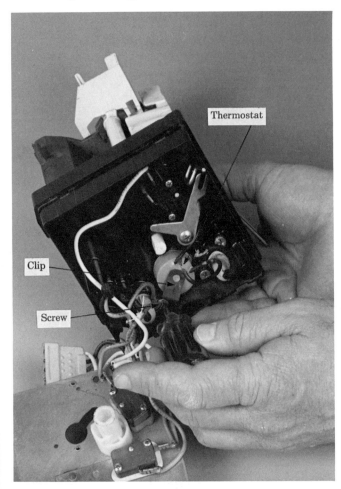

Figure 316 — Remove Screw that Secures Cycling Thermostat to Support Housing

When replacing a defective thermostat, you must apply a substance such as Vaseline or silicone to the thermostat base to restore the good thermal contact that will help the icemaker perform properly.

Install the replacement cycling thermostat by mounting it in the same position as the defective cycling thermostat that was removed. Follow closely the installation steps provided. If no installation steps are provided in the part replacement kit, reverse the above steps.

## To Replace Holding Switch

Unplug refrigerator power cord. Using hand tools, remove the icemaker from the freezer section of the refrigerator *(Figure 301)*. Remove the front cover from the icemaker. Remove the component plate that is secured to the icemaker support housing. Remove the screws that secure the holding switch to the icemaker support.

Remove the electrical wires from the terminals on the support housing and remove the holding switch *(Figure 318)*.

Install the part replacement holding switch by mounting in the same position as the faulty switch that was removed. Follow closely the installation steps that are provided in the part replacement switch kit.

## To Replace Icemaker Drive Motor

Using hand tools, remove the icemaker from the freezer section of the refrigerator *(Figure 301)*.

Remove the front component plate that is secured to the icemaker support housing. Locate the drive motor and remove the screws that secure the drive motor to the icemaker support. Remove the electrical wires from the drive motor terminals and remove the drive motor *(Figure 319)*.

Install the replacement drive motor by mounting in the same position as the faulty drive motor that was removed. Follow closely the installation steps that are provided in the part replacement drive motor kit. If no installation steps are provided in the part replacement drive motor kit, reverse the above steps.

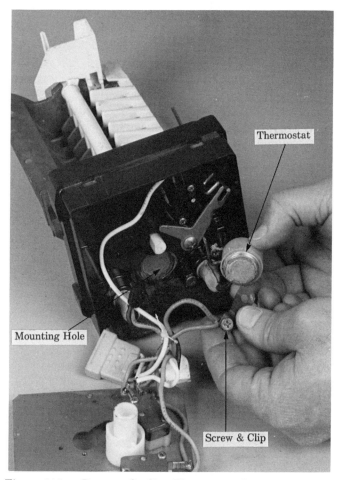

Figure 317 — Remove Cycling Thermostat from Icemaker

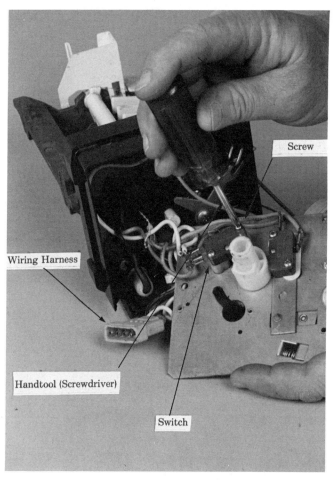

Figure 318 — Remove Holding Switch from Icemaker

133

Figure 319 — Removing the Refrigerator Icemaker Drive Motor

## To Replace Support Housing

Unplug refrigerator power cord. Using hand tools, remove the compact icemaker from the freezer section of the refrigerator *(Figure 301)*.

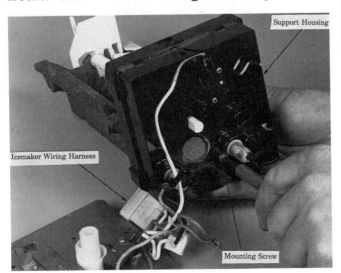

Figure 320 — Remove Screws to Replace Support Housing

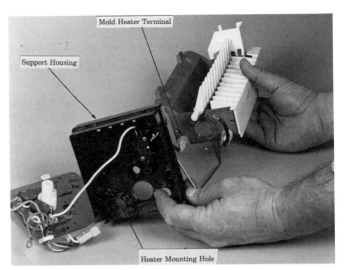

Figure 321 — Remove Support Housing from Mold Heater

Remove the screws that secure the component plate to the support housing. Next, remove the wiring harness that is attached to the switches on the component plate. NOTE: When removing the switch wires, note the sequence in which they were removed because they are to be reinstalled on the same terminals of the switches after replacement of the support housing.

Remove screws that secure the support housing to the mold heater. *Figure 320* shows screws being removed so that support housing can be removed.

As screws are removed, the support housing is removed by pulling forward so that it is dislodged from the terminals of the mold heater *(Figure 321)*.

Install the part replacement support housing in the same position as the faulty housing that was removed. Follow the instruction steps that are provided in the part replacement support housing kit. If no installation steps are provided in the part replacement support kit, reverse the above steps.

## To Replace Mold Heater

Unplug refrigerator power cord. To replace the icemaker mold heater, follow the installation steps that were discussed in the section "To Replace Support Housing," *Figures 320 and 321*.

## To Replace Shut-Off Arm

Unplug refrigerator power cord. Using hand tools, remove the compact icemaker from the freezer section of the refrigerator *(Figure 301)*.

Figure 322 — Removing Shut-Off Arm from Icemaker Support Housing

Remove the screws that secure the component plate to the support housing. Remove the shut-off arm spring that is attached to the lever arm. The shut-off arm can now be removed by routing the arm through the mounting hole of the support housing. *Figure 322* shows the shut-off arm being removed from the icemaker support housing.

Install the part replacement shut-off arm in the same position as the faulty shut-off arm that was removed. NOTE: When reinstalling the component plate, make certain that the shut-off arm is properly installed in the mounting hole of the component plate. If improperly installed, the icemaker will produce small portions of ice or the icemaker will not make ice.

# 6

# The Automatic Dishwasher

We felt that the simplest way to organize this service guide to help the do-it-yourselfer solve a problem was to organize it in the following manner:

- Show pictures of and describe all the components that make up the system.
- List specific problems (or failures) and suggest other symptoms that will help isolate the problem.
- List components to be checked in the proper sequence to isolate the faulty part.
- Give step-by-step replacement instructions for removing and replacing the faulty part.

In this chapter, the under-the-counter automatic dishwasher problems, diagnosis, and repair will be discussed. Because they are so similar, the automatic portable dishwashers will not be discussed in this service guide.

The automatic dishwasher is not only a time saver, it is one of the hardest-working appliances in the homeowner's kitchen. It is used on the average of two times per day. With this day-to-day workout, the dishwasher will eventually experience a failure. When a failure does occur, it is usually of a minor nature, and the home repairman can easily diagnose the problem and fix it himself.

One of the most common complaints is that dishes are not clean when they are removed from the dishwasher. When this occurs, it is possible that the soap is not being dispensed from the soap dispenser as the timer advances through the dishwasher cycle. It is also possible that the dishwasher is not getting enough water in the tub cavity to properly clean the dishes.

When the machine is turned ON and nothing happens, it could be no more than a burned or loose wire to the door switch.

It is usually not necessary to remove the dishwasher from its space when servicing it. Access to the working components is gained by removing the panel located at the bottom of the unit. Once the lower panel has been removed, the components are in full view. Problems like a burned wire to the heating element or a broken water inlet valve can be discovered by a simple visual inspection.

If a water leak is noticed, turn OFF the electricity at the circuit breaker or fuse panel *(Figure 1)* before servicing the dishwasher. REMEMBER THAT THE HOME REPAIRMAN MUST TAKE EXTREME CAUTION: ELECTRICITY IS VERY DANGEROUS AND IF NOT HANDLED PROPERLY CAN BE AN INSTANT KILLER.

By following the testing procedures as outlined in this guide, the home repairman should be able to diagnose most common dishwasher problems and in most cases fix it himself at little or no cost.

## THE DISHWASHER—HOW IT WORKS

The automatic dishwasher starts the cycle once the homeowner has placed the dishes in the dishwasher and the timer is pushed in or pulled out to ON. With the unit ON, electricity flows through the timer contacts to the water inlet valve solenoid. As the solenoid opens, hot water flows through the inlet valve, the inlet hose, and then into the dishwasher tub cavity.

With the dishwasher running, hot water is sprayed through the lower spray arm to the upper spray arm (if used) by the drive motor that is attached to the pump assembly. As the spray arm revolves, the water pressure sprays hot, soapy water onto the dishes. This spraying pattern is continual as long as there is water in the tub cavity and the drive motor is running. When the timer advances to the end of wash or rinse cycle, the dishwasher drive motor stops running. After a brief pause, the drive motor reverses in direction. The wash water is now removed from the tub cavity by the pump assembly, which pumps the water out of the dishwasher and down the drain.

The heater element is energized through the timer assembly. It is ON during the dishwasher cycle. This high-wattage heater dries the excess water that has collected on the dishes during the wash cycle. When the timer has advanced to the end of cycle, or when the unit reaches OFF, it is safe to open the dishwasher door and remove the clean dishes.

## AUTOMATIC DISHWASHER COMPONENTS

### Timer

The timer assembly *(Figure 323)* is located in the control console area at the front of the dishwasher. It controls the sequence during the dishwasher cycle. The assembly consists of a small electrical motor that drives a pinion gear, meshed with a drive gear in the timer

Figure 323 — Typical Timer Used In a Dishwasher

assembly. This assembly consists of the cam wheels that rotate slowly, causing the cam to make contact with switch levers which, in turn, "opens" and "closes" electrical circuits to perform the various functions of the automatic dishwasher. *Figure 323* shows a typical timer used in the dishwasher.

### Timer Knob

The timer knob *(Figure 324)* is located on the control console. It is attached to the timer assembly and is used for selecting a cycle.

### Timer Dial

The timer dial *(Figure 325)* is also located on the control console. It is attached to the timer assembly and has a pointer showing the cycle that has been selected.

### Selector Switch

The selector switch is located in the control console area at the front of the dishwasher. The selector switch *Figure 326* is pushed in or pushed out to select different types of washes: for example, a long wash or a short wash. The switch is also used to select whether the dishes are to be dried by the heating element or air dried.

Figure 324 — Dishwasher Timer Knob

Figure 325 — Dishwasher Timer Dial

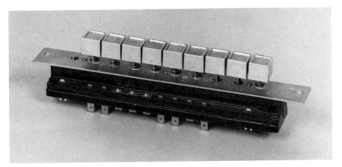

Figure 326 — Selector Switch

## Door Switch

The door switch *(Figure 327)* is located in the control area at the front of the dishwasher. The switch is a protective device that stops the dishwasher drive motor when the door is opened.

## Detergent Dispenser

The detergent dispenser *(Figure 328)* is located inside the dishwasher door. The detergent is placed in the dispenser compartment. The door is held closed by a catch or magnet. It opens during the dishwasher cycle and releases the detergent into the tub cavity.

## Heater

The heater element *(Figure 329)* is located in the tub cavity. It serves two functions during the dishwasher cycle: 1) The heat generated by the high-wattage element heats the water to a temperature of 140 degrees F. The water in the dishwasher tub has to be kept at

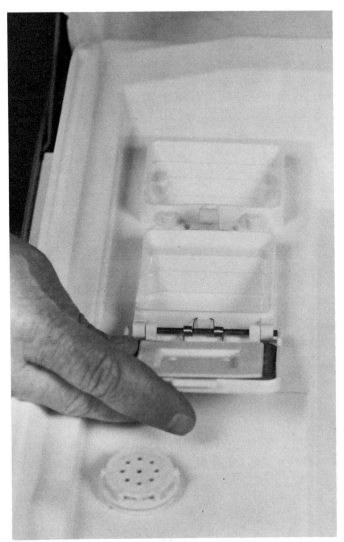

Figure 328 — Detergent Dispenser

this temperature or higher, so the hot water can dissolve the detergent. The dishes are thereby assured of being clean when they are removed from the dishwasher. 2) The element generates heat after the water is removed from the dishwasher. This heat helps dry the excess water that has accumulated on the dishes during the wash cycle.

Figure 327 — Dishwasher Door Switch

Figure 329 — Typical Dishwasher Heater

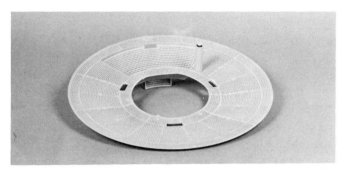

Figure 330 — Dishwasher Filter Guard

## Filter Guard

The filter guard *(Figure 330)* is located in the tub cavity. It is a protective device to assure that large objects and foreign matter do not pass through the dishwasher pump assembly. If this debris were to enter the pump, the internal components could be damaged.

## Filter Screen

The filter screen *(Figure 331)* is located in the tub cavity. As water sprays around the tub in a circular motion, it falls onto the dishes. Debris and scraps of food then settle on top of the filter screen. The food is thereby trapped in the screen and has no way of being sprayed back onto the clean dishes.

## Water Inlet Valve

The water inlet valve *(Figure 332)* is located at the bottom of the dishwasher. Water enters the dishwasher tub cavity through the water inlet valve. When a cycle is selected and the timer knob is turned ON, electricity energizes the solenoid valve coil that controls the supply of water entering the dishwasher.

## Spray Arm

The spray arm *(Figure 333)* is located in the tub cavity. Water passes through the jets of the spray arm as

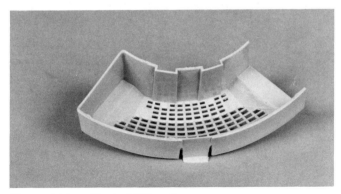

Figure 331 — Typical Filter Screen

Figure 332 — Typical Water Inlet Valve Used in Dishwashers

Figure 333 — Typical Dishwasher Spray Arm

the drive motor is running. Water pressure through the spray arm jets creates a circular motion that sprays hot soapy water onto the dishes to clean them.

## Overfill Switch

The overfill switch *(Figure 334)* is a microswitch that is operated by a float and is located in the tub cavity.

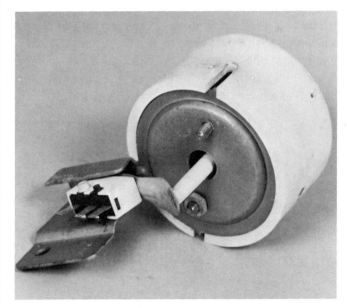

Figure 334 — Dishwasher Overfill Switch

Figure 335 — Typical Dishwasher Rack

If water entering the dishwasher were not cutoff by the timer, the overfill switch would break a circuit causing the water supply to cutoff.

## Dishwasher Rack

The dishwasher rack *(Figure 335)* is located inside the dishwasher tub cavity. Dirty dishes are placed in the rack so that they can be washed.

## Starting Relay

The starting relay is usually located inside the control console. The starting relay *(Figure 336)* is an electro-mechanical device that is used to start the dishwasher drive motor. As electricity flows, the relay energizes the start winding of the drive motor until the motor is almost up to speed. The relay then breaks the electrical circuit to the start winding and the dishwasher drive motor continues to operate on its RUN (or motor) winding. It follows the same procedure when the drive motor reverses direction.

Figure 336 — Typical Dishwasher Starting Relay

## Pump Assembly

The pump assembly *(Figure 337)* is connected directly to the motor. It is driven by the dishwasher drive motor. Internally housed in the pump assembly are two impellers. As the drive motor runs, one impeller (wash) turns in one direction, pumping water to the spray arm. The drive motor then reverses direction, which causes the other impeller (drain) to spin in the other direction, and wash water is pumped from the dishwasher.

## Drive Motor

The drive motor *(Figure 338)* is located under the tub cavity. The dishwasher drive motor drives the wash impeller in one direction while washing the dishes. The motor then reverses direction as the drain impeller pumps out the wash water.

## DIAGNOSING PROBLEMS

The most common dishwasher problems and their most obvious failing sequence are covered in the following discussion. This discussion should aid in diag-

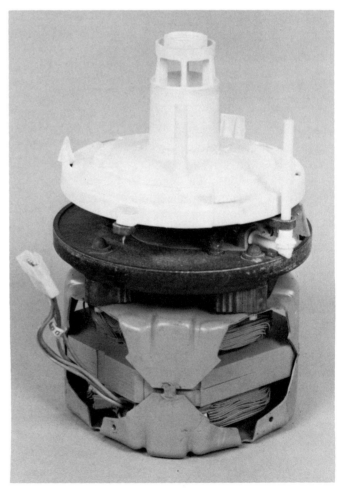

Figure 337 — Dishwasher Pump Assembly

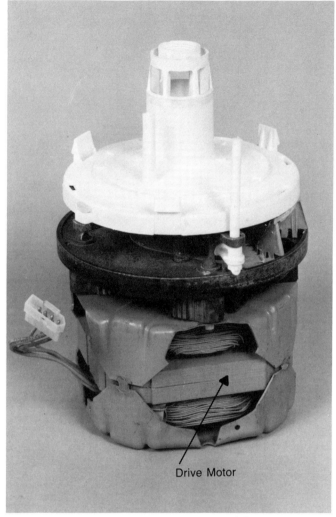

Figure 338 — Typical Dishwasher Drive Motor

nosing and pinpointing what is wrong with your automatic dishwasher. Also, listed are repair procedures to correspond to the failure symptom.

## DISHWASHER WON'T PUMP OUT WATER

Specific failure symptoms include: 1) Dishwasher has a full tub of water at the end of the cycle. 2) Dishwasher only partially drains and leaves water in tub at end of cycle.

Remove the lower panel *(Figure 339)*. Locate the pump drain hose and see if a kink in the hose is evident. If so, *(Figure 340)*, remove the kink and check the dishwasher for proper operation. If the dishwasher now pumps the water out, you found the problem — a kinked drain hose. If little or no water is being pumped out, the problem is in the dishwasher pump assembly.

## Using Test Equipment

To avoid any incorrect readings when using the

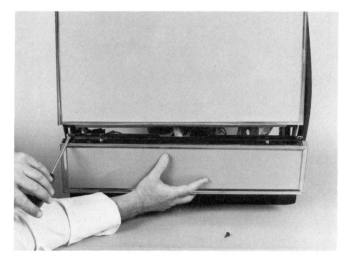

Figure 339 — Removal of Dishwasher Lower Panel

volt/ohmmeter, When making continuity checks with the volt/ohmmeter, always turn OFF the electricity at the circuit breaker panel *(Figure 1)*. Live voltage checks made with the volt/ohmmeter in a continuity position will damage the meter movement.

## Check Dishwasher Plumbing

A simple check to make for stopped-up or backed-up plumbing is to remove the lower panel from the dishwasher *(Figure 339)*. Locate the drain hose that is attached to the pump assembly base coupling *(Figure 341)*. Remove the drain hose from the coupling with hand tools *(Figure 342)*. Place the removed drain hose in a suita-

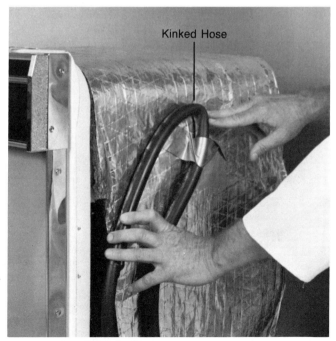

Figure 340 — Kink in Hose

141

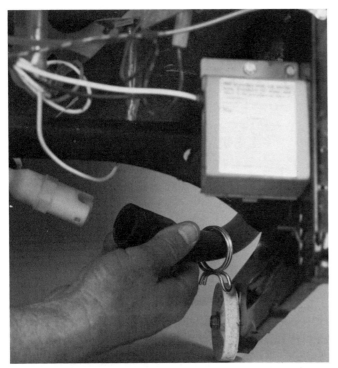

Figure 341 — Removing Hose Clamp Attached To Pump Assembly Base Coupling

ble container or bucket *(Figure 343)*. Turn the dishwasher timer dial to a pump out increment on the timer assembly dial. Turn the dishwasher to ON. With the drive motor running, water should now enter the container. If water pumps into the container, the problem is not with your dishwasher but the plumbing system. A plumber would have to be called to locate and clear the blockage. If no water collects in the container, the

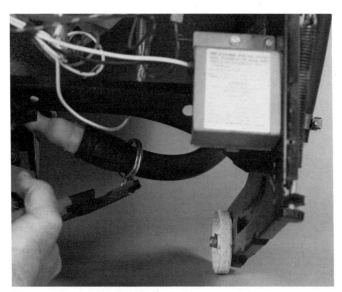

Figure 342 — Removing Drain Hose From Coupling With Hose Clamp Pliers

Figure 343 — Placing Hose In a Container

problem is a defective component in the pump assembly, or a kinked drain hose.

### Check Drive Motor Pump Assembly

To check the pump assembly, it is necessary on most dishwashers to remove the drive motor and pump assembly from the dishwasher. NOTE: The removal and installation of the internal components of the pump assembly will be discussed in the repair procedures of this chapter.

### Check Timer Assembly

With the dishwasher timer knob in the OFF position, slowly move the timer dial in a clockwise rotation until a pump-out increment is found on the timer dial. With the knob pushed in or pushed out, to ON, the drive motor should start to run. After the motor has run for approximately three minutes, open the dishwasher door to see if the wash water has pumped out. If the tub is empty, the timer assembly is skipping increments in the cycle. The timer will have to be replaced. NOTE: Never turn the dishwasher timer knob while the drive motor is running or while the timer assembly is in the ON position. It will damage the timer assembly and require replacement.

142

## Check Drive Motor

It would be difficult for the home repairman to accurately make an operational test of a dishwasher drive motor. A special dishwasher test cord is required to properly check the drive motor. Most motor or appliance repair shops offer these services. If a drive motor is found to be defective, it would be necessary to replace the drive motor to restore the dishwasher to proper operation.

The drive motor windings, however, can be tested for continuity by using the volt/ohmmeter. With the volt/ohmmeter "zeroed" and the selector switch set to the RX-1 scale, place one probe of the volt/ohmmeter on one terminal of the motor connector and the remaining probe on another terminal of the motor connector. If the winding to be tested shows continuity, the volt/ohmmeter will show full-scale deflection (or 0) ohms *(Figure 344)*. Check the remaining motor terminals with the volt/ohmmeter for an open or shorted winding.

The drive motor starting relay is also tested for continuity by using the volt/ohmmeter. Set the selector switch on the RX-1 scale. Place one probe of the volt/ohmmeter on the terminal of the relay winding. Place the remaining probe on the terminal to end of relay winding. If the winding tested shows continuity, the volt/ohmmeter will show full scale deflection, or 0 ohms. A NO continuity reading would indicate a defective motor relay — replace it.

## REPAIR PROCEDURES

Turn OFF the electricity at the circuit breaker panel *(Figure 1)* before servicing the dishwasher. Exercise care

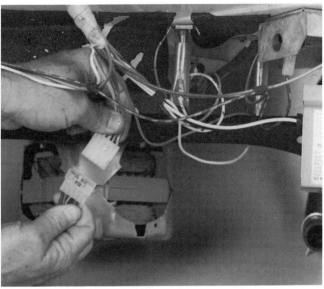

Figure 345 — Wiring Harness Being Removed From Motor Connector

when moving the dishwasher from its space. The leveling legs can easily damage the floor.

## To Replace Drive Motor Pump Assembly

Turn OFF the electricity at the circuit breaker panel. Remove the screws that secure the lower panel to the dishwasher cabinet *(Figure 339)*. Disconnect the drive motor connector from the harness wiring. *Figure 345* shows a wiring harness being removed from the motor connector. Remove the hose clamp from drain hose that is secured to drive motor base coupling *(Fig-*

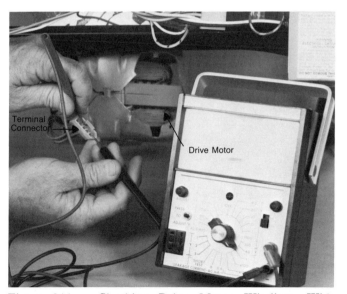

Figure 344 — Checking Drive Motor Windings With Volt/Ohmmeter

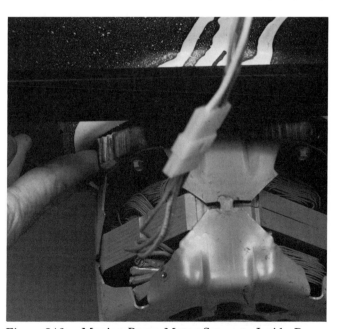

Figure 346 — Moving Pump Motor Supports Inside Pump Base

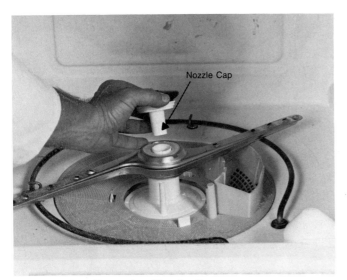

Figure 347 — Removing Nozzle Cap

*ure 341)*. Remove drain hose from coupling *(Figure 342)*. NOTE: When removing drain hose, place a small pan or towel under the motor base coupling. It is possible that when hose is removed water could spill onto the floor.

Next, move the motor pump supports inside the pump base *(Figure 346)*. Open the dishwasher door. Remove the nozzle cap that secures the lower spray arm to the pump assembly *(Figure 347)*. Remove the spray arm from the pump assembly housing *(Figure 348)*. Locate the filter guard and remove by pressing inward on the two sides *(Figure 349)*. Remove the filter screen by pulling upward *(Figure 350)*. Pull upward to remove the motor and pump assembly *(Figure 351)*.

NOTE: In the above discussion, the pump assembly was not secured to the tub cavity with screws or

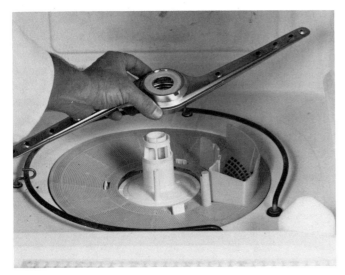

Figure 348 — Removing Spray Arm

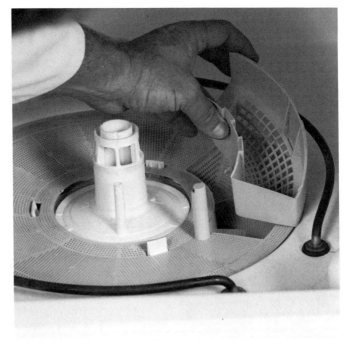

Figure 349 — Remove Filter Guard

bolts. In some dishwashers, however, the pump assembly may be attached to the tub cavity using clips or screws to avoid water leaks.

When servicing the dishwasher pump assembly internal components, it is necessary to disassemble the pump assembly. The following discussion describes the removal and installation of the wash and drain impellers

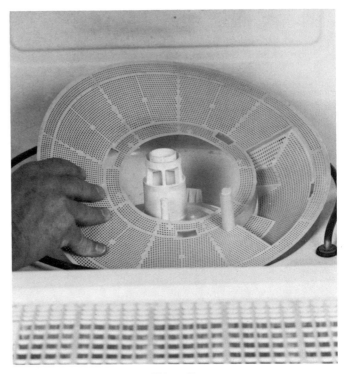

Figure 350 — Removing Filter Screen

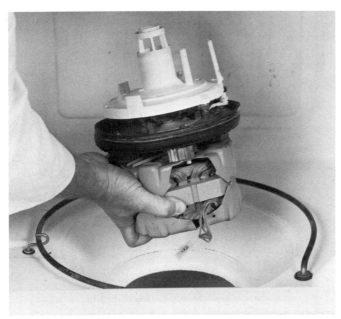

Figure 351 — Removing Pump Motor Assembly

of a typical dishwasher pump assembly. Note: An impeller that has been damaged by glass or other debris will not perform the job as well as when it was new. A damaged drain impeller will cause the wash water to: 1) Pump out very slowly. 2) No water will be pumped out of the dishwasher tub cavity.

**Wash Impeller** — To remove the impeller, the

Figure 353 — Removing Impeller Screw Lock

pump assembly top housing will have to be removed. Remove the housing key way and turn the housing in a counter-clockwise direction and remove *(Figure 352)*. Using a screwdriver, straighten out the impeller screw lock *(Figure 353)*. Remove the screw that secures the wash impeller to the pump housing and remove wash impeller *(Figure 354)*. Using a screwdriver, remove the screws that secures coverplate to base assembly and remove coverplate *(Figures 355 and 356)*.

**Drain Impeller** — To remove the impeller, follow the procedures above for the wash impeller. After removal of the coverplate, remove the shim that is attached to top of drain impeller (it has to be reinstalled in the same position after new impeller part replacement). Using two screwdrivers remove the impeller by pulling off the motor shaft in an upward direction *(Figure 357)*.

Install the above replacement impeller parts by mounting in the same place and position as the faulty impeller parts that were removed. Follow closely the

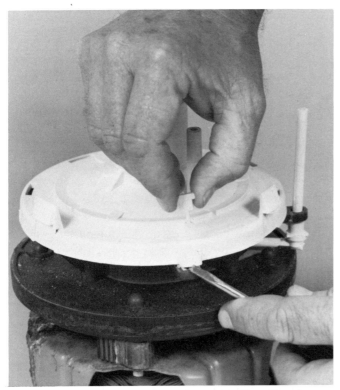

Figure 352 — Removing Pump Assembly Top Housing

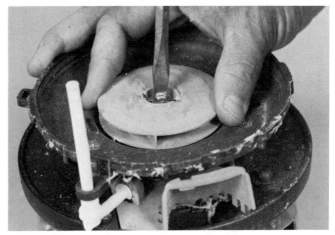

Figure 354 — Removing Screw That Secures Housing to Wash Impeller

145

Figure 355 — Removing Screws From Pump Housing Base

Figure 357 — Removing Drain Impeller From Motor Shaft

Figure 356 — Removing Screws To Coverplate

installation steps that are provided in the replacement part impeller kits. If no installation steps are provided in the replacement part impeller kits, reverse the above steps.

To Replace Timer Assembly

Turn OFF the electricity at the circuit breaker panel *(Figure 1)*. Remove the timer knob by turning counterclockwise *(Figure 358)*. Grasp the edges of the timer dial *(Figure 359)* and pull forward off the timer shaft. NOTE: When reinstalling dial, it is important to position the dial on the flat spot of the timer shaft. If not installed properly, the dishwasher will not program properly during the cycle.

Using a screwdriver, remove the two end caps that secure the console panel to the dishwasher cabinet *(Figure 360)*. Remove the screws at the top and bottom that secure the console panel to the cabinet *(Figure 361)* and remove console panel *(Figure 362)*. Using a screwdriver, remove the screws that secure the timer assembly to door frame *(Figure 363)*. With screws removed, pull the timer forward, remove wiring harness from timer con-

Figure 358 — Removal Of Timer Knob

nector *(Figure 364)* and remove timer assembly *(Figure 365)*.

Install the replacement timer assembly by mounting in the same position as the defective timer assem-

Figure 359 — Removing Timer Dial

Figure 360 — Removing End Caps From Console Panel

bly that was removed. Follow instructions provided in the replacement timer assembly kit. If no installation steps or procedures are available, reverse the above steps.

### To Replace Drive Motor

To replace the dishwasher drive motor assembly, refer to "Dishwasher Won't Pump Out Water" section of this chapter.

### To Replace Motor Relay

Turn OFF electricity at circuit breaker panel *(Figure 1)*. Refer to Repair Procedures under the "Dishwasher Won't Pump Out Water" section of this chapter for removal of timer, knob, dial, and console assembly. Next, remove screws that secure motor relay to dishwasher cabinet. Remove wires to relay terminals and remove relay *(Figure 366)*.

### DISHWASHER LEAKS WATER ONTO FLOOR

Specific failure symptoms include: 1) Water on floor near dishwasher. 2) During dishwasher cycle, water accumulates on left or right side of dishwasher lower panel.

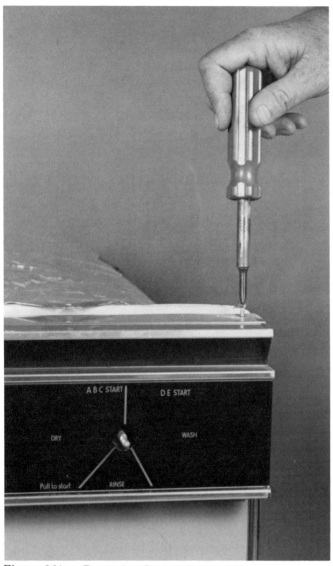

Figure 361 — Removing Screws From Console Panel

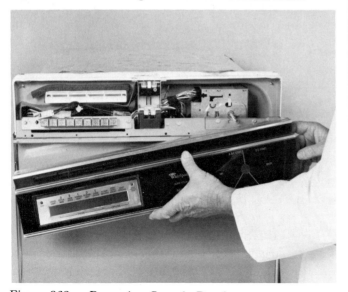

Figure 362 — Removing Console Panel

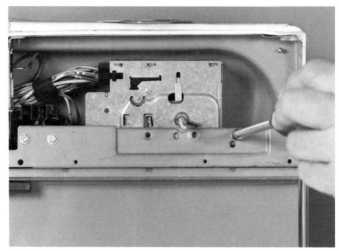

Figure 363 — Removing Screws Securing Timer To Door Frame

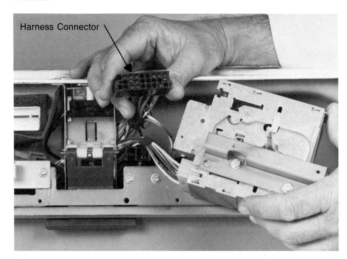

Harness Connector

Figure 364 — Removing Timer Wiring Harness

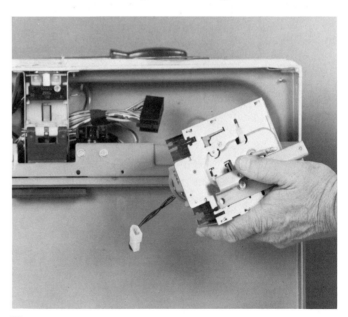

Figure 365 — Removing Timer Assembly

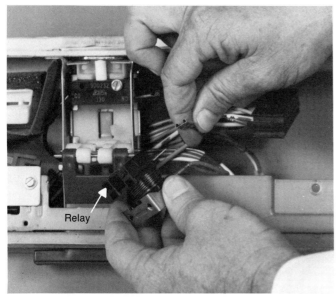

Figure 366 — Removal Of Motor Relay

To locate the cause of the problem, remove lower panel *(Figure 339)* and check for broken plumbing drain connections, water inlet valve, broken or cracked hoses (drain and inlet), or drive motor and pump assembly motor seal. If a hose or a faulty part is found, replace it. Check that door is closing properly.

Using Test Equipment

To avoid any incorrect readings when using the volt/ohmmeter to test a suspected dishwasher defective component part, always "zero" the ohmmeter scale of the volt/ohmmeter before making any continuity checks. See your operating instructions.

When making continuity checks with the volt/ohmmeter, always turn the electricity OFF at the circuit breaker panel *(Figure 1)* because live voltage checks will damage the meter movement.

Check Dishwasher Plumbing

Remove the dishwasher lower panel *(Figure 339)* and visually inspect the plumbing for water under the dishwasher. Vibrations made by the drive motor during the wash cycle can sometimes cause soldered connections in the plumbing to develop water leaks. To correct this problem, a qualified plumber should be called. Welding equipment and special skills are required to make these repairs.

Next, all hoses (drain and inlet) should be checked for damage. Hoses that have become brittle or cracked should be replaced with new ones. Also, hoses that show signs of hairline cracks should be replaced with new ones.

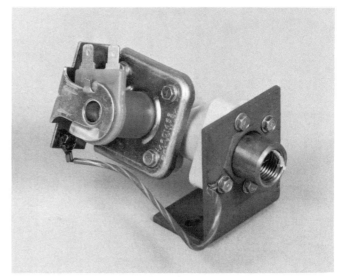

Figure 367 — Water Inlet Valve

Check Water Inlet Valve

With the water supply ON, locate the water inlet valve *(Figure 367)*. If water is noticed on the floor or around the tub cavity, check for a hairline crack in the valve body *(Figure 368)*. A cracked valve body will cause a fine mist of water to be sprayed onto the drive motor, tub cavity, and other components. The water inlet valve will have to be replaced. If water droplets are visi-

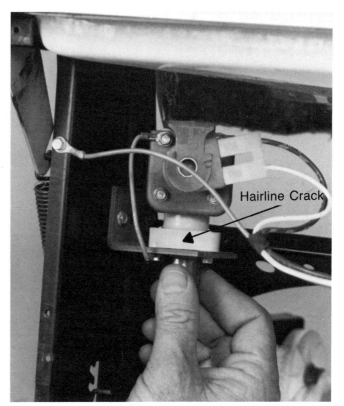

Figure 368 — Hairline Crack In Water Inlet Valve

149

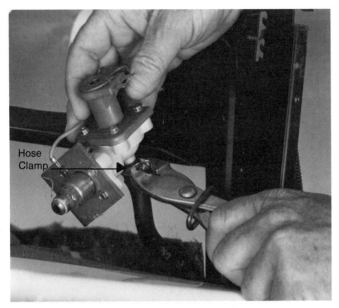

Figure 369 — Water Inlet Valve Hose Clamp

ble on the floor or under the water inlet valve, it is possibly caused by a loose inlet hose clamp that is attached to the valve body for signs of water stains and rusty screws *(Figure 370)*. If rust and water stains are noticed, the water inlet valve will have to be replaced. A final check should be made of the tubing that attaches to the water inlet port of the water inlet valve. Hand tools should be used to tighten nut or connections to avoid all water leaks.

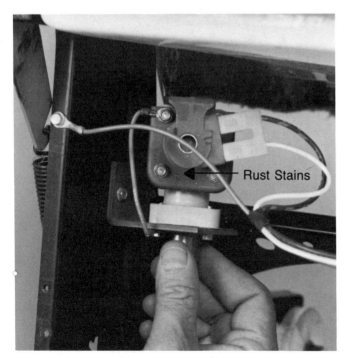

Figure 370 — Rust Stains On Water Inlet Valve

## Check Drive Motor Pump Assembly

Turn ON the electricity to the dishwasher at the circuit breaker panel *(Figure 1)*. Turn the timer dial to a timer increment where the drive motor will start to run. Turn the timer knob to ON. Remove lower panel *(Figure 339)*. Locate the drive motor and look for signs of water stains on or around the base of the drive motor *(Figure 371)*. If stains are noticed, they are caused by a defective pump assembly seal. It is recommended that the drive motor be replaced since the pump seal has allowed water to enter the drive motor windings, which has damaged the motor internally.

## REPAIR PROCEDURES

Turn OFF the electricity at the circuit breaker panel *(Figure 1)* before servicing the dishwasher. Exercise care when moving dishwasher from space. The leveling legs can easily damage the floor.

Figure 371 — Water Stains On Drive Motor Pump Base

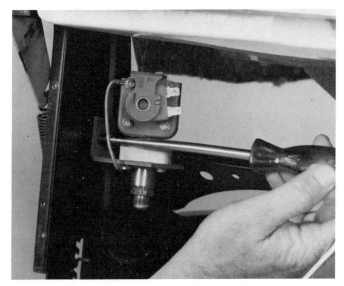

Figure 372 — Removing Screws Holding Inlet Valve To Cabinet

## To Replace Water Inlet Valve

Turn OFF the water supply to the dishwasher. Turn OFF the electricity at the circuit breaker panel *(Figure 1)*. Remove the lower panel *(Figure 339)*. Remove the plumbing tubing that is attached to valve inlet port. Remove the screws that secure the water inlet valve to the dishwasher cabinet *(Figure 372)*. Remove the inlet hose clamp *(Figure 373)*. Remove the wiring harness

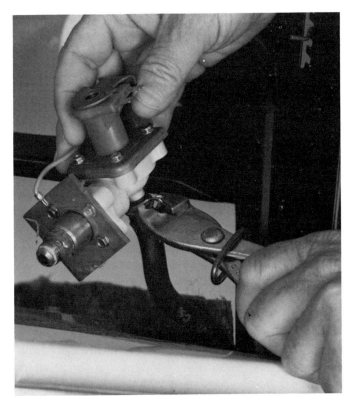

Figure 373 — Removing Inlet Hose Clamp

from the solenoid coil *(Figure 374)* and remove water inlet valve.

NOTE: When reinstalling the inlet hose clamp on the replacement water inlet valve, do not install the hose clamp in the original groove from which it was removed *(see Figure 49)*. A water leak could result. Install the replacement water inlet valve by mounting in the same position as the faulty inlet valve that was removed. Follow instructions that are provided in the replacement inlet valve kit. If no installation steps are provided, reverse the above steps.

## To Replace Drive Motor Pump Assembly

To replace the drive motor pump assembly, refer to "Dishwasher Won't Pump Out Water" section of this chapter.

## DISHWASHER DOES NOT FILL WITH WATER

Specific symptoms include: Little or no water enters the dishwasher tub cavity. To find the cause, first check to be sure the water supply is ON.

## Using Test Equipment

To avoid incorrect readings when using the volt/ohmmeter, always "zero" the ohmmeter before making any continuity checks on dishwasher components. See operating instructions that came with your volt/ohmmeter.

When making continuity checks with the volt/ohmmeter, always turn the electricity OFF at the circuit

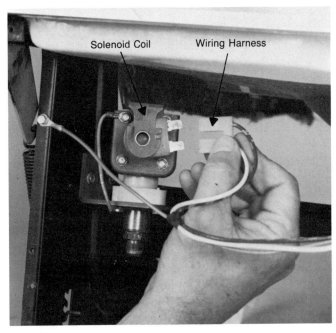

Figure 374 — Removing Wiring Harness From Solenoid Coil

breaker panel *(Figure 1)*. Live voltage checks will damage the meter movement.

## Check Dishwasher Plumbing

With the water supply ON, remove the lower panel *(Figure 339)*. Place a towel or shallow container on floor to absorb water. Loosen the nut that secures the dishwasher water tubing to the inlet port of the water inlet valve. If water collects immediately in the towel or container, it can safely be assumed that the water pressure is adequate and the plumbing system is not clogged or stopped up. If little or no water collects in the container, the water line gate valve could be defective or there is a problem in the plumbing system. A qualified plumber should be called to fix the problem.

## Check Water Inlet Valve

Turn the water supply OFF. Remove the lower panel *(Figure 339)*. Loosen and remove nut that attaches water tubing to water inlet valve inlet port. With tubing removed, check for corrosion and debris that has accumulated inside the tubing and inlet valve inlet port. Tap the nut and along the tubing wall to loosen corrosion inside the tubing. Continue this procedure until all corrosion has been removed from the water tubing. Place the tubing in a container or bucket and turn the water supply ON. The reason for this test is to make sure there are no restrictions in the water line, and also to thoroughly flush the corrosion deposits from the water tubing. Turn the water supply OFF. Reinstall the water tubing to the water inlet valve inlet port. Turn the water supply ON. Select a cycle on the timer dial where the dishwasher starts to fill with water. If it starts to fill with water — you fixed it. The problem was corrosion inside the water tubing or inlet valve water inlet port. If the dishwasher still does not fill with water, an additional electrical check will have to be made.

Next, test for electrical power to the water inlet valve from the dishwasher timer assembly *(Figure 375)*. Using the volt/ohmmeter, set the meter on the 150-volt scale and attach the two test leads of the volt/ohmmeter to the two terminals of the water inlet valve solenoid coil to be checked. Turn the water supply ON. With the test leads attached to the solenoid terminals, select a cycle on the dishwasher timer dial where the dishwasher starts to fill with water. Push in or pull out the timer dial. You should get a voltage reading of 110-125 volts A/C on the volt/ohmmeter scale. If you get a reading, this would indicate that electricity is available from the dishwasher timer assembly to the water inlet valve.

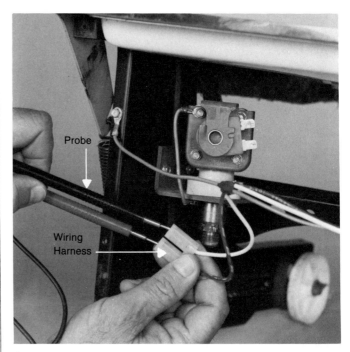

Figure 375 — Check For Voltage To The Water Inlet Valve With Volt/Ohmmeter

However, the absence of water flow means the water inlet valve is defective and you would have to replace it in order for the dishwasher to fill with water.

If you get a no voltage reading on the volt/ohmmeter, you will have to check for a possible defective timer assembly. Also, check for possible broken or burned wires from the timer assembly to the door switch. A check should be made for a defective door switch. Also, check for broken or burned wires from the door switch to the water inlet valve.

## Check Door Switch

Turn the electricity OFF at the circuit breaker panel *(Figure 1)*. Remove the timer knob by unscrewing it in a counter-clockwise direction *(Figure 358)*. Remove the dial by pulling forward *(Figure 359)*. Remove the caps *(Figure 360)*. Remove the screws that secure the console panel to the cabinet *(Figure 361)* and remove panel *(Figure 362)*. Locate door switch. NOTE: A defective door switch will keep the dishwasher from filling with water because electricity is not capable of reaching the water inlet valve. Using the volt/ohmmeter, set the meter on the RX-1 scale. Connect one probe from the volt/ohmmeter to one terminal of the door switch. Check for continuity by depressing (push in) the plunger of the switch with the fingers. The volt/ohmmeter should show full scale deflection, or 0 ohms *(Figure 376)*. This check would indicate that the switch is not defective. If you

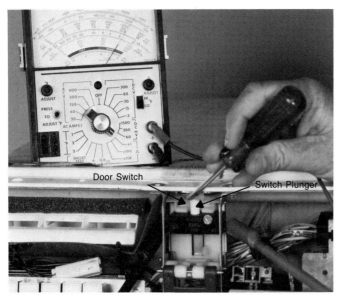

Figure 376 — Checking Door Switch For Continuity

do not get a continuity reading, the switch is defective — replace it.

NOTE: Probes placed incorrectly on the terminals of the switch terminals will result in inaccurate readings leading to a misdiagnosis of the door switch.

### Check For Broken or Burned Wires

Turn the electricity OFF at the circuit breaker panel *(Figure 1)*. A suspected broken or burned wire(s) can be checked with the volt/ohmmeter. NOTE: A broken or burned wire(s) that connects to dishwasher components will cause it to not fill with water because electricity is not capable of reaching the water inlet valve. Set the volt/ohmmeter on the RX-1 scale. Connect one probe from the volt/ohmmeter to the terminal of the wire to be checked. Trace the wire to the component that it connects to. Remove the wire from the component terminal. Attach this wire to the remaining probe of the volt/ohmmeter. The volt/ohmmeter should show full scale deflection or 0 ohms *(Figure 377)*. This would indicate that the wire is not defective. If you do not get a reading, the wire is defective and it will have to be repaired or replaced.

### REPAIR PROCEDURES

Turn the electricity OFF at the circuit breaker panel *(Figure 1)* before servicing the dishwasher. Exercise care when removing the dishwasher from its space because the dishwasher legs can easily damage the floor.

### To Replace the Dishwasher Plumbing

When a major plumbing defect is suspected, it is recommended that a qualified plumber be called to fix the problem. The replacement of deteriorated plumbing requires knowledge, special tools, and welding equipment that are usually not available to the home repairman.

### To Replace the Water Inlet Valve

To replace the water inlet valve, refer to "Dishwasher Leaks Water Onto Floor" section of this chapter.

### To Replace Door Switch

Turn the electricity OFF at the circuit breaker panel *(Figure 1)*. Remove the timer knob *(Figure 358)*. Remove timer dial *(Figure 359)*. Remove the caps *(Figure 360)*. Remove screws that secure console to cabinet *(Figure 361)* and remove panel *(Figure 362)*. Remove the screws that secure the door switch to the door latch assembly *(Figure 378)*. Remove the wiring harness wires from the switch terminals and remove door switch.

Install the replacement door switch by mounting in the same position as the faulty door switch that was removed. Follow closely the installation steps and instructions that are provided in the replacement door switch kit. If no installation steps are provided, reverse the above steps.

### To Replace Broken or Burned Wires

Turn the electricity OFF at the circuit breaker panel *(Figure 1)*. While the dishwasher drive motor is running, it vibrates excessively. This constant vibration over a period of time can be responsible for wires vibrating

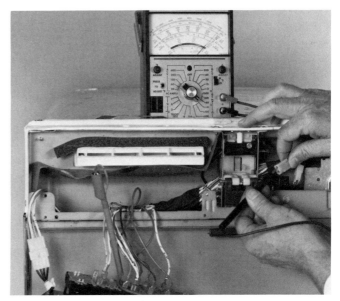

Figure 377 — Checking Continuity Of Wire With Volt/Ohmmeter

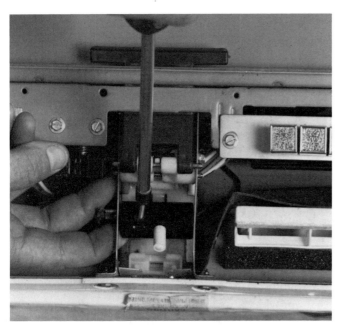

Figure 378 — Removing Screws To Door Switch

off or breaking at the terminal connections. In this case, a new solderless connector will have to be installed on the broken wire. NOTE: These connectors can be purchased at any hardware store. Every homeowner that does home appliance repairs should have an assortment of solderless connectors and a crimping tool.

*Figure 379* shows how a crimping tool is used to connect a new solderless connector to a broken wire. Wires that are burned and have bare spots in the insulation should be repaired or replaced.

## DISHWASHER STOPS IN CYCLE

Specific failure symptoms include: 1) The dishwasher won't complete the dishwasher cycle. 2) The dishwasher has a burning smell during the cycle.

Check the dishwasher wiring for a possible loose connection where it connects to the house wiring.

Check for a circuit breaker in the circuit breaker panel that is defective.

### Check Timer Assembly

Check the dishwasher timer assembly for erratic operation. If the dishwasher suddenly started when the timer dial is pushed to the ON-OFF position, the timer assembly ON-OFF contacts are defective internally. You will have to replace the timer assembly in order for the dishwasher to program through the cycle properly.

The timer switch contacts that supplies voltage to the drive motor are checked in the same manner as the automatic washer. See *Figure 94* in Chapter 2.

### Check Dishwasher Drive Motor Pump Assembly

With the electricity turned ON and the timer assembly pushed in or pulled out, to ON, slowly move the timer dial in a clockwise direction. If the dishwasher starts to run, but after a period of five to fifteen seconds or up to an hour, starts to smoke in the area of the drive motor, the drive motor is damaged internally. To restore the dishwasher to proper operation, the drive motor would have to be replaced.

A suspected faulty drive motor should be removed from the dishwasher. "To Replace Drive Motor Pump Assembly" in this chapter.

To check the drive motor windings for continuity, refer to "Dishwasher Won't Pump Out Water" section of this chapter.

### Check Circuit Breaker

Turn the electricity ON at the circuit breaker panel *(Figure 1)*. Select a cycle on the dishwasher timer dial to where the drive motor starts to run. Push in or pull out the timer knob and start the dishwasher. Observe how long the dishwasher runs during the cycle. If it stopped during the cycle and did not come back ON, a defective circuit breaker would have to be suspected.

Remove the screws that secure case to circuit breaker panel *(Figure 1)*. NOTE: Some homes have fuse panels instead of circuit breaker panels. Fuses and circuit breakers are discussed in detail in the "Electrical Testing" section of this service guide. With the case removed, check the panel for a breaker (15 amp) that

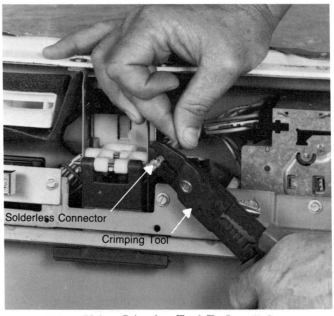

Solderless Connector

Crimping Tool

Figure 379 — Using Crimping Tool To Install Connector

tripped from the ON to OFF position. Reset the circuit breaker to the ON position. Restart the dishwasher and observe how long the drive motor runs during the cycle. If it runs for a few minutes and stops and does not come back ON, you have isolated the problem — a defective circuit breaker. It will have to be replaced in order for the dishwasher to operate properly.

Check for a burning odor in the area of the circuit breaker panel. If an odor is noticed, it must be found and isolated quickly because a circuit breaker that has overheated can be responsible for a major house fire.

## Repair Procedures

Turn the electricity to the dishwasher OFF at the circuit breaker panel *(Figure 1)* before servicing the dishwasher. Exercise care when removing the dishwasher from its space because the leveling legs can damage the floor.

## To Replace Timer Assembly

Refer to "Dishwasher Won't Pump Out Water" section of this chapter.

## To Replace Drive Motor Pump Assembly

Refer to "Dishwasher Won't Pump Out Water" section of this chapter.

## To Replace Circuit Breaker or Fuse

It is not recommended that the home repairman undertake the replacement of a suspected defective circuit breaker or fuse when a known failure occurs.

In cases, however, where the home repairman has more than a basic knowledge of electricity, the following procedures must be followed when replacing a defective circuit breaker or fuse:

- Turn the electrical power to the circuit breaker or fuse OFF.
- Remove one or two wires that are attached to the circuit breaker. Fuses are screwed out in a counter-clockwise direction.
  Pull up and snap out the defective circuit breaker.

## THE HOME REPAIRMAN SHOULD WORK AROUND ELECTRICITY WITH EXTREME CAUTION. IT CAN BECOME AN INSTANT KILLER.

Install the replacement circuit breaker or fuse by mounting in the same position as the defective circuit breaker or fuse that was removed.

## DISHWASHER WON'T START

Specific failure symptoms include: 1) When the dishwasher is turned ON, nothing happens. 2) When the dishwasher is turned ON a "buzzing" sound is heard.

To find the cause of this problem, first check to be sure the electricity is turned ON at the circuit breaker panel *(Figure 1)*. Next, check to see that the dishwasher timer knob is pushed in or pulled out to the ON position when selecting a cycle.

### Check Dishwasher Terminal Box

A check should be made with the volt/ohmmeter to check if voltage is available to the dishwasher wiring. A voltage check is made by setting the volt/ohmmeter on the 150 A/C scale and placing one probe of the volt/ohmmeter on one wire that supplies voltage to the dishwasher. Place the other probe on the remaining wire. The meter should read 110-125 volts *(Figure 380)*. This would indicate that electrical power was available from the circuit breaker panel to the dishwasher terminal box.

### Check Circuit Breaker or Fuse

If the above check showed no voltage at the dishwasher terminal box electrical wires, the problem could be a defective circuit breaker or fuse, house wiring burned or broken from circuit breaker panel to terminal box. If a defective circuit breaker or fuse is suspected, it would be recommended that a qualified electrician perform these repairs. Refer to "Dishwasher Stops In Cycle" in this chapter for procedure to check a defective circuit breaker or fuse.

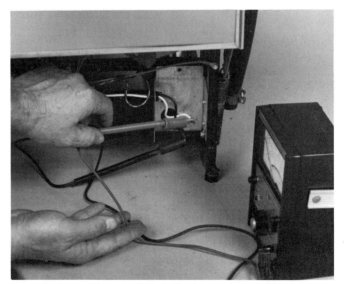

Figure 380 — Voltage Check To Dishwasher Wiring

### Check For Broken or Burned Wires

Turn the electricity OFF at the circuit breaker or fuse panel *(Figure 1)* before servicing the dishwasher. To check for broken or burned wires, refer to "Dishwasher Does Not Fill With Water" section of this chapter.

### Check Selector Switch

Turn electricity OFF at the circuit breaker panel *(Figure 1)*. Refer to the "Repair Procedures" in this chapter for removal of the selector switch.

Check to see that selector switch (push button) is not in the half-way position. In this position, it is possible the dishwasher will not start when making a cycle selection. Fully depress the button when selecting a cycle.

To check the selector switch, set the volt/ohmmeter on the RX-1 scale. Connect one probe from the volt/ohmmeter to one terminal of the selector switch. Attach the remaining probe to another terminal of the switch. Check for continuity by depressing the button of the selector switch. The volt/ohmmeter should show full scale deflection or 0 ohms *(Figure 381)*. This check would indicate this terminal of the switch is not defective. If you get NO continuity, the switch is defective — replace it. NOTE: A selector switch (push button) contains several terminals. Check each terminal connector with the volt/ohmmeter. Each terminal should show continuity when the switch button is depressed. If one of these checks shows NO continuity, the switch is defective — replace it.

### Check Door Switch

Turn the electricity OFF at the circuit breaker or fuse panel *(Figure 1)* before servicing the dishwasher. To check the door switch, refer to "Dishwasher Does Not Fill With Water" section of this chapter.

### REPAIR PROCEDURES

Turn the electricity OFF at the circuit breaker panel *(Figure 1)* before servicing the dishwasher. Exercise care when removing the dishwasher from its space as the dishwasher legs can easily damage the floor.

### To Replace Dishwasher Terminal Box

It is usually not necessary to replace the dishwasher terminal box. The electrical wiring, however, sometimes requires replacement. Wires that are brittle or burned should be replaced. When wires are tied together they should be secured by wire nuts. NOTE: It is not

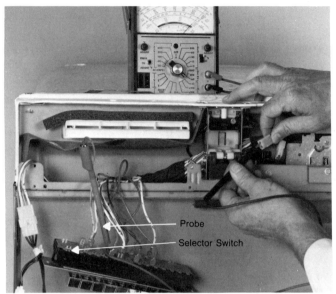

Figure 381 — Checking Selector Switch With Volt/Ohmmeter For Continuity

recommended that electrical wires be tied together with electrical tape. The tape can melt from extreme heat and be responsible for the dishwasher to not operate properly.

### To Replace Circuit Breaker or Fuse

It is not recommended that the home repairman attempt to replace a known defective circuit breaker or fuse. For additional information, refer to "Dishwasher Stops In Cycle" section in this chapter.

### To Replace Broken or Burned Wires

To replace broken or burned wires, refer to "Dishwasher Does Not Fill With Water" section in this chapter.

### To Replace Selector Switch

To replace door switch, refer to "Dishwasher Does Not Fill With Water" section in this chapter.

### To Replace Selector Switch

Turn the electricity OFF at the circuit breaker panel *(Figure 1)*. Remove timer knob, dial, end caps, console screws, and console. Refer to "Dishwasher Won't Pump Out Water" section of this chapter for the removal of these components. Remove the screws that secure the switch to cabinet. Remove the wiring harness wires from the switch and remove switch *(Figure 382)*.

Install the replacement selector switch by mounting in the same position as the faulty selector switch that was removed.

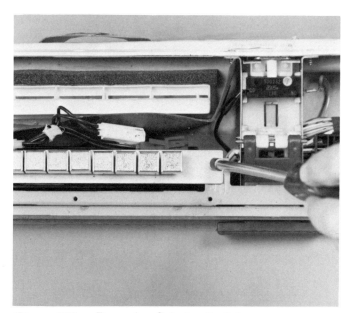

Figure 382 — Removing Selector Switch

## DISHWASHER NOT DRYING DISHES

Specific failure symptoms include: 1) Dishwasher stops before the drying cycle. 2) The dishes are not dry when removed from the dishwasher.

When this problem is noticed, it is often not the fault of the dishwasher. The homeowner simply did not close the dishwasher door. A partially closed door will prevent the dishwasher from making electrical contact. When closing the door, make sure that the door shuts properly before starting the dishwasher.

### Using Test Equipment

To avoid any incorrect readings when using the volt/ohmmeter always "zero" the ohmmeter scale (see your operating instructions) before making any continuity checks.

When making continuity checks with the volt/ohmmeter, always turn OFF the electricity at the circuit breaker panel *(Figure 1)*. Live voltage checks made with the volt/ohmmeter in a continuity position will damage your volt/ohmmeter.

### Check Dishwasher Plumbing

Check for stopped-up or backed-up house plumbing. Open dishwasher door and check to see if water is standing in the tub cavity. For additional information, refer to "Dishwasher Won't Pump Out Water" section in this chapter.

### Check Drive Motor Pump Assembly

To check the dishwasher pump assembly, it is necessary on most dishwashers to remove the drive motor and pump assembly from the dishwasher. Refer to Repair Procedures, "Dishwasher Won't Pump Out Water" section in this chapter.

### Check Timer Assembly

To check the timer assembly, refer to "Dishwasher Won't Pump Out Water" section in this chapter.

### Check Heater Element

Turn the electricity OFF at the circuit breaker panel *(Figure 1)*. Remove the lower panel *(Figure 339)*. Remove the wires that are attached to the heater terminals. Using the volt/ohmmeter, set the meter on the RX-1 scale. Connect one probe from the volt/ohmmeter, set the meter on the RX-1 scale. Connect one probe from the volt/ohmmeter to one terminal of the heater element. Attach the remaining probe to another terminal of the heater element. The scale of the volt/ohmmeter should show full scale deflection or 0 ohms *(Figure 383)*. If you do not get a continuity reading, the heater element is defective — replace it.

## REPAIR PROCEDURES

Turn the electricity OFF at the circuit breaker panel *(Figure 1)* before attempting to service the dishwasher. Exercise care when removing the dishwasher from its space as the dishwasher legs can easily damage the floor.

### To Replace the Dishwasher Plumbing

When major plumbing problems are suspected, it

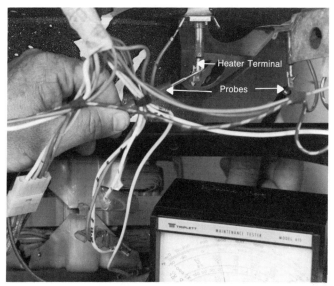

Figure 383 — Checking Heater Element For Continuity With Volt/Ohmmeter

is recommended that a qualified plumber be called to make the repairs. The replacement of deteriorated plumbing requires knowledge, special tools, and welding equipment that are usually not available to the home repairman. For additional information, refer to "Dishwasher Won't Pump Out Water" section in this chapter.

## To Replace Drive Motor Pump Assembly

To replace the pump assembly, refer to "Dishwasher Won't Pump Out Water" section in this chapter under "Repair Procedures."

## To Replace Timer Assembly

To replace the timer assembly refer to "Dishwasher Won't Pump Out Water" section in this chapter.

## To Replace Heater Element

Turn OFF the electricity at the circuit breaker panel *(Figure 1)*. Remove the dishwasher lower panel *(Figure 339)*. Remove the harness wires attached to the heater element terminals. Remove the nozzle cap that secures the lower spray arm to the pump assembly *(Figure 347)*. Remove the spray arm from the pump assembly *(Figure 348)*. Remove the screws that secure heater element to the tub cavity and remove element.

Install the replacement heater element by mounting in the same place and position as the faulty heater element that was removed.

Edited by Cherie R. Blazer